Theoretical Biology

International Library of Psychology
Philosophy and Scientific Method

ʒ

Theoretical Biology

International Library of Psychology Philosophy and Scientific Method

GENERAL EDITOR   C K OGDEN, M A.
(Magdalene College, Cambridge)

PHILOSOPHICAL STUDIES .	. by G. E MOORE, Litt D
THE MISUSE OF MIND .	. . by KARIN STEPHEN
CONFLICT AND DREAM	. by W. H. R RIVERS, F R S
PSYCHOLOGY AND POLITICS . ,	by W. H R RIVERS, F R S
MEDICINE, MAGIC AND RELIGION	by W. H R RIVERS, F R S
TRACTATUS LOGICO-PHILOSOPHICUS	by L. WITTGENSTEIN
THE MEASUREMENT OF EMOTION	by W WHATELY SMITH
PSYCHOLOGICAL TYPES ,	by C. G JUNG, M D , LL D.
SCIENTIFIC METHOD . . ,	. by A. D. RITCHIE
SCIENTIFIC THOUGHT .	by C D BROAD, Litt D
MIND AND ITS PLACE IN NATURE . .	by C D BROAD, Litt D
THE MEANING OF MEANING . by C K OGDEN and I A RICHARDS	
CHARACTER AND THE UNCONSCIOUS .	by J H. VAN DER HOOP
INDIVIDUAL PSYCHOLOGY .	by ALFRED ADLER
CHANCE, LOVE AND LOGIC .	by C S PEIRCE
SPECULATIONS *(Preface by Jacob Epstein)* .	by T E. HULME
THE PSYCHOLOGY OF REASONING . .	by EUGENIO RIGNANO
BIOLOGICAL MEMORY . .	by EUGENIO RIGNANO
THEORETICAL BIOLOGY . .	by J VON UEXKÜLL
THE PHILOSOPHY OF MUSIC .	by W POLE, F R S
THE PHILOSOPHY OF 'AS IF'	. . by H VAIHINGER
THE NATURE OF LAUGHTER	by J C GREGORY
THE NATURE OF INTELLIGENCE . .	by L L THURSTONE
TELEPATHY AND CLAIRVOYANCE , . .	by R TISCHNER
THE GROWTH OF THE MIND	. . by K KOFFKA
THE MENTALITY OF APES .	by W KÖHLER
PSYCHOLOGY OF RELIGIOUS MYSTICISM . .	by J. H LEUBA
RELIGIOUS CONVERSION . .	by S DE SANCTIS
THE PSYCHOLOGY OF A MUSICAL PRODIGY .	by G REVESZ
PRINCIPLES OF LITERARY CRITICISM .	, by I. A. RICHARDS
METAPHYSICAL FOUNDATIONS OF SCIENCE	by E A BURTT, Ph D
COLOUR-BLINDNESS . . .	by M COLLINS, Ph D
THOUGHT AND THE BRAIN .	by H PIÉRON
PHYSIQUE AND CHARACTER	by ERNST KRETSCHMER
PSYCHOLOGY OF EMOTION .	by J T MacCURDY, M D
PROBLEMS OF PERSONALITY.	*in honour of* MORTON PRINCE
PSYCHE . .	by E. ROHDE
PSYCHOLOGY OF TIME ,	by M STURT
THE HISTORY OF MATERIALISM	by F. A. LANGE
EMOTION AND INSANITY . .	. by S THALBITZER
PERSONALITY .	by R G GORDON, M D
EDUCATIONAL PSYCHOLOGY .	by CHARLES FOX
LANGUAGE AND THOUGHT OF THE CHILD	by J PIAGET
CRIME AND CUSTOM IN SAVAGE SOCIETY	by B MALINOWSKI, D Sc
SEX AND REPRESSION IN SAVAGE SOCIETY .	by B MALINOWSKI, D Sc
COMPARATIVE PHILOSOPHY . . .	by P. MASSON-OURSEL
PSYCHOLOGY AND ETHNOLOGY	by W H R RIVERS, F R S

IN PREPARATION

THE LAWS OF FEELING .	. by F. PAULHAN
THE PSYCHOLOGY OF CHARACTER . .	by A A. ROBACK
CONVERSION . . .	by S DE SANCTIS
THE ANALYSIS OF MATTER .	by BERTRAND RUSSELL, F.R S
STATISTICAL METHOD IN ECONOMICS	by P SARGANT FLORENCE
THE PRIMITIVE MIND . . .	. by P RADIN, Ph D
SOCIAL LIFE IN ANIMAL WORLD .	. by A ALVERDES
COLOUR-HARMONY . .	by JAMES WOOD
THE THEORY OF HEARING	by H HARTRIDGE, D Sc
SUPERNORMAL PHYSICAL PHENOMENA	. by E J DINGWALL
THE INTEGRATIVE ACTION OF THE MIND	by E MILLER
PLATO'S THEORY OF KNOWLEDGE	by F M CORNFORD
PRINCIPLES OF PSYCHOPATHOLOGY	by WM BROWN, M D., D Sc
THEORY OF MEDICAL DIAGNOSIS	by F G CROOKSHANK, M D
LANGUAGE AS SYMBOL AND AS EXPRESSION	by E SAPIR
A HISTORY OF ETHICAL THEORY	by M GINSBERG, D Lit
THE PHILOSOPHY OF LAW . .	by A L GOODHART
PSYCHOLOGY OF MUSICAL GENIUS .	. by G REVESZ
MODERN THEORIES OF PERCEPTION .	by W J H SPROTT
SCOPE AND VALUE OF ECONOMIC THEORY	by BARBARA WOOTTON
MATHEMATICS FOR PHILOSOPHERS .	by G H HARDY, F R S
THE PHILOSOPHY OF THE UNCONSCIOUS .	by E VON HARTMANN
THE PSYCHOLOGY OF MYTHS .	by G ELLIOT SMITH, F R S
THE PSYCHOLOGY OF MUSIC	by EDWARD J DENT

Theoretical Biology

By
J. VON UEXKÜLL

NEW YORK
HARCOURT, BRACE & COMPANY, INC.
LONDON: KEGAN PAUL, TRENCH, TRUBNER & CO., LTD.
1926

Translated by
D. L. MACKINNON, D.Sc.

PRINTED IN GREAT BRITAIN BY
THE EDINBURGH PRESS, 9 AND 11 YOUNG STREET, EDINBURGH

CONTENTS

27274

PREFACE

NATURAL SCIENCE falls into two parts, doctrine and research. The doctrine consists of dogmatic assertions, which contain a definite statement concerning Nature. The form these assertions take often suggests that they are based on the authority of Nature herself.

This is a mistake, for Nature imparts no doctrines: she merely exhibits changes in her phenomena. We may so employ these changes that they appear as answers to our questions. If we are to get a right understanding of the position of science vis-à-vis of Nature, we must transform each of the statements into a question, and account to ourselves for the changes in natural phenomena which men of science have used as evidence for their answer.

Investigation cannot proceed otherwise than by making a supposition (hypothesis) in its question, a supposition in which the answer (thesis) is already implicit. The ultimate recognition of the answer and the setting up of a doctrine follow as soon as the investigator has discovered in Nature what he considers a sufficient number of phenomena that he can interpret as positive or negative on the lines of his hypothesis.

The sole authority for a doctrine is not Nature, but the investigator, who has himself answered his own question.

A man may have assimilated the conclusions of natural science in the form of doctrine, and may know how to employ them in speculation, according to the rules of logic; but he still knows nothing whatsoever

concerning Nature—or at any rate, infinitely less than
does any peasant or gardener who is in daily intercourse
with her.

Peasants and gardeners, however, are not students of
Nature, unless they happen to have acquired the art of
interrogation.

This art forms the gateway to all knowledge in natural
science. In biology it is associated with quite especial
difficulties, and so it should occupy the central position
in the whole doctrine.

In the present book I have endeavoured to frame the
theoretical considerations concerning biology, in such
a way that there can no longer be any doubt that, in
their very nature, biological doctrines always remain
unsolved problems.

*In Nature everything is certain; in science everything
is problematical.* Science can fulfil its purpose only
if it be built up like a scaffolding against the wall
of a house. Its purpose is to ensure the workman a
firm support everywhere, so that he may get to any
point without losing a general survey of the whole.
Accordingly, it is of the first importance that the
structure of the scaffolding be built in such a way as to
afford this comprehensive view; and it must never be
forgotten that the scaffolding does not itself pertain to
Nature, but is always something extraneous.

From time to time it will always be necessary to
renew the scaffolding. And in the present book an
attempt of the kind is made.

The reason for this attempt is that hitherto all the
problems dealing with conformity with plan in living
Nature have been used simply for the denial of any
such conformity. Along such lines it is impossible to
make any advance. It used to be assumed that the great
majority of animals arose by spontaneous generation

out of an appropriate mixture of substances. Investigation taught us that all animals develop from the egg,
and that every cell arises from another cell.

Thus "omnis cellula e cellula" became doctrine. But
it was still assumed that the very first living things of
all must have arisen from a primordial flux. In this
way the attempt was made to get rid of conformity with
plan as a natural factor.

The primordial flux, which was supposed to have
been in existence in remote antiquity, now persisted
merely as an idea, and so could neither be proved nor
disproved by experiment. Accordingly, we have to
find other methods in which to attack the question as to
whether in living Nature there are independent factors
acting in accordance with plan: we must hearken to
Nature while she acts in this way, and to the negative
statement we must oppose positive evidence.

In recent years this evidence has so accumulated that
we may regard the question as practically settled. To
the phrase "omnis cellula e cellula" we may add,
"everything expressing plan is derived from something
else that is also in conformity with plan."

And this means that a new scaffolding is needed for
biology: the old scaffolding, borrowed from chemistry
and physics, will suffice no longer. For chemistry
and physics do not recognise conformity with plan in
Nature. Biology, however, consists in the setting up
of a scaffolding of doctrine that takes account of this
conformity as the basis of life.

There is a difficulty in the way of this construction,
and it is that the concepts of which the scaffolding is
made are not directly accessible, but can be got only
through a new interrogation.

As a rule, the text-books that arrange facts under a
definite scheme may be read in any sequence: but with

the present book this will not work. In order to understand the whole structure of the scaffolding, the reader must go through this book in the given sequence. Then at the end he can decide whether the scaffolding is defective and needs improvement, or whether he prefers not to accept it at all.

INTRODUCTION

BIOLOGY at the present day claims not merely a certain domain of the will, but also the possession of a peculiar theoretical basis of its own, which is in no way deducible from the fundamental concepts of physics and chemistry.

The need for elaborating the theory of biology made itself felt relatively late. So long as biological studies, such as zoology and botany, confined themselves to description, they needed, it is true, special methods for attaining to a clear arrangement of the great mass of facts, but they did not require a special theoretical foundation.

The investigation of the processes in the living organism followed the description of forms; and for that the basis furnished by chemistry, physics and mechanics sufficed. And so it came about that men learnt to regard the living organism as a physico-chemical machine.

The correctness of this view has been questioned indeed more than once by those investigators who have studied the connection between subjective processes and objective phenomena. In the course of their work they met with life-factors that would not permit of subordination to physico-chemical laws. But the name which, following the trend of the times, men gave to this science, expressed the hope that this ideal might be reached in the future. Physiological psychology means that psychology is to be treated according to physiological principles.

What turned the scales in this direction was the weighty opinion of a physicist of genius. Helmholtz, by perfectly logical methods, reduced all the objects surrounding us to sense-qualities pure and simple. The sense-qualities are the ultimate elements of our intuition, and, as such, are quite independent unities, which are indivisible, and capable of change only in their intensity. Transitions, such, for instance, as orange, which we find between red and yellow, depend on two qualities sounding out simultaneously.

Now Helmholtz explained the qualities as signs of an external phenomenon which proceeds parallel with their change. This external phenomenon remains forever unknown to us. By his famous "trust and act," as the philosophy to be drawn from this latter conclusion, he actually declared the bankruptcy of physiological psychology.

For if the external laws of Nature are forever withdrawn from our knowledge, then the proof that our psyche is under their control can never be adduced.

What Helmholtz required of us was the belief in the existence of natural laws which are entirely independent of us. This requirement was readily complied with. For the average thinker there is an end to everything, if we no longer try to believe in force and matter!

Up to this point the physical laws had been no more than hypotheses; now they acquired the authority of an article of faith, which was enthusiastically spread abroad by the lesser deities.

But it was very unsatisfactory for research to be obliged to base its entire structure on an article of faith which was in no way better than the dogmas of the Church. And that merely because Helmholtz saw in the sense-qualities subjective signs of the actual phenomenon.

It was certainly a misleading assumption, but in no way necessary. As Helmholtz himself taught, the objects that surround us are constructed from the sense-qualities; and indeed, one person uses some sense-qualities for the making of objects, and another uses others. So for him they are nothing but signs or indications for his subjective use, and they assert nothing whatever with regard to a phenomenon that is independent of him.

Helmholtz indeed acknowledged that all objects must appear different to each subject; but he was seeking the reality behind appearances. Many have done this before him : but he differed from his predecessors in supposing that what lies behind appearance is not the "Weltgeist," but the physical laws of the universe. That is a matter of taste.

Helmholtz remained consistently a physicist even in extremes, and his exceptional genius paved the way for materialism, whether he would or no, since it invested physics with an unmerited halo.

No attempt to discover the reality behind the world of appearance, i.e. by neglecting the subject, has ever come to anything, because the subject plays the decisive rôle in constructing the world of appearance, and on the far side of that world there is no world at all.

All reality is subjective appearance. This must constitute the great, fundamental admission even of biology. It is utterly vain to go seeking through the world for causes that are independent of the subject; we always come up against objects, which owe their construction to the subject.

When we admit that objects are appearances that owe their construction to a subject, we tread on firm and ancient ground, especially prepared by Kant to bear the edifice of the whole of natural science. Kant set the subject, man, over against objects, and discovered the fundamental principles according to which objects are built up by our mind.

The task of biology consists in expanding in two directions the results of Kant's investigations :—(1) by considering the part played by our body, and especially by our sense-organs and central nervous system, and (2) by studying the relations of other subjects (animals) to objects.

To make things easier to understand, I shall first of all endeavour to reproduce in current biological terminology the main results of Kant's line of research.

It is Kant's undying merit to have discovered an organisation in our subject, and to have revealed its principles. ("Subject" is used to include all the mental and spiritual powers.) There is here an internal conformity with plan, which, however, is revealed only when the subject becomes active. And so we must observe the subject while, as its activity dictates, it is in process of receiving impressions and making use of them.

The impressions received by the subject always consist of sense-qualities, which it then arranges and connects into unities, which we call objects. Accordingly we have to distinguish in every object between two things :—(1) the sense-qualities, which Kant called the *material*, and (2) the arrangement imposed on them by the mind, which he called the *form* of knowledge.

Undoubtedly, before any single piece of knowledge can be received, its form must be already prepared in the mind. But these forms change in the course of experience. Kant did not concern himself with those forms of knowledge which are of such great importance biologically ; he restricted himself to those which must have preceded all experience whatsoever. In this way, he proposed to lay the foundations of the principles that apply to every human being (quite independently of what other mental gifts he may have), by means of which he turns his experience to account. And thus Kant endeavoured to establish the universal and essential laws, uninfluenced by any psychology whatsoever, according to which each mind collects experiences. This led him to set up the two intuitional forms of space and time, which are necessary for every experience.

And if these seemingly simplest of the forms in which the mind finds expression, have, since Kant's day, become susceptible of further analysis, this merely means that the principle of analysis, as employed by him, has proved to be a discovery even more brilliant than was supposed.

THEORETICAL BIOLOGY

CHAPTER I

SPACE

KANT writes, " Space is merely the form of all appearances of the outward senses, i.e. the subjective conditioning of sensibility, by which alone intuition of the outside world is possible for us." The biologist would express this in the following way,—" The existence of space is dependent on the inner organisation of the subject's personality, which clothes the sense-qualities in spatial form."

This spatial form, however, is not the same throughout the various domains of sense, and it requires separate consideration for each

If when we are listening, the accompanying tactile sensations of the ear are cut out, we get a condition in which the auditory sensation remains quite normal but the direction from which the sound comes can no longer be estimated. In the same way, we can separate the sensations of smell and taste from the sensations of touch which accompany them, and then ask ourselves, " What do these pure sensations tell us about space ? " The answer must be that they tell us very little indeed. For the qualities of these senses are merely projected ; they are not localised In this primitive " what-lies-outside-ourselves " there are no places, no directions and no forms. We may call this " what-lies-outside-ourselves " space, but it must be remembered that

1

A

we are dealing with quite another kind of space from that of
which we usually speak.

Moreover, we must bear in mind that the sense-qualities,
and especially that of hearing, are not destitute of arrangement, although they be cut off from space. The whole
musical scale is an example of systematic arrangement,
although there is no preconceived image of it among the
objects of experience. The order of the sounds is determined
a priori as the expression of our subjective organisation, which
precedes all experience.

The order in which we receive at once each note as it
sounds, an order that determines with certainty its relationship to all other musical sounds, is an " intensive methodical-
ness " peculiar to our mind. It is, to use Kant's words, a
" transcendental form " of our intellect, vis-à-vis of which
the individual sounds constitute the " material " of knowledge.

A very momentous question now faces us,—" How can
the intensive design of the psyche and the extensive design
of the brain be combined as concepts ? " We shall often
meet this question again.

Turning again to space, we perceive that the two spatial
senses par excellence are sight and touch. And yet it is not
in virtue of their specific qualities that they are space-forming.
Colours, for instance, have a very remarkable relationship-
arrangement one with the other, as we know from the complementary colours ; but this has nothing to do with spatial
relations. There must be other qualities in addition which
are space-forming.

Local signs. The existence of specific spatial qualities
was deduced by Lotze and demonstrated experimentally
by Weber.

If the two points of a pair of compasses are set one centimetre apart and are then drawn down the back, beginning
at the neck, the person experimented on at first feels the two

points quite distinctly, and then they gradually approach one another until they fuse.

How does this come about ? How is this movement of approach so clearly detected ? The sensation of pressure does not alter in the least ; the only thing that does alter is the accuracy with which the skin of the back is able to detect the distance between the two points of pressure. From this we may confidently infer that, as well as sensitiveness to pressure, we also have in our skin a power of localisation.

The theory developed from such experiments states that we have in our skin outspread nerve-endings which envelop the whole surface of the body ; and these are not, so to speak, focussed on specific stimuli, but respond to every kind of stimulus The terminal nerve-expansions are distributed in areas which vary quite considerably in size. Each area allows one quality to sound, which imparts a definite local colour to the qualities of touch and temperature.

The areas are measured by determining the distance apart at which the two compass-points are instantly felt as two distinct points of pressure. In this way, it has been shown that the areas are by far the smallest and most numerous in the finger-tips and the tip of the tongue.

The qualities emanating from these areas are called *local signs*. Investigation of the local signs proves very difficult, because we have to disregard the specific stimulus that accompanies them ; this requires great concentration of attention, and it can be done with certainty only at a few places on the skin I find that when I shut my eyes and gently stroke the small hairs on the back of my hand, this brings best to my consciousness the alteration of the local quality But merely a light touch on the skin of the thigh gives one some insight into the relations of the local signs one to another. They are best compared with the musical scale. Imagine a piano with the keys in seven rows, one above another ; in the horizontal rows the sounds would be arranged according to octaves, while each vertical row would hold the sounds of one octave.

By means of such a piano we can most easily demonstrate the twofold relationship which each local sign has to its neighbours. For with the local signs two types of relationship can be shown. If the nervous areas are stimulated one after the other throughout the length of one of our limbs, the local signs come into play in a definite and related series, which, repeating itself with every lengthwise stimulation, may lead to some confusion. Another type of relationship-series appears when the stimulation acts transversely. These two types are never confused with one another.

Now, with normal stimulation, as, for instance, when you press the ball of a finger on the edge of the table, the local signs play a quite subordinate rôle to that of the touch-qualities ; and, in virtue of this, their fixed relation-series can the better be appreciated, for the touch-qualities have got no arrangement of the kind. We might indeed go so far as to say that the same touch-quality really always repeats itself, and changes only in intensity. So we transfer the arrangement of the local signs to the touch-qualities, and are enabled thereby to feel that these are arranged not only step-wise with relation to one another, but also in rows alongside one another.

And it is only now that we understand in its full significance the profound truth of Kant's dictum that space is merely a form of sense perception. For what enables us to apprehend touch-sensations as extended is not the new quality of the local signs, but the form of their arrangement, which is extension itself.

The existence of a quality which is merely consonant with the local signs and yet independent of them, and which gives information as to the place of stimulation, could be proved in the case of the sense of touch only by demonstrating that at different places on the skin the sensation of touch remained the same, whereas the local signs changed. It is easier to get this proof by using the retina of the eye. The individual elements of the retina are not all directed on the same colour-quality, though they are all directed on the same local quality. No one will deny that at the place he is regarding any colour whatsoever may appear, and therefore place and colour are factors independent of one another. And from the outset we were able to assume that the touch-qualities might everywhere be different.

If we turn our eyes skywards and do not move them, what we see looks like a uniform blue surface . if we look earthwards in the same way, all manner of surfaces present themselves, arranged together in series. Each surface is complete in itself, but the unity of the whole visible world is nevertheless preserved. It remains always the same, how-ever much the coloured fields of view may alter, because it is based on the simultaneous sounding of all the local-signs, a consonance which tells us of the enduring presence of the extended.

In contrast to the visible, the palpable is never simul-taneously apprehended in all its parts. The palpable is felt as unity because the same touch-sensations return at each stimulation.

We compared with the musical scale the interrelations of the local signs, since the musical scale likewise forms a con-nected relationship. The degree of the relationship between the individual sounds is determined by their resemblance : by that we determine the qualities that are just appreciable between them. This determination is rendered easier by the recurrence of the resemblance at each octave.

It is not nearly so difficult to determine the relationship of the local signs, because here a new quality comes in, the quality of direction. When, as we have seen, stimulation is applied at different points on the skin, it is easy to show that there are two different kinds of relationship ; the quality of direction, however, does not appear. We have only to think of the " pins-and-needles " feeling that comes when a limb " goes to sleep " ; we then localise very exactly the individual pricklings in our skin by means of their different qualities, but we have absolutely no sensation of direction

The sensation of direction comes in only when one local sign strikes up while the others most nearly related to it have not yet quite died away ; with " pins-and-needles " this does not happen. In " pins-and-needles " we feel the change in the quality very precisely ; but what we call " motion " is only that change in the quality which is connected with the quality of direction.

To simplify the description, I will call that which connects the local signs a direction-sign. It would seem that all the local signs of the skin, wheresoever situated, are invariably connected with their neighbours by two direction-signs only ; we had best call these " transverse-signs " and " longitudinal-signs."

On closer investigation, we observe that the direction-signs have a very important property which distinguishes them from all local signs, i.e. they are reversible. Without losing its character as transverse-sign or longitudinal-sign, every direction-sign will serve for " hence " as well as for " hither."

No quality known to us has this power ; the order in which the qualities appear can be reversed, but the individual quality itself never can. On that account, it is open to question whether in direction we really have to do with genuine qualities, or whether we are not merely dealing with an especially clearly expressed sequence of local signs.

Fortunately it is possible to give an unequivocal answer to this objection, for we know of direction-signs in quite another domain in which there are no local signs at all. I refer to muscular sensations. In all muscular sensations, which arise during muscular contraction, direction-signs always appear, and they are so strong that they sometimes drown the sensations proceeding from the muscles or the joints Muscular sensations are so badly localised that there is no question of their being the cause of the delicate and precise sensations of direction As soon as direction-signs accompany muscular sensations, we speak here also of " movement ", and, more explicitly, of our own movement.

Direction-signs determine movement in the outer world as well as in ourselves . we therefore divide them into " other signs " and " self signs." Since movements of other bodies are accomplished outside, and our own movements inside of our own body, we may also speak of *outer* and *inner* direction-signs. The chief distinction between the two kinds of direction-sign consists, however, in this, that the one is accompanied by a reception, the other by an action ; the one is purely sensory, the other sensory-motor.

The inner direction-signs for our own movement are of three kinds, i e back and forth, up and down, left and right. Arranged in series, the direction-signs admit of every order of movement that is possible

We contrast the individual sounds, as the material of sensation, with the musical scale, as their sensation-form, a form which comprises in itself the possibility of all sounds and at the same time their necessary arrangement In like manner, we shall contrast with the individual local signs as material, " the extended " as form : and with the direction-

signs as material, " motion " as their sensation-form, because
within it every possible direction is contained.

THE PLANES OF DIRECTION

When we close our eyes and picture what-lies-outside-ourselves as filled with series of direction-signs, we become aware
that the series are arranged not merely with relation to one
another, but that each series occupies a fixed place. This is
surprising, since our inner direction-signs (we are dealing
only with these here) are quite free from local signs, and
what-lies-outside-ourselves has in itself no places whatsoever.

How comes it then that we are nevertheless able to assign
its fixed place to every direction-sign ? On closer inspection
it appears that we are able to split up what-lies-outside-
ourselves into three pairs of halves—(1) right and left, (2)
above and below, (3) before and behind. We intersect what-
lies-outside-ourselves by means of three bisecting planes,
which cross one another in front of our heads. The attentive
observer will notice that, while what-lies-outside-ourselves
remains at rest, the system of the three planes shifts as
the head moves.

As a magnet arranges iron-filings, so the direction-signs
of the same kind place themselves on the bisecting plane that
belongs to them, along the lines of this marvellous magnet.
And thus a kind of three-dimensional canvas is formed, in
which the movements actually performed appear like threads
of coloured wool.

It is only by the insertion of the three planes of direction
that what-lies-outside-ourselves becomes " space " as we know
it and make use of it. It is nothing but a pure form, ready to
receive all our sense-qualities, and these become linked up
with it directly or indirectly. Space is a perfect unity—a self-

contained law. Moreover, it has no limits, for every perceivable movement is of necessity linked up with a direction-sign, which determines its position in space.

If we recognise in what-lies-outside-ourselves the possibility of movement, then space as the connection of this possibility with the planes of direction, will be true " form,"—namely, possibility and law.

IDENTITY OF THE OUTER AND INNER DIRECTION-SIGNS

Space, as we have just defined it, furnishes directly the " scaffolding " for our own movements, for the muscle-feelings in all movements that are actually performed can always be coupled with direction-signs   We must now show how the other qualities make use of this scaffolding and are influenced by it   This influence shows itself most clearly on the direction-signs which are connected with the local signs and give us information about movement in the outside world

The outer direction-signs, of which we distinguish two kinds, i e. transverse and longitudinal, are directly transformed into the corresponding inner signs, according to the position that their local signs take up with relation to the planes of direction   When I detect the stroking on the back of my hand, I get, over and above the sensation of touch, the direction-signs, " Along . . . along   .   along " and so forth. These direction-signs can be transformed every time into the direction-signs, " Forward . . . forward . .   forward " and so on, or " Up   up   . . up "   ., " To the left . . . to the left . . . to the left " . . . or into the reversed signs corresponding to these, according to the position which I give my hand.

If my eyes are shut, I know very little about the position of my hand, on account of the imperfectly localised sensations in the muscles or joints. (Everyone knows that if you shut your eyes and try to touch one forefinger with the other, you often go wide of the mark) As soon, however, as the first local sign is aroused which is connected with the sensation of touch, I become quite clear about the relations of this local sign with the three planes of direction ; I am " orientated." If now, at the moment when a series of local signs sounds, the outer direction-signs belonging to them correspond, these latter at once get their relation to the planes of direction, and transform themselves into inner direction-signs , but they do this without assuming the character of our own movement-sensations, because muscular sensations are lacking.

The consequences of this identification of outer with inner direction-signs are very important, for they enable us to bring to a common measure our own movements and movements in the outside world. If I run the ball of one finger along the edge of the table, the inner and outer direction-signs begin to sound together ; but they are opposite signs If the outer signs are " To the left . . . left . . . left," the inner signs are " To the right . . . right . . right." Then the effect of the inner and outer signs, as an indication (index) of move-ment, is nullified and I am aware only of my own movement. The inner direction-signs unite with the outwardly transferred touch-sensations, and I get the impression of my own move-ment of touch along an unmoved object.

(Whereas muscular feelings are referable to the condition of one's own body, the sensations of touch with their very precise local signs, serve as indications for properties of the outside world)

Each local sign instructs us concerning one spot in our own body, but it is the direction-signs which determine its position in space. This fact is very obvious in the case of our fingers while they touch things and are all the time chang-ing their position. The tip of the forefinger has become extra-

ordinarily sensitive to touch, and by its agency we test not
so much the nature of the external resistance (for that we
use in preference the ball of the finger) as its position in space.
In so doing, we ignore what the local signs have to tell us
about the place of our body; to give us that, the inner
direction-signs link up directly with the sensations of touch,
and the sensation of " pressure there " no longer means
pressure on the forefinger, but pressure at that point in space.

It can easily be shown that the determination of the point
in space depends simply on the voluntary direction-signs,
i.e. on the direction-signs connected with muscular activity
called forth by our nerve impulses: The proof of this is as
follows. Make the little finger bend itself over to the inner
side of the adjacent ring-finger; then shut your eyes and
press the edge of a card on the balls of both fingers; you
will feel one straight edge. Now with the other hand move
the same finger across the ring-finger (scarcely further than it
was able to go unaided), hold it firmly in this position with
the ring-finger, and now press the same card on the balls
of the fingers : if your eyes are shut, you will this time feel
two cards   The illusion disappears when the eyes are opened,
because the eye at once makes the correction.

To the same cause is referable the well-known experiment
of transforming one ball into two by touching it simultaneously with the index- and middle-fingers crossed over
one another.

From all of which it may confidently be inferred that the
very definite sensations coming from the joints and their
ligaments, although themselves localised, have no direction-
signs to inform us as to the position of the finger   The

muscular sensations are feeble in comparison with these sensations in the joints ; consequently, we feel the finger-move-
ments within the finger itself, although the muscles that
produce the movements lie in the forearm. The muscular
sensations become distinct only when we clench the fist ; but,
in that case, there are no sensations of direction

This sort of thing indicates that the direction-signs are not
indissolubly bound up with muscular sensations, but with
the impulses that initiate movement. I see further evidence
of this in the fact that when we swing our arms to and fro
there is a summation of the sensations in the two limbs, but
a subtraction of the direction-signs ; and this leads us to the
fact that we can distinguish two different kinds of innervation—one for muscular action and one for movement. When
we seize an object, we are innervating a muscular action ;
when we move it to another place, we are innervating a movement In somewhat more complicated movements which
we perform with ease, we should be greatly embarrassed if
we consciously ordered the individual muscular actions to
follow one after the other. It is easy for us to write the
numeral 2 on a slate, with our eyes shut ; but we have no
idea what muscular action we set a-going in order to do it.

It was Helmholtz who pointed out that we must have
innervation-sensations for the impulses belonging to a central
sense-organ As soon as we bring them into relation with
the impulses, the inner direction-signs appear in quite a new
light. We innervate muscular actions either by a single
impulse, as in clenching the fist (in which case we ignore the
direction-signs), or else we innervate them by an impulse-
sequence, as in writing (in which case we are conscious only
of the direction-signs)

The following experiment gives us some information as to
the rôle played by the direction-signs in innervation. First
with the right hand and then with the left write slowly in the

air the numeral 3 : you will get two numerals in their correct position. Now quickly give to both hands simultaneously the order to write a 3, and instead of 3 3 you will get Ɛ 3, i e. two numerals, of which one is the mirror-image of the other. This is not surprising, since the muscles of the two arms, although alike, are arranged mirror-wise with relation to one another. The experiment merely shows that the nerve impulse is divided between the two arms to carry out the same movement, and that the movement is performed without reference to the different arrangement in the left arm.

Every muscular action is connected with a direction-sign. For the right hand we have learnt by now to make the impulses succeed one another in such a way that the direction-signs thereby sounding produce the numeral 3. When we initiate the same series of muscular actions in the left arm, the mirror-image of the numeral 3 must result

Nevertheless we are somewhat surprised, because we get none of the effects we expected from the left arm. Before the act of writing, we picture to ourselves more or less clearly the numerals 3 3, and we find now that the result does not correspond with this preconceived image We should feel the same astonishment, if, when we wanted to play a familiar tune on a piano, we found that the strings of the piano were arranged in reversed sequence

From this experiment we may infer that the preconceived image, however exactly formed, does not directly innervate the muscles of the left arm. The preconceived image consists, in the best instances, of carefully ordered memory-signs which are arranged extensively like the actual direction-signs. In contrast to this, the innervation that initiates the movement consists of separate impulses which follow one another *in time.* For the arrangement in time of different factors we shall employ the current term for a succession of sounds— " melody."

The melody of the impulses is quite unknown to us, but it enters directly into our consciousness when we perform the actual movement and the direction-signs resound, or when we play off their memory-signs in our imagination.

As soon as the movement begins, direction-signs appear which give us information not as to the muscles that are in action, but as to the path that is followed in space. So we learn that the left arm is following a different path from the right. In thus far, we are justified in describing the direction-signs as signs of the innervation that has come into action For the performance of a simple muscular contraction we do not require the melody.

SPACE AS LAW

As we know, Kant established the doctrine that we have information about space before we have any experience, because, as the form of intuition, space must precede every experience. But space does not differ therein from the other forms of sense-perception; the musical scale is in existence as soon as the first sound is perceived, and the first colour seen already has its complementary colour before ever that enters our perception. The relations, regulated by law, which one sound bears to all other sounds, and those which one colour bears to all other colours, must be investigated, it is true, in experience, but they precede all experience and merely reveal their nature with the beginning of the first experience.

The reason why an exceptional position is accorded to space in contrast to other forms of sense-perception, is quite other. All sense-qualities that are not connected with our movements are called forth by impressions from outside, which are entirely independent of our own activity. Only those qualities which accompany our own movements are quite independent of the outside world, and hence of any external experience. It is just these qualities, and more especially the direction-signs, that have space as their necessary form. On that account, we can develop the whole theory of space without the assistance of external experience ; and since all the other qualities come directly or indirectly into relation with space, we may say that space precedes all experience as the form of intuition common to all experience, and that the laws regulating it, which we investigate through the inner experiences of our own movements, were a priori there in their entirety.

But with space, not merely do its laws precede external experience, but so also does the science of these laws. This explains the exceptional part played by the figures in plane geometry. These figures that we draw are not outlines of objects, but imperfect symbols of our own movements ; by the attempt to commit to paper by means of lines the series of direction-signs, we study the relation of these movements to one another.

It is clear that plane geometry precedes external experience, but equally clear that plane geometry is a creation of internal experience We should be led into serious error if we were to assume that somehow, by means of memory-signs in the imagination, we could establish a science that would inform us as to what actually happens. An actual phenomenon, whether external or internal, can only be recognised in itself.

While it is true that there can be an idea of space into which the memory-signs can be thrown, yet space itself is not an idea. Space is an essential component of our organisation, and, as such, an actual law of nature, valid subjectively as well as objectively

In order to give us some insight into our own organisation, Kant made *apperception* the central point of his doctrine. Apperception is the activity lying at the root of all perception. Only when it is in action can we learn anything about the organisation of our subject, which else lies shrouded in utter darkness. Whatever the perception, the activity is of the same kind ; different qualities are constantly being associated into unities The power of the subject that exercises this apperceptive activity is for ever creating new structures ; in its very nature, it is a formative force.

The material for this construction is furnished by the qualities ; the laws governing the construction are the forms. From force, material and law the organisation of our subject becomes revealed to us.

Hence we are justified in calling space a law, since it is the most general form of sense-perception ; and since the activity of our mind is the only part of Nature directly known to us, its laws are the only ones that we can justifiably call laws of Nature. The determination which space imposes on all objects is undoubtedly a law of Nature.

This determination according to law, imposed by space on all objects, is, as we have seen, twofold :—(1) possibility of movement and (2) position with regard to the three planes of direction. From this consideration arises the question whether space, although it represents a fundamental law for all objects, may not itself be merely a creation by apperception.

THE ORGAN THAT GIVES DIRECTION IN SPACE

The clue put into our hands by Kant to enable us to penetrate the mystery of the organisation of our subject, depends on a conclusion drawn from the activity of the subject itself as to its own constitution, and hence leaves unsolved many questions as to the nature of that organisation. In contrast to this, the organisation of our body lies exposed before our eyes, and does not have to be revealed by conclusions drawn from its activity.

Organisation means a unity in which the different parts are combined into a whole through the agency of a common activity This holds good for the organisation of our body as well as of our mind. Now the different activities of the mind are so closely connected with the activities of the various organs of the body (sight with the activity of the eye, hearing with that of the ear, and so forth), that we draw the following conclusion :—in some way or other, each organ of the body corresponds to an organ of the mind. Through the manifold experience of every day, we learn that the suppression of an organ leads, as a consequence, to the suppression of an activity of the mind.

Here we see a way in which we may solve the twofold problem of space Let us try to find an organ of the body whose removal influences our space-forming activity, either by destroying the direction-signs or by suppression of the planes of direction.

Cyon established the much-contested theory that the semicircular canals of our ear stand in relation to the three planes of direction It is impossible to perform the decisive experiment on ourselves. We cannot put this mysterious organ out of action by stopping up the external auditory meatus, as we can put the eye out of action simply by closing the eyelids. We are obliged therefore to resort to ambiguous animal experiment. We must first ask ourselves what visible disturbances of the outside world would appear in our own case if we were suddenly deprived of the direction-planes of our own space, and then find out whether animals deprived of their semicircular canals show corresponding disturbances.

The planes of direction permit of our transforming the relative position of a movement in space into an absolute position, because the individual direction-signs, by reason of their fixed relation to the planes, appear like separate stitches sewn in a firm canvas. Removal of the semicircular canals

B

would mean the removal of this canvas and would deprive movements of their fixed position in space.

In order to imagine the injury you would suffer from such a loss, shut your eyes, and with your hand quickly bring a flat object, such as a book, from a distance to the boundary between right and left, then to the boundary between above and below, and finally to that between before and behind. You can then convince yourself of the exactness with which the bounding planes are found, and where they intersect. We carry around with us near the tip of the nose an invisible co-ordinating organ as the basis of our movements, which is quite unaffected by all the influences of the outside world and by the position of the rest of the body. The loss of this basis would undoubtedly have the most injurious effect on the certainty of our movements.

The planes of direction influence most of all the movements of our eyes; their loss would therefore be felt there most. We determine the position of the various objects in space by extremely rapid movements of the eyes; these movements start from the middle position, and go to and fro. It is easiest to verify the continually repeated return of the eye to the middle position by watching a person who is looking at rapidly passing objects. The to-and-fro movement of his eyes is known as normal nystagmus. Very different is the abnormal nystagmus which we observe in animals that have lost their semicircular canals: here the eyes roll continually to and fro from one corner of the orbit to the other, as though they were seeking for the lost median position. Animals in that state prefer to remain in the dark, and only very gradually do they re-acquire their normal eye-movements.

The picture they present corresponds in all details with the condition we should be in if we were suddenly deprived of the direction-planes It is only through knowing the planes of direction that we are always able to bring our eyes back

exactly to the starting-point, and, in this way, to determine
the position of various objects in space   If, in looking for
objects, we were to roll our eyes from side to side in a completely uncontrolled way, intolerable confusion would result,
from which we would flee away into darkness.   Only very
gradually, by having recourse to the external direction-signs
with their local signs, could we learn again how to orientate
ourselves in space

Since it has been demonstrated that, after removal of
single semicircular canals, disturbances in the movements
occur in quite definite directions, I consider that Cyon's
theory is proved in its essential point.   From his theory, Cyon
has drawn the conclusion that the directions of space are to
be reckoned among the sense-qualities, and that space in
Kant's sense should not be put with the forms of intuition,
for it itself must first be formed   In this I see only an
apparent contradiction   If, with Kant, we make the con-
structive activity of the subject the very centre of our consideration, then we can very well imagine that the business
of construction (and apperception is nothing more or less
than this) first creates the forms of intuition, and then proceeds to make use of them.   As has already been emphasised,
we know nothing about the real organisation of our mind.
Only through the activity of experience are the three factors
revealed which Kant discovered, namely shaping power,
material and law.   With the beginning of experience, these
three first form space as a form of intuition, and space then
yields the general laws for all further experience   Undoubtedly we know more about the forming of space than
Kant did ; but everything he said about space as the means
whereby we construct external experience, retains its full
value.

With the first movement of our limbs, our inner experience begins, and the first direction-signs are manifested.

Space is at once formed, and it is made up of the possibility of movement in all directions (which possibility is the most general relationship-form of the direction-signs) plus the planes of direction ; the actual movements are traced out in space as definite series of direction-signs.

Thus it seems to me that the theories of one of the most gifted of physiologists are really in full accord with Kant's doctrine , it is only now and then that his enthusiasm over-shoots the mark.

ILLUSORY MOVEMENTS

When we look at the world with one eye, and at the same time move the eye-ball to and fro with a finger, the objects surrounding us begin to swing to and fro at the same rate ; whereas, when the movements of the eye are performed by our own muscles, the objects remain stationary. Passive and active shifting of the eye, then, produces entirely different results. From this experiment Helmholtz concluded that the innervation of the eye-muscles is made known to us by special qualities of a central sense. We call these qualities direction-signs. The experiment tells us even more ; it shows us that any displacement of the retina is alone sufficient to give us information about movement. When an image of an object shifts on the retina, this invariably gives an impression of a movement , and this whether it is the object that has shifted, or the retina itself.' The appearance of the local signs in continuous series produces in the retina, just as in the skin, the impression of movement in the outside world. We become conscious of our own movement only through the movement of our muscles.' Our own movement is re-vealed to us by the inner direction-signs which accompany our impulses when the muscles are stimulated.' The outer direction-signs tell us about movement in the outside world ; they come into being with the sounding out and dying away of adjacent local signs.

Helmholtz's experiment shows that the two kinds of direction-sign which we have distinguished from one another, are really identical, for only identical but opposed signs can annul one another.

We also arrived at this conclusion from our discussion of what happened when we slid the balls of our fingers along the edge of the table ; but with the movements of our limbs, the sensations in the muscles and tendons play so large a part that we cannot lose the feeling of our own movement. With the eye, however, the subsidiary feelings become quite inconspicuous ; and so here the opposed signs can completely cancel one another, and we get an impression of rest.

It is only through the eye that we become certain that motion is not merely a derived concept, but that, just as space is the form of the co-existence of the direction-signs, so motion represents the form of the sequence of the direction signs , accordingly the appearance of the first direction-signs presupposes space as well as time

The production of a second kind of illusory movements of objects depends on the assumption that each retina is like a chess-board on which a game of chess is being played. How is it that the two games simultaneously played come to our consciousness as one ? This is explained by identical fields of the two chess-boards having the same local signs , and two different things can never happen simultaneously at the same spot   Now, while looking at an object, turn one eye slightly outwards (it is not every one who can do this) ; the fields of sight will shift towards one another, and the outline of the object, which in the one eye keeps its original place, in the other begins to shift. The shifting is not perceived through the outward movement of the eye that has been moved ; of this we can convince ourselves by covering the eye that has remained still.

If we imagine the retinæ to be superimposed on which an image is to be thrown, and let one retina be shifted laterally by its eye-muscles, the image no longer falls on identical retinal spots, and must appear double, because now there are two identical places everywhere. The movement that appears when this happens is not perceived by the retina that has shifted, for on it the two kinds of direction-signs balance one another ; it is perceived by the stationary eye, which has not followed the impulse The displacement of the stationary retina relatively to the one that has been moved is not balanced by inner direction-signs, and consequently must appear as movement in the outside world

That outer direction-signs should appear even when the image has not been moved shows that these also are independent central qualities like the inner direction-signs, which in all points they essentially resemble. Similar direction-signs (inner and outer) appear sometimes in association with muscular actions, sometimes with local signs, and either combine together or else cancel one another.

Hence the remarkable fact that, though when we look around us, the images of objects on the retina continually stimulate fresh local signs, we do not always notice this, and the objects do not leave their places : consequently, they acquire a position in space which appears to be independent of us. If the direction-signs did not balance one another in this way, the world would lose all its repose ; in place of its calm, there would be an intolerable dancing about of objects, such as we experienced when we moved the eyeball with the finger.

To sum up briefly :—We get knowledge of the direction-sensations or direction-signs from two different sources. Firstly, they may appear on appropriate excitation of the local signs ; and secondly, through the innervation of our muscular activity. In both cases, these sensations show the same very important property of reversibility, which is made possible by reciprocal cancelling of the direction-sensations. From this we conclude that both kinds of direction-signs, in spite of their different origin, are united in one and the same central sense-organ. This central sense-organ for the direction-signs is in close connection with the semicircular canals of the inner ear.

POINT AND ATOM

Having brought the analysis of the basal elements of biology thus far, we are in a position to explain some problems of fundamental importance. It was Helmholtz, as we know, who pointed out that in a world of human beings having cylindrical lenses, the axiom of plane geometry, in accordance with which the shortest distance between two points must be a straight line, would not hold good. We can now explain this paradox, for we can show that there are two sorts of straight lines, one of which invariably obeys the axiom, while the other does not.

If we understand by " line " a series of direction-signs, then undoubtedly the straight line (i e the sequence one after the other of all the similar direction-signs) is the shortest course, i e. the one that requires the smallest number of direction-signs to get from one point to another. Every deviation from the straight course by bringing in direction-signs of other kinds, will sooner or later lead to the interpolation of the opposed sign ; and such a course must be reversed again if the goal is not to be missed Each détour, by this interpolation of other signs and then their correction, increases the number of direction-signs employed.

If, on the other hand, we understand by " line " a series

of optically created local signs, then it is obvious that, since
image-forming on the retina is under the influence of the
optical apparatus, occasionally a completely distorted image
of the line can arise   The optical line is subjected to all the
vicissitudes of external experience, and from these an axiom
can never be drawn as it can from internal experience.

Just as there are two kinds of lines, so also there are
two kinds of points. As is generally known, we distinguish
the immaterial (mathematical) point from the material
(physical) point. The mathematical point is defined as the
place where two lines intersect. In this case, by " line " is
understood a series of direction-signs   The mathematical
point, consequently, has no extension.

The physical point, or atom, is no other than local sign +
sense-quality   Only by establishing this, can we explain the
inner contradictions of this primary element of physics,
and at the same time the necessity for its application.   The
local sign is the smallest quantity of space known to us that
possesses no form, for in order to create a form several local
signs are needed.   For the same reason, the atom, as its name
implies, is indivisible.

The local sign is not itself material, but it is to be found
only in conjunction with other sense-qualities which serve as
characteristics of matter.   The local sign is the smallest
spatial receptacle for each kind of matter, but it itself possesses none of the properties of matter.   (It is neither blue
nor red, neither light nor heavy.)   Nevertheless, the local
sign governs all the spatial laws of matter, because it is the
only bearer of matter in space   This description of the local
sign is at the same time a complete enumeration of the properties of the atom.

From this it follows that to define the atom as the primary
element of all kinds of matter is wrong   It is possible that
all substances are composed of one primary element ; only

experience will teach us whether this is so.   But it is certainly
not an axiom.

All that is certain is that every physical analysis must proceed from this indivisible, smallest space-receptacle, without
form or substance ; and it must end there, because at that
point our own organisation has set the limit to investigation.
So long as by the aid of optics we are enabled to magnify the
smallest particles of matter yet known, just so long will our
local signs go on creating fresh atoms.   The limit to this is
purely practical   There is no theoretical limit to the practical
application of local signs.

Summarising, we may make the following definitions :—
As the point of intersection of two series of direction-signs, a
mathematical point is a point in space that has no extension ;
a local sign is the smallest spatial magnitude ; an atom, as
the association of a local sign with a sense-quality, indicates
a material point in space

GLANCING AND SEEING

By this time we have been able to establish an almost
complete parallel between the functions of touch and sight.
We even speak metaphorically of " sweeping " objects with
the eye.   But this very expression gives the clue to where
the difference between touch and sight is to be sought.
" Sweeping " an object means a movement of the hand or
eye in which only a few local signs come into activity.   When
the eye is moving we call the employment of limited local
signs " glancing," and when the eye is stationary, " staring."

In contrast to this, we describe the collective employment
of all the local signs as "looking."   We know of no parallel
process for the act of touch, where all the local signs in
the skin come into activity simultaneously

In order to make glancing possible, a special contrivance

in the retina is affected ; this is the yellow spot, in which
lie special nerve-endings, the cones With this part of the
retina, which is at the same time the region of sharpest vision,
we " sweep " objects with a glance.

When we read, the eye has to follow the guidance of the
lines of letters and figures ; we do no more than " glance."
Through the frequent repetition of the same sequence of
direction-signs, this sequence of symbols fixes itself firmly in
our memory like a melody, and enables us not only to recognise the known letter when we see it again but also to create
an image of it in our mind Finally, by copying the letter,
we establish the melody of the direction-sign so firmly that
the impulse-sequence for the muscles of the arm follows in
the manner that the melody prescribes , then we are able to
write. In a previous experiment, we convinced ourselves
that the same impulse-sequence in our two arms, of which
one is the mirror-image of the other, gives rise to a reversal
of the direction the line takes. As a matter of fact, when
once we have learnt to write with the right hand, we can
straightway produce mirror-writing with the left—given, of
course, that the left hand is not by nature too clumsy.

The same process that is gone through in learning letters
of the alphabet, occurs over and over again when we observe
objects. We " sweep " with the yellow spot the outlines of
objects over and over again until within ourselves a melody
of direction-signs is established. We use this melody in
order to recognise the objects again , on the other hand, we
use it very seldom or very imperfectly for reproducing them
in our imagination as the melody of memory-signs. Thus
it comes about that we are but imperfectly informed as to
the number and affinities of the impulse-sequence , we have
no means of recognising them directly, and we know them
only indirectly through the medium of the melody of the
direction-signs.

The artist as he draws is the only man who can let the melodies of the direction-signs become really vivid in his imagination. He must do this if by the direction-signs of his eye he is to control the impulse-sequences guiding his hand long enough for the melody of its direction-signs to become so strong that it gives unerring control.

If we admit that in the greatest artists the power of reproducing the melody in the imagination, and so of controlling the hand, is carried to the furthest limit of what is possible, then the finished drawing furnishes us with a criterion for our own melodies, for the lines of the drawing show us the essential features of an object much more clearly than we saw them in the object itself. Hence we may conclude that in an artist the melodies are far purer and far stronger than in ourselves, and on that account they enable him to recreate in a way that we should find impossible.

Our inferiority is not referable merely to our lesser talent ; the carelessness of our observation of the external world is evident enough and it leads to the construction of second-rate melodies. How many people there are who content themselves with constructing a single melody for all trees ! A melody like this must be quite meaningless since it suppresses all those differences which are characteristic of the forms of various kinds of trees. No doubt the widespread use of writing, which governs our every step, especially in towns, is responsible for turning our attention from natural objects. We become aware of this when we try to find our way about a city where the directions are posted up in unfamiliar letters Most people are then deprived of signs by which to guide themselves, for to them one house looks like another, and one street like another.

The melody of direction-signs which observation of outline gives, furnishes us with one of the chief characteristics from which objects are built up. As a rule, only part of this melody need sound in order for us to recognise the object again. For many objects we must form several melodies if we want to recognise them at the first glance. If we have not done this for one side of the object, we do not recognise it, but content ourselves with saying that something is there whose outline stirs no melody when our glance rests on it.

We are faced here with the astonishing fact that we are completely ignorant as to one of the main characteristics of objects, certainly no less important than colour or smell, and become conscious of it only when we make use of it, and then in virtue of the accompanying quality. We employ impulse-sequences all the time, and yet they remain concealed, like the impulses to our larynx when we sing ; of these we become conscious only when they are translated into sounds, either in reality or in our imagination.

Here we get to know a very real factor in our organisation, a factor which, in order to become apparent, must find expression either in time as a melody of sounds, or in time and space as a melody of direction-signs We can do no more than observe its operation and establish its existence. As soon as we attempt to classify it in the organisation of our subject, or ask ourselves whether we can find something that represents it in our brain, it eludes us

What is so tantalising is that we formed the melodies from the impulse-sequences themselves ; assuredly, knowledge of the letters of the alphabet is not inborn. Neither can we content ourselves by saying that the melody is just a rule or a method of systematising which we then impose on the sequence of direction-signs, a rule that simply cannot exist apart from the phenomenon with which it is associated. No, the impulse-sequence forms the sign-series quite on its own, and without reference to whether we are cognisant of it or not.

All we can do is to establish the fact that, after frequent

repetition of similar series of sound-qualities or direction-signs, an X is formed in our mind, and this X combines into a single unity the entire sound-sequence or sign-sequence. As soon as the first notes sound or signs appear, this unity reveals its presence as an already existing whole, and then, when the sounds or direction-signs are re-created, it prescribes their sequence.

When we look at a familiar object or listen to a piece of music that we know, we learn nothing except that a unity corresponding to them is already present in our mind All we discover is the fact that this unity is already completely formed ; we learn nothing about the unity itself or about the process of construction by which it was formed. And accordingly, this unity, which we have called " impulse-sequence," is itself a living, active factor, which, when we reproduce the signs or sounds, sets its mark on the qualities under its control.

So it appears that the most important processes of life are gone through in complete obscurity, although on our side of appearances. One thing we can affirm with confidence ; the secret of the world is to be sought not behind objects, but behind subjects.

LOOKING

In music, we distinguish between melody and symphony. By " melody " we understand the orderly sounding of musical notes one *after* the other ; by symphony, their sounding *together*. When combined, melody and symphony give us harmony. In glancing at objects, we drew a comparison between certain regularly recurring series of direction-signs and melodies ; we might describe as the symphonic theory of looking the rules that are revealed when all the optical local signs are consonant.

As raw material for perception, the sum-total of our

optical local signs furnishes us with but one plane, which is composed of surfaces, mutually influencing one another as to colour, form and luminosity. Strange to say, Helmholtz, while describing as laws the rules that influence luminosity and colour, relegated to the realm of optical illusion all the rules he investigated concerning the influencing of shape and size.

Thus it has come about that such phenomena are still treated as " curiosities," and in this province we are without the groundwork for a theory of symphony. And yet it is possible to recognise at the first glance general rules which serve to unify and simplify the impression we receive of the whole. When we look at an object, the eye is guided most easily along the two chief directions of space ; every tailor knows that clothes with longitudinal stripes make the wearer look slighter, and that transverse stripes, on the other hand, make him look broader. The eye attempts to render parallel all lines that do not deviate too far. The branching of leafless trees seen against the sky takes on the simplest possible pattern.

This compensating activity of the eye can be observed most clearly and interestingly by filling up the blind spot in the retina. Hold at arm's length in front of the right eye a silver-knobbed walking-stick, keeping the left eye shut ; then, holding the knob level, move it towards the right : you will find that, if the eye is kept still, the knob disappears completely at one point. In its place appear the lines, shadows or pattern of what is the background for the time being. When the blind spot is filled up, the optical imagination always completes the surfaces only, and never the object.

Though in the twilight our imagination transforms trees and bushes, or in the day-time the shapes of clouds, into the most surprising objects, yet the optical imagination is exceedingly limited in its activity. Nothing new ever appears in the

blind spot ; the surfaces surrounding it simply grow together
We get the impression all the while that quite a different
kind of imagination is at work here, an imagination completely
lacking the power to form shapes

In any case, the fact that we are continually filling in
an anatomical hiatus with an adaptable product of the
imagination quite independent of our will, sets us thinking,
for here what is bodily and what is spiritual clearly have the
same origin   And this is a strong indication that bodily
things, like spiritual, are merely manifestations of the same
unknown natural force.

In the physiological text-books we find collected all that
is worth knowing about the reciprocal influences of light,
dark and coloured surfaces ; but this wealth of material has
not yet been utilised for a symphonic theory of sight. Yet
in Goethe's works are to be discovered the foundations for it,
and set forth with his incomparable originality. But the
physicists rate Goethe as an amateur, and accordingly the
majority of physiologists likewise treat his views with con-
tempt. The reason for this misunderstanding lies in the
fundamentally different standpoints from which physics and
biology regard the world.

In the world of the physicist there are only objects, which
react on one another through the medium of space ; in the
world of the biologist there are only appearances, which react
on one another through the medium of the subject.

According to the physical theory, wave-like vibrations of
different diameters pass outwards from all objects ; each
of these different kinds of waves corresponds to a certain
colour-value   It is, however, a great mistake to suppose
that this explanation fits in with even the simplest facts.
If we cut out of the spectrum all the colours except pure red
and pure green, and illuminate with these alone the same
colourless surface, that surface will appear white. If we mix

a blue-green paint with a yellow-green, the mixture is green, even when, in the colours we started with, the green admixture was so faint as to be scarcely perceptible. The reason for this is that blue and yellow when mixed give white, and only the green comes out as colour.

We call the pairs of colours that unite to give white, complementary colours. Every coloured surface has the power to call forth its complementary colour in its environment, and also, when its own colour disappears, to take on the complementary colour. To explain this, the physiologists are obliged to assume special arrangements in the retina of the human eye, since physical theory is at complete variance with this phenomenon. The reciprocal reaction of coloured surfaces plays an important part in nature : for instance, the shadows of trees on a yellow road seem blue, and cloud-shadows on the blue-green sea appear reddish.

Nowadays there can no longer be any doubt that in the distribution of colours in the world the subject plays the decisive rôle. But feeling with Goethe, we can well imagine the scorn he must have had for the physicist who utterly refused to consider such a thing.

It is worth while to pause for a moment and inquire why it is that physics is bound to deny the theory. The official physical theory stands or falls with the dogma of the absolute reality of space. According to this theory, one object cannot affect another except by means of actual changes in space. The complementary effect of coloured surfaces, however, is nothing of the kind ; nothing at all happens in the objective world that could be accounted for in such a way. For example, two coloured surfaces so placed that there can be no mutual irradiation, nevertheless influence one another. On the other hand, there are in the subject actions and reactions according to law, which account for the complementary phenomena.

Through its belief in the absolute existence of an objective world, physics has come to a deadlock. It overlooks the fact that the only realities it recognises—namely, the atom and its motion in space—are subjective qualities, which, like all qualities, permit of only a limited application, The atom as the primary element of matter, which, in its very nature, is discontinuous, is referable to the local sign, and motion, which is continuous, to the direction-sign, Both these qualities have meaning and justification just so long as we are dealing with changes in space   If we tried to apply them, for instance, to the musical scale, which is not arranged with relation to space, the result would be sheer nonsense. We transfer even the source of sound to space ; and yet no one would take a symphony for an objective phenomenon having any reality apart from the subject. It is the same with colours   although one coloured surface can irradiate another through space, just as a sound can awaken an echo, and physical changes thereby appear in space, yet these spatial processes tell us nothing about the laws according to which the qualities will intermingle.

The peculiarity of colours as opposed to sounds lies merely in this, that even when they remain separate from one another in space (in two contiguous surfaces), yet they influence one another according to the non-spatial laws of their affinity   Physics will not hear of such a thing ; but biology may, for why should not two spatial impressions influence one another within the same subject ?

SPATIAL VISION

Hitherto we have confined ourselves to considering the symphonic relations that are discoverable in space as we see it. We turn now to the symphony of space-magnitudes, as it reveals itself to the eye

C

One of our greatest observers, the sculptor Hildebrandt, advanced the theory that in all works of art, in painting as well as in sculpture, the foremost plane should be the chief plane, starting from which the eye must travel into the distance and the depths; for in looking at Nature it behaves in the same way.

The physiological cause of this kind of vision is to be found in the structure of the accommodating apparatus of our eye. The lens of the eye is focussed for near vision by the active pull of the lens muscles. Distance sight is brought about by relaxation of the muscles, whereby the lens apparatus, in virtue of its elasticity, returns automatically to the position of rest. Both in contraction and in relaxation of the muscles, direction-signs appear, which are brought into relation with the corresponding plane of the apparatus that orientates us in space.

During active focussing of the lens on nearer and ever nearer objects, whole groups of direction-signs reach our consciousness together, and, as it were, in jerks: whereas when we focus slowly from near to far objects, the individual direction-signs appear one after the other in a uniform series; and as this is done without effort, it leaves behind it an harmonious impression.

This is spatial vision. Looking at solid bodies begins only near at hand, when the two eyes noticeably converge and begin to observe objects from two sides. That it really is the convergent movement of the eyes which directly produces our " plastic vision," we can prove if we look through a modern stereoscopic telescope. This also enables us to look at objects from two sides, but we do not get plastic vision; instead of that, the object becomes broken up into a number of planes lying one behind the other. In this case, all the conditions are present that accompany normal plastic vision, but the convergent movement of the eyes is lacking.

Soon, however, we learn to forget this deficiency, for other features come to our aid, which enable us to see objects as spatial magnitudes and not as surfaces, and this without our eyes converging. We may sum up these features—penumbræ, shadows, etc.—as object-signs. How great is the effect of object-signs can be shown by a well-known physiological experiment ; on any coin it is possible to make the relief appear as a concavity, and vice versa, if, unknown to the observer, we reverse, by means of a mirror, the way the light falls.

Moreover, in looking through the stereoscope, we must first acquire plastic vision by supplying the lack of convergent movement with object-signs.

In such cases we have to do only with the symphony of space-magnitudes : and here we must draw attention to a further peculiarity of the human eye which has far-reaching consequences. In the distribution of the nervous areas for the local signs, our retina shows a clear division into an upper and a lower half. The half that we chiefly use, since our sight is essentially concerned with objects on the ground, shows a greater wealth in local signs than the half we use for looking at the sky. That is why still, inland lakes, in which the surrounding trees are clearly reflected, produce such a fairy-like impression ; in the reflection, the trees appear richer in detail and therefore higher and the sky seems further off, because the images of these things are perceived by a greater number of local signs than in direct vision

The peculiar shape of the firmament, which rises steeply from the horizon and then flattens out into the form of a watch-glass, depends on the same thing.

In the blue and cloudless sky, devoid of all the object-signs that would make us aware of the curve, we see, if we look at it through our hollowed hand, a level blue surface, always running parallel to the main direction-plane of our head. If, on the contrary, we see a bit of blue sky through a small window placed high up, the blue surface runs vertically downwards parallel to the window-frame.

The size of objects is just as dependent on how much of the whole field is visible. To illustrate this, we must retrace our steps a little.

In normal vision, what is presented to the eye is not all equally definite, for when the lens is focussed for distance, the outlines of objects close at hand are vague, and vice versa. If we focus our eyes first on the nearest objects, and then, little by little, on the more distant, the direction-signs that appear in the process give us the sensation of gliding into the depths, until the muscles are relaxed. As this happens, we perceive in succession object-signs which serve as indications of distance. But other special signs of distance come in, as Leonardo da Vinci long ago pointed out. For instance, the gradually increasing admixture of white with all the other colours serves as a criterion of distance.

When the muscles are quite relaxed, then, thanks to the distance-signs, objects very far off appear to lie not all in one plane but placed behind one another.

The eye, when it is looking, always tries to penetrate into the furthest distance until the limit of all object-signs is reached; and it stops there only because it must This uttermost, objectless region which surrounds the whole visible world, is never the horizon, but always lies beyond that. On a dark night, the sky may be the limit ; but by day that very seldom happens, for as soon as the firmament appears as a definite covering, we seek behind it the region without objects.

This region devoid of objects comes most clearly to our consciousness when we look at the starry sky on a dark night , then it spreads out immediately behind the stars as the final and invisible.

It is not empty space, for even empty space is filled with

our direction-signs. The space of the direction-signs is, in its very nature, a magnitude of motion, whereas the objectless offers us the absolute calm that we are forever seeking behind all motion.

The objectless is not the form of the direction-signs, but of pure local signs,—i.e. it is the extended.

The absolutely motionless, extended objectless is not nothingness, for nothingness has no extension ; it corresponds rather to the Buddhist's Nirvana It is invisible and non-apprehensible, yet of necessity always present, and it has immense value as "atmosphere," since it serves as background for all form and all motion, a background towards which the seeking eye ever strives.

The extended is always felt to be the same distance away, and so it serves as a fixed basis from which our eye can estimate the magnitudes of space. When we look around us at a varied landscape, the horizon and the sky which rises up from it seem on different sides to be set at very different distances from us. Sometimes the difference in the distance is so great that we imagine the whole sky must be gathered into folds.

When we ask how it comes that, on one side the horizon is so near, and, on the other so far away, we can prove to ourselves that this difference lies in the object-signs being relatively few or many.

Every traveller must have noticed that a high snow-peak seen from afar over a wide plain seems relatively small, and he surveys all its foot-hills and narrow valleys as though they were mere ridges and cracks in the mountain-base If he goes away from the mountain and follows up a narrow valley, the snow-peak begins to rise up above him to unsuspected heights

In Naples I have often been much struck by noticing that Vesuvius, as seen in its full extent across that incomparable bay from the heights of Posilippo, seems very far off and not remarkably high. If, on the other hand, one turns into a street that leads towards Vesuvius, the mountain is suddenly quite close at hand and of gigantic size.

We get a most disconcerting effect of this kind if from Monte Pincio we turn our eyes towards St Peter's, far away across the great expanse of Rome with all its countless streets, palaces, piazzas and bridges. Then the great church appears to rise in the far distance not so very high above the Eternal City. But if we step back about fifteen metres from the balustrade, so that, for our eyes focussed on the distance, it is brought into sharp relief and at the same time covers the town, then almost immediately behind it the magnificent building rises up in overwhelming size. At the same time the horizon also seems to come nearer.

Now, in all these cases, it is not the retinal image of the object that has become larger ; it has actually become smaller . and yet, in spite of that, the object appears to us nearer and larger. Nor has it moved away from the horizon ; the horizon has approached us along with it. What has happened is that the object has moved away from the extended and objectless, towards which it now stands in a new relation.

Since it is without objects, the extended possesses no sort of feature by which we can measure its magnitude or divide it up into parts. It has the effect always of an indivisible whole, to which different objects stand in different relations The observer, however, is always at the same distance from the extended. If the objects change their distance from the observer, then, according to the number of distance-signs they present, their relation to the extended simultaneously changes

The extended has no definite order of magnitude, but is in itself magnitude. Everything that approaches it, or seems to approach it, must consequently get smaller and smaller.

When we look at it in this way, we begin to understand

the otherwise mysterious fact that the rising moon appears large while it forms part of the horizon, but after it has risen and taken its place in the plane of the stars, which is so near the extended, it may shrink to a quarter the size it was at first.

Between our ego, which has no extension at all, and the absolute magnitude of the extended (as the pure form of the local-sense) which embraces the whole world-picture, space lies outspread, as the absolute possibility of motion. All three factors—the ego, space and the extended—are pure forms of intuition, which stand throughout in close relation to one another, and form, as it were, the scaffolding for the whole of intuition. As such, they constitute a unified, indivisible whole, invisible, it is true, but, by means of laws, fitting into its set forms all that our eye can see.

Beginning with ourselves, there are three phases of vision by means of which we penetrate space—(1) the phase of plastic vision, which lasts so long as the convergent move-ments of the eyes are appreciable, (2) the phase of direct spatial vision, while the accommodation-muscles remain active and direction-signs enable us to perform movements in the third dimension, and (3) the phase of indirect spatial vision, in which, for estimating distance, we rely on the indications offered by object-signs and distance-signs.

Now, since object-signs were made use of even in the first phase to form material shapes, when they appear alone, as in the third phase, they create there also the plastic forms of objects. Thus the whole of space appears filled with plastic objects, even to its furthermost limits, where the world of objects ends and the extended begins

Since it is a form of intuition, the frame of the extended adapts itself to every kind of vision and without altering its own size, whether we observe the starry heaven with the naked eye, or with a huge telescope screw down the moon and stars towards ourselves. When we do this, we increase only the image on the retina ; our relation to the extended remains what it was

This way of regarding the universe is essentially different from that of the astronomers, who merely pile up infinite space around us By so doing, they disintegrate the unity of the cosmic picture and substitute a dead abstraction for the living reciprocal action of intuition.

The extended forms, as it were, the invisible canvas on which the panorama of the world surrounding each one of us is painted, for it gives harmony and form to the local signs which bear the colours. Vis-à-vis of the world-panorama there is no other standpoint than that of our own subject, for the subject, while observer, is at the same time the builder of his world. An objective picture of the world that shall fit all subjects equally well is of necessity impossible.

THE SPACE OF ANIMALS

The biologist will find much interest in applying to animals what he has learned from study of human beings, and in asking himself the question, " What does the space look like that surrounds animals ? "

He cannot do as the physicist, i e. regard the space of human beings as the only reality and, without more ado, transplant animals into that he must make a detailed inquiry concerning the factors from which the space is composed where lives the particular animal he is studying at the moment In order to do this, he must first make a clear diagram of the visual space of a human being, and this diagram can then be modified according to the faculties of the animal under investigation

To make this diagram, stick together three circular pieces of card-board at right angles to one another, to represent

the three planes of direction. Around the point of intersection of the three planes place a number of increasingly
larger and larger hollow spheres. The small spheres nearest
to the centre are very close to one another. With the size of
the spheres, the distance between them increases, until the
last and largest stand quite by themselves. The distance
from one sphere to the next represents in each case a " step-
into-distance " Near the eye this is short, while direction-
signs got by convergent movement of the eyes permit us to
estimate the distance exactly. The step-into-distance becomes longer in the region which is sensed only by the aid of
the direction-signs of the muscles of accommodation : it
becomes very long as soon as criteria of distance alone can
be made use of in forming the estimate. Since the step-
into-distance stands for the interval recognisable at a given
moment between two points in the dimension of depth,
it does not matter by what means the measurement is
carried out.

Each sphere has just as many places on it as there are
local signs available Hence there are much fewer to the
same surface of the larger and more distant spheres than
there are on the smaller ones close at hand The number
of the angles at the centre is fixed by the local signs, and
the angle determines the size of surface on the various sphere-
planes.

While the same " place " in space means a series of tiny
surfaces lying one behind the other on all the spheres (and
present in equal number on all of them), the " position "
determines where the " place " lies on any one sphere. The
point in space which has both place and position is fixed with
certainty, (1) by the number of spheres (or steps-into-distance)
that lie between it and the centre, and (2) by the number of
places (or smallest surfaces) that separate it from the nearest
planes of direction : this number gives at the same time the

number of direction-steps for the human eye when it is moving.

This is how space appears as we make use of it in vision. But since we are able to transfer ourselves in thought with this intuited space to every place we look at, we transform space into a continuous series of places Space as we think of it is the space with which the physicist deals, while intuited space as we look at it is the space of the biologist. The two are fundamentally different from one another

It is only intuited space that comes into consideration in investigating animals. We shall try to decide whether animals have three, two or one plane of direction, or whether they have none at all and perhaps substitute for them the line of the horizon. Further, we shall investigate the means which animals have at their disposal for making steps-into-distance. Lastly, we must discover the number and the distribution of the places in animal space. Only when all these factors are known, can we affirm that we have gained an insight into the spatial world of animals.

Every spatial animal world, however limited as regards places and steps-into-distance, and even though it be without planes of direction, is nevertheless surrounded by the pure extended, which, as necessary form, precedes all space-creating. The extended lies immediately behind the last step-into-distance. So the space peculiar to each animal, wherever that animal may be, can be compared to a soap-bubble which completely surrounds the creature at a greater or less distance. The soap-bubble of the extended constitutes for the animal the limit of what for it is finite, and therewith the limit of its world ; what lies behind that is hidden in infinity.

In entering on the attempt to establish these matters concerning the space of animals, we make no declaration as to the manner in which the animal consciously intuits space

—such speculations are left to the psychologist : we restrict ourselves to the forms of space-intuition to which we, as observers, are confined

MATTER AND FORCE IN SPACE

Normally the three phases of spatial vision shade into one another by imperceptible degrees   As regards the first two phases, this is at once understandable, for while the eyes are performing their convergent movements, the accommodation-apparatus is also in action, so that things seen as solid bodies may be brought into the right distance.

But both kinds of activity have their limits, and if the axes of the eyes are parallel and the accommodation-muscles are relaxed, object-signs and distance-signs must come in, in order to make spatial vision for long distance possible. These signs owe their existence to no special arrangement of the optical apparatus, but have to be acquired by us through oft-repeated experience ; sometimes they must even be learnt anew   I remember very well how, the first time I went out after a severe attack of typhoid fever, the street, at about fifteen or twenty paces in front of me, swayed to and fro like a great, flat, gaily-painted plate   Houses, trees and people, although of different sizes, and the sky with them, lay all in the same plane, and seemed to hang free in space.

Only by degrees did they separate from one another, and the extended, which connècted them together, moved back to the outermost limits of space.   The explanation of this was that my glance, passing from the nearer objects to the more remote, was hampered within the space of accommodation through perpetual re-focussing by the muscles of accommodation, and when it had to deal with more distant objects, seemed, thanks to their distance-signs, to come up against fresh resistance.

In doing this, my normal vision was restored—the sort of vision that corresponds to a movement of touch by the hand as it comes against objects, now close by, now further away ; as it does so, the direction-signs orientate us as to the position of the obstacles in space. With our glance, as with our hand, we come up against more and more remote obstructions until we get to the horizon, behind which lies the extended, offering no resistance.

In our visual space every coloured surface, of whatever kind it may be, constitutes a check, lying either close at hand or far away. All arouse the same sensation, namely that of an obstacle, like the resistances which present themselves to the groping hand   In virtue of this, they get the character of material things, which, taken generally, mean nothing but actual obstructions.

And so it comes about that we describe as substances all things that prove their reality as obstacles. Without prejudice to this common property of all forms of matter, the various substances can evoke the most manifold qualities of the senses of sight and touch. And since we project all the other sense-qualities as well, and comprehend all their effects as coming to us from the outside, we connect these likewise with the forms of matter in space, as the only realities known to us outside those residing in our own subject.

The content of the space surrounding us consists of motion and resistance. The localising of the various resistances is necessary for the movement of our own body in space. It is much more important than an awareness of objects. For each rapid movement we must have accurate information as to the place where a resistance lies, if we are not to injure ourselves ; and we will avoid an apparent obstacle rather than come up against a real one.

We are not yet ready to discuss accurate conception of form, for that pertains to the construction of objects. All we have to do is to get quite clear as to which places in space are filled with resistance and which are not.

The resistances in space are all resistances of bodies, i.e. they are three-dimensional. They all, without exception, have a body, quite independently of the qualities they possess Therefore they may all be described as collections of material points or atoms. How the atoms are referable to local signs has already been discussed.

Matter is always in motion, and since substances cannot all be at the same time in the same place—i.e. cannot possess the same local signs—they get in one another's way, and, in their movements, mutually influence one another.

We are able to resolve movements into series of direction-signs ; and so, if we regard only their spatial character and neglect their other qualities, it is possible to refer all sub-stances to local signs and direction-signs. The great advan-tage of this is that all reciprocal actions of substances in space can be measured and reckoned, and can be brought under mathematical formulæ.

Physics has striven towards this goal, with admirable results. It has succeeded in subjecting to its mathematical formulæ the reciprocal action of all the qualities of matter, in so far as these are of a spatial nature.

Physics succeeded first with sounds, because matter was present in the form of air, the movements of which carried the waves of sound from place to place, and made it possible to convert the theory of sound into a theory of air-vibrations. Indeed, Helmholtz went so far as to explain dissonances as perturbations of the sine-waves. In so doing, he transgressed the limits set him by the spatial factors. The effects of sound-qualities on the subject have their own par-ticular laws, which have absolutely nothing to do with the laws of space ; and it is these, and these only, that can be formulated mathematically.

It was more difficult to bring colours under mathematical formulæ . that became possible only when physicists assembled under the concept of "light" the spatial influencing of coloured surfaces on one another, and in addition discovered the ether, a new medium, constructed on the analogy of air, and transmitting light-waves.

Newton had got out of the difficulty in a more primitive manner, by assuming that little coloured spherules were projected through space. The ether, however, proved itself a much better aid to the analysis of the action of light.

As we have already shown, the subjective effects of colour can never be referred to spatial laws, because they have laws of their own ; and only a thorough-going separation of the spatial laws of light from the subjective laws of colour can obviate the confusion still prevailing in optics.

With the help of the ether it also became possible to bring under observation the spatial laws of heat. As concerns the subjective laws of heat, we owe our information to Johannson Heat consists of three qualities—warm, cold and hot If part of our skin is touched simultaneously by two objects, one of which calls forth the sensation "warm" and the other that of "cold," the sensation "hot" results.

From this we may conclude that we have only two nerve-ending apparatuses in our skin—one for warm and one for cold,—and that the combined simultaneous stimulation of both produces "hot." Of this subjective law, the physicist knows nothing, and moreover it is not necessary that he should ; he is concerned with investigating the radiation of heat,—i.e. with etheric vibrations or the conduction of heat.

As regards the phenomenon of smell, the theory of emergent, chemically active spherules is still held, because the air-currents determine their path. Their subjective effects, i.e. odours, consist, as with the qualities of taste, in the drowning of one quality by another.

The hypothesis of the ether has had very important consequences, for it has enabled us to bring together under law actions in space that would otherwise have remained inexplicable—as, for instance, in the theory of electricity and magnetism   But we must not forget that the assumption of a medium that binds together everything in space is in no way a necessary postulate for the biological theory of space. Local signs may quite well be connected by direction-signs alone, without its being necessary to fill in the gaps with local signs transformed into atoms, which is the purpose served by the etheric medium.

It is important to establish this, for, in the theory of gravitation, the hypothesis of the connecting medium has completely broken down, and we have got no further than the action of masses at a distance, according to Newton.

Undoubtedly, physics has succeeded in referring to local signs and direction-signs almost all the spatial actions of matter, since it banished from its calculations (though only with very great difficulty) a quality which in the beginning was regarded as the cause of all material activities, namely, " force."

Force is primarily nothing but a sensation that is connected with the movements of our muscles. As an inevitable conclusion, the muscular sensation was exalted into the cause of the movement of our limbs, and then transformed into the cause of all movements whatsoever.

When we lift an object, we measure our force by the muscular sensation, but we also ascribe to the object an equal and opposite force, which we overcome.

For a long time, physics worked with the concept of force as the cause of motion and as the cause of the inhibition of motion. Weight, elasticity and hardness were defined as forces. Moreover, there were forces of chemical tension, magnetic and electrical forces   A non-spatial quality was thereby brought into spatial activities, and this enormously increased the difficulty of defining concept clearly.

Only through the explanation that motion was the sole cause of motion was the concept of force gradually eliminated from physics. The word itself fell out of use, and in its place was substituted the word *energy*, which merely indicates the kind of motion   The movements of substances carried out in space were described as kinetic energy ; by potential energy, we understand motion stored up within substances.

The law of the conservation of energy completed the theoretical basis of physics, for it cleared the domain appertaining to that science of all that was extraneous, and taught us to regard all material activities in space as isolated and thus accessible to mathematical formularisation.

Since the physico-chemical laws are, jointly and severally, spatial in kind, it is only for practical reasons that I have hitherto opposed them to the subjective laws of the domains of sense : I certainly do not wish to ascribe to them any higher reality, for that they do not possess. By referring material processes to local signs and direction-signs, the subjective nature even of these phenomena is demonstrated beyond question, and the place of the so-called objective natural sciences within biology becomes evident.

Henceforth we are in a position to repudiate easily the contention of the materialists or monists, which claims that in the world there are only two realities—force and matter. For if they are asked why local signs and direction-signs should be more real than colours and sounds, they will certainly not be able to give any answer. Biology is quite able to save the world from sinking to the low level to which blind overestimation of physics is trying to reduce it.

OBJECTIVE AND SUBJECTIVE

As we advance, oui investigations increasingly compel us to seek a clear definition of the concepts " objective " and " subjective."

We have shown that, in Kant's sense, there is no such thing as absolute space on which our subject is without influence. For both the specific material of space, namely local signs and direction-signs, and the form this material assumes, are subjective creations. Without the spatial qualities and the bringing of them together into their common form that apperception makes possible, there would be no space at all, but merely a number of sense-qualities, such as colours, sounds, smells, and so forth ; these would, of course, have their specific forms and laws, but there would be no common arena in which they could all play their part

We may satisfy ourselves as to this, and yet the distinction between objective and subjective has a real meaning, even if it be admitted from the first that there is no such thing as absolute objectivity.

Even if we were cognisant of our subjective direction-signs which accompany the movements of our muscles, we should know nothing of an objective world, but would be surrounded merely by a subjective space.

Music furnishes us with a means of making a representation of subjective space. When we are so much under the influence of music that, forgetting the origin of the sounds and whether they come from this instrument or that, we give ourselves up to the rhythm, the subjective direction-sounds are aroused in us without there being any accompanying movement of our body ; and these, together with the sounds, seem to fill the space belonging to them.

It was Helmholtz who once pointed out that music creates sensations of movement ; and in all languages the popular

D

description of sounds as " high " and " low " bears this
out.

In order to make very vivid what is meant by existence in
subjective space, let us think of ourselves as condemned to
move by swimming about in water, without eyes or organs of
touch. In such a case, we should learn nothing from our
swimming movements beyond the changing claims of our
subjective direction-signs ; we should learn absolutely nothing
about forward movement in space.

Now if we imagine ourselves as having an eye that can
release colour-sensations but not local signs, still that would
alter nothing with regard to subjective space ; the sensations
of red, green, blue and yellow would indeed arise, but the
colours would remain properties of our subject, and the inner
world of the subject means likewise the world as a whole.
We ourselves would be emitting simultaneously sound and
colour and filling the whole of space with our person. It
would be impossible to draw a distinction between thoughts
and feelings, on the one hand, and sense-perceptions on the
other, because the latter could not become properties of
objects. We should then be solipsists, in the real sense of
the word.

As soon as local signs appear, the world is transformed
in a flash ; space acquires places to which colours can attach
themselves, and from the sensations of colour develop coloured
surfaces. No longer do colours appear and then disappear, as
our eye roams to and fro. The red circle over there remains
red, even if we are no longer looking directly at it. And by
so doing, it has acquired an objective existence independent of
the optical activity of the subject ; on the other hand, it
remains dependent on its position in a space that has now
become objective

The same thing happens with the other sense-qualities.
The red circle that we touch remains hard, even when we no

longer put out our hand towards it. It loses neither resonance nor flavour nor scent when we turn our attention towards other things. Even our own body receives a definite position in space, which it can alter by moving the limbs in a certain way.

While our body becomes objective in this way, like all other objects of the external world, our ego remains of necessity subjective ; for the ego, as the unity of apperception which builds up all the qualities into higher organisations, cannot have so much as a single local sign of its own

On the other hand, it is conceivable that our thoughts and feelings, which we group together as a whole under the name of soul, might bear local signs, for they also are stirred up by outside impressions, like the melodies and harmonies that we construct from hearing sounds. If this were the case, then with it the contrast between body and soul would disappear, a contrast which indeed does not exist in the subjective world It is a mistake to maintain that the soul must be entirely non-spatial, for many of our feelings—such, for instance, as longing—readily connect themselves with subjective direction-signs, and so enter subjective space. If thoughts and feelings had local signs as well, we should be able to develop an objective science of the soul, in addition to the subjective.

From all of which it is possible to derive, as sharply and clearly as we could desire, the definition we have been seeking for " objective " and " subjective." Every quality is objective only so long as it remains in connection with a local sign ; it becomes subjective as soon as this connection is broken. The local sign, when considered by itself, is purely subjective ; as soon as it enters into association with any quality whatsoever, it becomes objective place

CHAPTER II

TIME

THE MOMENT-SIGN

JUST as certainly as that there is no such thing as absolute space, so also is it certain that there is no such thing as absolute time ; for both space and time are merely forms of our human intuition.

But we have been able to show that it is nevertheless possible to maintain a distinction between objective and subjective space, by introducing the possession of local signs as the distinguishing feature.

We must now ask ourselves whether it is possible to establish the same difference for time. The advance we have made beyond Kant's doctrine consists essentially in the discovery of specific spatial qualities (local signs and direction-signs), and in the recognition that space is the form of its own material, just as the musical scale represents the form of the specific material of sounds.

For the discovery of a specific material for time we are indebted to K E. von Baer, who based his brilliant exposition concerning the subjective character of time on the moment as the specific time-quality Felix Gross has revealed the close connection between time and apperception, and we are now in a position to form for ourselves a clear picture of the nature of time.

Apperception is a life-process, carried out in phases, each of which manifests itself through a sense-sign ; this sign is the moment.

We must therefore employ the word moment-sign`
According to Kant, the unity of the apperception creates the
unity of our ego, which, although destitute of local signs, is
always furnished with a moment-sign.' As a consequence, all
psychic processes, feelings and thoughts are invariably bound
to a definite moment and proceed contemporaneously with
the objective sensations. Time envelops both subjective
and objective worlds in the same way, and, unlike space,
makes no distinction between them.

In order to understand in what respect we can nevertheless
distinguish between subjective and objective in time, we must
try to penetrate deeper into the nature of the moment-sign.

We have taken the local sign to be the smallest spatial
magnitude into which the various qualities were poured in
order to give us the atom : in like manner, we may compare ˥
the moment-signs with the smallest receptacles that, by being
filled with a content of various qualities, become converted
into moments as they are lived. Like the local sign, the
moment-sign remains constant in its magnitude and intensity,
changing only in its content.

We might be led to suppose that the content of the
moment-signs would distinguish between' their objective or
subjective character This is never the case. I may give
myself up to my thoughts, or plunge into contempla-
tion of a landscape , I may even engage in observation of
the movements of men and animals—the time that elapses
while I am thus occupied is always subjective. This indeed
is not surprising, for the same process of apperception is gone
through on each occasion, and with it appear its moment-
signs.

For whether we are looking at objects or formulating
thoughts, the same business of construction is initiated for
the forming of higher unities from simpler elements.

The duration of time that has passed—i e the length of

the series of moment-signs—we estimate with more or less
exactness ; but as soon as we turn our attention to a sound
repeating itself in the outside world, the degree of exactness
increases enormously. By contrasting them, we can then
estimate with unfailing certainty the number of unaccented
moment-signs (the so-called intervals) that lie between those
that are accented.

This enables us to set about making an exact measurement of time from a change of sound in the outside world ;
and when we have found it to be constant, there is nothing to
prevent us from employing this change of sounds as a time-
measurement in its turn. Even at the present day, watch-
makers correct by means of accented moment-signs the swing
of pendulum-clocks, which we then use to measure time.

We can also replace the external change of sound by
innervating our own muscles at equal intervals, dividing the
moment-signs into accented and unaccented by our own
regularly interrupted movement. We call this " beating
time."

Beating time is a subjective kind of time-measuring
which makes very great demands on the attention ; therefore
as a rule we rely on a change of sound that is independent of
our own effort, such as the stroke of the second pendulum,
which we describe as an objective measurer of time   Objective time-measurement has thrust subjective into the background in such a way that we have come to regard even
time itself as an objective phenomenon, and naturally this has
given rise to very serious mistakes.

Always and in every connection, time remains subjective,
since it is bound up with the process of apperception ; it is
only the measurement of time that can be termed objective,
in the case where the accentuation of the time-signs results
from a change in sound independent of our own activity.

The behaviour of a conductor and his orchestra will serve

as an interesting illustration of this   The conductor depends
for guidance entirely on his own subjective time-measurement, which he retards or accelerates by altering the intervals
and moving his bâton now quicker, now slower   The bâton
serves as an objective time-measurer for the instrumentalists,
and according to it they have to direct the bowing of the
violins and the blowing of the horns.

The ability to separate accurately the accented moment-
signs from the unaccented, and to vary this change itself, is
very differently developed in different people ; and this is
the reason why all men are not fitted to become conductors
of orchestras.

NUMBER

Every one possesses the power of beating time, even if
only in a primitive form, and this power is the basis of com-
putation   We are able to combine the individual time-beats
into groups, and to free them from one another in other groups.
In this respect also there are great differences in natural
talent.   There are people, wrongly called " lightning cal-
culators," who have a marked gift for constructing very
extensive and complicated groups.   This power has nothing
to do with real arithmetic, for real calculation depends on a
conscious working with numbers and not on a grouping
of beats

Number is not an inborn natural creation, but an artificial
product of the human mind, and it consists of an objective
sign with which we describe the individual beats, just as a
letter of the alphabet serves as the visible sign for a certain
sound.

In the beginning, number may have arisen by a man's
scratching lines alongside one another in the sand with his
hand as it beat time.   For even to-day, every school-child
begins in this way when he writes strokes on the slate at his

first arithmetic lesson. By doing so, we succeed in making a
connecting-link between the magnitudes of time and those of
space, and we call this connecting-link " number."   For just
as the beat consists in the alternation of accented with unaccented moment-signs, so the row of strokes consists likewise
of accented and unaccented local signs   The series of Roman
numerals approaches the original type most nearly, except that
in it every fifth stroke has a special shape, so as to facilitate
by group-formation a rapid comprehensive survey.   The series
of Arabic numerals has a special sign for each stroke from 1 to
9, and thereby offers important advantages for group-formation   For each Arabic numeral signifies not merely a certain
stroke in the series, but also the whole group beginning with
the first and ending with the stroke in question

It is interesting to find that, at first, group-forming by
writing lingered behind group-forming by special words for
the numbers ; for spoken Latin, unlike written, possessed ten
different designations for the numbers from 1 to 10.

The method often employed for giving children an idea of
number by beginning with objects is really too circuitous.   If
one tries to teach a child that 3 apples and 1 pear together
are 4 fruits, that may only lead to confusion ; for what the
child really ought to learn—namely, to combine in groups its
own regularly recurrent activity—is made more difficult for
it by having its attention turned from the subjective beat to
objective things

The following will help us to a more profound understanding of the processes described.

If you consider the numerical series represented by any
long row of strokes as the symbol for a series of beats which
can be extended at will, it becomes evident that the making
of numbers even in this elementary form requires very great
abstraction.

Let us inquire how this abstraction is effected   On the

one hand we have a sound recurring at intervals ; on the other, an optical phenomenon, the stroke, likewise recurring at intervals What common basis admits of these two things being interchangeable ?

It is evident that what they have in common can only be the same change in the process of apperception, a change which appears both when we hear and when we look at written strokes. Since the process of apperception always releases a series of moment-signs, in both cases a change in the filling up of the moment-signs must appear. No attention is given to the fact that the content of the moment-signs is very different in the two cases ; all that is felt as the same subjective act is the regular alternation of filling up and emptying the moment-signs.

The same subjective act also appears when we innervate our muscles in beating time. In the course of apperception, it always happens that certain moment-signs are noted especially. We call this power of noting certain moment-signs more than others, " attention." And since we describe as rhythm any regularly recurring change whatsoever, we may in the last instance refer the power to form numbers to a rhythm of the attention. Now, according to the length of the interval, there are very different kinds of rhythm, which we distinguish from one another and are able to combine into unities. The so-called lightning-calculators have this faculty in an especially high degree.

To our attention it is a matter of indifference towards what sort of content it is directed—whether on objects, or sensations, or feelings. As soon as there appears a regular change in the attention, it can be subjected to the rule of the simplest rhythm, i.e. it can be counted This peculiarity gives to number its almost unlimited applicability.

CALCULATING AND ESTIMATING

Since it is possible to count up everything of which we can so much as form a thought, the resulting confusion has led to the development of the art of arithmetic, the first principle of which requires that we shall reckon together only those things that have the same denominator Thus it is inadmissible to add $\frac{1}{2}$ and $\frac{1}{4}$; $\frac{1}{2}$ must first be transformed into $\frac{2}{4}$, and then we may calculate that $\frac{1}{4}$ and $\frac{2}{4} = \frac{3}{4}$.

In the same way, we must not count up 3 apples and 1 pear straight away. The apples and pears must first of all be brought under the same conception of " fruit " ; then we may calculate that 3 fruits and 1 fruit = 4 fruits

So it appears that calculation is not merely a summing-up of the rhythms of the attention ; it also has regard to the content of the things to which the attention, stimulated by rhythm, is turned. Only by assuming like content can we institute a calculation having any real sense.

We take as the common denominator of regular movements the direction-sign ; as the smallest magnitude of movement that remains always constant. It is quite indifferent what name we give to the direction-sign.

The difficulty is greater when we try to subject to calculation regularly increasing intensity of a sensation. If, for instance, we hold a pail under a tap, we feel the steady increase in the weight ; we can estimate it approximately, but we are quite unable to calculate it. Even if we let the water run in intermittently, that does not help us, for, each time, the estimation of the increase in weight is so uncertain that we dare not use it as the common denominator for calculation

Weber has helped us out of this predicament in an ingenious way, by employing as the common denominator the feeling of just perceptible increase in weight and introducing for it the concept of " threshold." By so doing, he has

been able to compare subjective sensation of weight with
the objective process, and to set up a fundamental law. It can
be shown, that is to say, that the same amount of water
poured in by no means always corresponds to the same threshold, but that the amount of water required to overcome the
threshold increases proportionally to what has been poured
into the pail. If, for instance, there was one cubic decimetre
in the pail, the addition of only one cubic centimetre was
necessary to overcome the swell ; if there were already two
cubic decimetres of water in the pail, two cubic centimetres
would be required for doing the same thing.

The law according to which the threshold increases proportionally to the magnitude of the stimulus, finds its application in all the domains of sense, so long as the qualities undergo
any increase in their intensity.

FILLING UP THE MOMENT-SIGNS

In looking at a picture, it is important to choose our
position so that it corresponds to the position from which
the artist looked at his painting. Only then shall we employ
on the picture the same number of local signs as he himself
used. If we go to the right distance from the picture, the
objects represented in it seem to us correct ; that is to say,
they appear within the same optical angle as that in which
the painter looked at them It is this angle, however, that
decides the quantity of local signs stimulated.

If we go too near the picture, we see details that we are
meant to overlook, because we are using more local signs on the
representation than the painter used on the thing he was representing As a consequence, the picture gets broken up into
brush-strokes It is vain to expect that the object depicted
will display more intimate details than the actual object
itself does.

If the observer goes too far away, he loses details, for he now uses fewer local signs than the painter put there, and the full effect of the picture is not realised.

How is it that we can go so much closer to the pictures of the older Dutch school (from Van Eyck to Holbein) than the view-point of the painter permits, without what is represented being robbed of its verisimilitude ? And how comes it that the things represented, if we look at them from the right standpoint, seem much more real on the picture than the things themselves do, showing us details much better than we could detect them at a corresponding distance ?

My answer to such questions is that these great painters had at their disposal a much larger number of local signs than we This enabled them to break up the world into a much greater number of " places," and these furnished them with many more object-signs The world of these artists was larger and richer than ours.

On the other hand, it is undeniable that, with the work of some of the more modern painters, the man looking at the picture can see nothing but brush-strokes, from which, even with the best will in the world, he is unable to form objects. Putting aside cases of sheer arbitrariness, this can only mean that the painter has fewer local signs than the observer.

Let us assume that the observer has 10 visual cones to a square millimetre of retina, and that each of these cones stimulates one local sign ; then the painter of the rich world would have 100 cones to the same unit of surface, and the painter of the poor world only 1.

The aim of all this argument is merely to make it easier for us to use the same ideas with regard to time ; and we shall now proceed to do so We have seen that the same picture of the world, when broken up into more numerous places, must of necessity be richer and larger ; in like manner, life must be appraised, not according to the number of years that it covers, but by the number of moments lived through. The life of two human beings who were born on the same day and who died on the same day, may be very different as regards duration and in richness in experience, even if their fates be identical. Let us take an instance. While the second-pendulum swings to and fro once, A lives through 10 moments, B, on the other hand, through 20 ; the life of B will accordingly last twice as long and will be twice as full as the life of A.

If we assume that the stimulation of the moment-sign is connected with the combustion of a certain quantity of oxygen in the brain, then A burns up his oxygen more slowly than B

As the local sign represents for each human being the absolute measure for space, so the moment-sign gives him the absolute measure for time   It is only when we compare two individuals with one another that the two measures become relative ; but we must not conclude from this that there is such a thing as a real space with its absolute measurement, and a real time with absolute measurement. The attempt to introduce absolute space and absolute time comes from the observer who is investigating the relativity of two subjects necessarily taking as the basis of comparison his own time and his own space.

The illusion of absolute time is heightened by objective measurement of time, which tries to read off from the same clock everything that happens in the world from the Pole-star to the Southern Cross. As is well known, the most modern physical theories have shaken this doctrine to its foundation.

K. E. von Baer has given us a very striking description of the change that would come over our picture of the world if the number of our moments, which at present extends over 80 solar years, held the content of only eight years, or of one year, or of one day, or of one hour ; and of what would become of our knowledge of the world we live in, if the same number of moment-signs had to cope with the content of from 800 to 8000 solar years.

These speculations of von Baer's teach us that, assuming sensory activity to remain unchanged, our world of movement would come to a standstill, if its duration were abbreviated or lengthened beyond a certain point.

Let us take as an example the spoke of a wheel, the turning of which we can clearly recognise, and let us first slow down the motion, and then speed it up. The movement is of the same kind throughout, but in the first case we accompany it with many moment-signs and in the second with few ; nevertheless, in both the movement ceases. If the spoke goes round as slowly as the minute-hand of a watch, it seems to stand still all the time, because the change in its position is so slight that we do not perceive it   If we let the spoke whirl round very quickly, we see nothing in the wheel but a uniform clear area, which, as the revolutions continue, persists as a sort of thin veil.

The same thing would result if we were to crowd the world phenomena into very short duration, or if we were to stretch them out very greatly, so that in the first case they were framed, as it were, by too many moment-signs, and in the other by too few.   If there are too many frames, the pictures that succeed one another are too much alike ; if there are too few, the content of many pictures is squeezed into one.   In the first case, a ball thrown into the air would stand still ; in the second, the sun would describe a gleaming curve across the sky.

The rule runs as follows :—a moment ceases to be perceived if its gradient is either too steep or too level

THRESHOLD

In order to expose the causes of these laws, we must have recourse to the idea of threshold, as originated by Weber. Threshold means the just perceptible difference between two intensities of a quality. It can be used in the same way, however, to mean the difference perceptible between two qualities. If we compare together two adjacent local signs, it appears that the difference between them is so slight as to be inappreciable, i.e. it lies below the threshold. If that were not so, and if each local sign lay alongside the next without there being any intermediate steps, the whole world would consist of coloured points It is only because the difference between two adjacent local signs is imperceptible that the world-picture is continuous, for continuity means nothing but an imperceptible transition, in contrast to one that is abrupt.

The same holds good for direction-signs, whether they be objective or subjective It is merely because the difference between two adjacent direction-signs lies below the threshold that a movement appears to be continuous.

The continuity of time depends also on this state of things. If the moment-signs were perceptibly separated from one another, our life would proceed by tiny, separate jerks.

For a continuous movement to be appreciable at all, several conditions must be fulfilled Not only must the movement include more than two direction-signs if it is to be perceptible, but the direction-signs must stand in the right relation to the moment-signs If all the direction-signs are comprehended within two moment-signs, then the whole path traversed is interpreted as a synchronous unity, and the movement is suppressed

But even if there be a sufficiently large number of moment-signs as well as of direction-signs, the movement may yet pass

unperceived ; as, for instance, when one direction-sign falls
on several moment-signs. The movement then remains below
the threshold, because the content of one moment-sign is not
appreciably distinguishable from that of its predecessor ; for
the observer, this means that nothing changes.

It is only when, in a series of moments, several direction-
signs coincide with one moment, that their content is differentiated and movement is perceived.

The rule that a movement is perceptible only when its
gradient is neither too steep nor too level, is rendered intelligible through the introduction of threshold ; moreover,
this concept makes it more clearly defined. Movement must
be slow enough for all the direction-signs to occur within
three moment-signs, and yet it must be fast enough for at
least two direction-signs to occur within each moment-sign.
If these conditions are unfulfilled, then no movement is
initiated ; everything is stationary.

CALCULATION OF THE RULE OF MOTION

In order to make susceptible of calculation the relations
between these fundamental qualities of space and time, it is
necessary to consider them as world-factors. So long as we
consider local signs, moment-signs and direction-signs as mere
qualities of our mind, they remain three non-comparable
magnitudes. But each of these elementary magnitudes has
its task to perform in the world, and then it comes into correlation with the other magnitudes, which can be expressed in
numbers.

For all three qualities, the task prescribed is the same.
Each serves as the smallest receptacle or the smallest frame
for other qualities which, only by being so enclosed, become
part of the cosmic system. Local, moment- and direction-
signs renounce all claim to being " content," and endow the

world with colour, scent and sound. It is entirely due to them
that an orderly construction of the world is possible ; and for /
that reason they may be called the elementary organisers of
the world. None of them ever alters in magnitude and
intensity ; and so they furnish us with, as it were, a stable
currency, which makes the world secure. This unchanging,
stable currency is the ideal denominator, employed in every
calculation concerned with measuring the world, whether as
regards space or time

It will make things clearer for us if, when we consider the
three qualities as elements of the mind, we employ a different
terminology from what we use when they are considered as
world-factors. We have already contrasted the place, as
the smallest indivisible world-factor, with the local sign
as the mental element ; in the same way we contrast the
moment with the moment-sign. It is only when we come
to the direction-sign that we find ourselves in a difficulty,
because the word " direction " does not contain the idea of a
very small entity. But since a series of direction-signs
signifies a definite progression in one direction, we can set
each direction-sign parallel with a step, and speak of direction-
steps. It is only close at hand that we are made aware of
direction-steps in the dimension of depth by means of direction-signs ; for greater distance we must make use of other
aids, such as distance-signs. Therefore it is appropriate in
such a case to speak of distance-steps.

Accordingly we shall describe moment, place and step as
the three factors of the cosmic order, to which in calculation
we must have recourse as the final, indivisible elements.

Since no one world is applicable generally, the three
world-factors have no universal value, but are restricted to
the special world of each subject ; and they must not be applied
directly from the world of one subject to that of another. In
order to make things more intelligible, we have made a kind

E

of compromise, and have chosen certain measurements of time and length, which we all employ in our own world as so-called objective measurements   If we are trying to get a real insight into the worlds of other subjects, we must each of us refer to these standard measurements the particular world-factors by which we measure things in our own world.

Since we are as yet without reliable measurements of the kind, I shall limit myself to indicating how, by means of the motion-formula, we may induce the length of the direction-step.   The length of the moment is estimated, on the average, as one-tenth of a second.   On the dial of a very large clock with minutes of one centimetre in length, the large hand begins to show appreciable movement when I am five metres from it.   Now, according to the rule of motion, at least two steps fall within one moment (= 0 1 seconds) ; so, if the movement is to be perceptible, in one centimetre 1200 must be made to the minute.   This gives 120 to the millimetre, and accordingly the length of each step is about 0·01 millimetre at a distance of five metres.

This is not the place in which to discuss the methods that enable us to make an exact measurement of the interval in space between one place and another, or the interval in time between one moment and another.   We shall merely point out that for the first time the possibility is indicated here of expressing in the conventional time- and length-measurements the absolute unity of measurement of the subjective worlds.

If we should succeed in bringing these absolute subjective measurements into harmony with the objective structure of our sense-organs, there would be some prospect of initiating, by a strictly scientific method, a comparative cosmology of human beings and the higher animals.   Let us take an instance.   Suppose that the distance from rod to rod in the human retina corresponds not only to the distance from one place to another, but also to the length of a direction-step in the human world, then a knowledge of the measurement-relations in the retina of an animal would give us a clue to the place, step and moment in the world of this particular kind of animal.

THE INFLUENCE OF ABSOLUTE WORLD-MEASUREMENTS ON OUR EXISTENCE

It is suggestive that, as the number of places in the world increases, so also does the size of the objects surrounding us, and their details correspondingly multiply. In such a case, the whole world seems to expand on all sides and become fuller We get some notion of this by looking through a magnifying-glass. But we must bear in mind that this artificial increase in size of individual objects takes place at the expense of their neighbours ; the magnification by the lens depends on small sections of the field of vision being perceived by more optical cones of the retina than in normal vision. If, for instance, I project the image of a horse-chestnut leaf on the visual surface of my retina, which normally would hold the entire tree, the tree itself will disappear from the field of view.

But that would not happen if I could give to my retina a correspondingly larger number of rods and cones. Then the whole section of space represented by the chestnut leaf would remain equally large in proportion to the whole optical surface, but it would include now as much detail as previously the whole tree did, and the tree itself would acquire a corresponding increase in detail.

In a world of such huge dimensions, crammed with innumerable details, quite valueless for the requirements of our existence, we should feel extremely ill at ease.

If we assume that the moments did not change, then the sun, whose forward gliding is, as things are, imperceptible to our eyes, would acquire colossal speed in order to cover, in the same length of time, the vast span of the heavens   The shadows of the giant trees would be in perpetual movement. The movements of all living objects would seem to us to be accelerated ; even the snails would hurry by at the speed of a trotting horse, and we ourselves would move about through this monstrous space as fast as express trains.

Assuming, on the other hand, that the moments correspondingly shortened, then all movements would remain of normal size, but for their execution the day would stretch out to excessive length, and soon we should no longer be able to cope with the strain imposed by this super-world.

If we imagine our powers also increased in the like direction, we should become super-men, as possibly—if but in a limited degree—the great artists and geniuses actually are.

Following up this line of argument, it is not difficult to construct for ourselves a picture of the " subter-man " with his miniature world.   And it would not be uninteresting to determine, by means of measurements, to which of the two types our individual fellow-men approximate most nearly.

In each case it will appear that the duration of the moment stands in close relation to the number of places and to the length of the direction-steps, and this relationship again depends on the power of the mind to form an estimate of the world.

How closely the world, in regard to its spatial and temporal dimensions, hangs together with our requirements and our faculties, can be demonstrated by innumerable examples I will refer to only one other instance—the beneficial effect it has on us that the tree-shadows in which we are resting also seem to be at rest ; on the other hand, every movement of the twigs produced by the wind or by a bird, reveals itself as a movement of the shadow, and awakens our attention   Thus what is going on close at hand is thrown into effective contrast with the repose that the imperceptible progress of the sun spreads over the world.

This connection, expressive of a plan, between the dimensions of the world, eternal both as to space and time, and our own everyday requirements, is easily explained if we remember that it is our own qualities which are the moment-signs, local signs and direction-signs providing the absolute measure for our world, and that eternity can be inferred from the form of the order-signs.

CHAPTER III

THE CONTENT-QUALITIES

THE POINT OF VIEW OF PHYSICS AND OF BIOLOGY

ACCORDING to the physicist, there is only one real world ; and this is not a world of appearance, but a world having its own absolute laws, which are independent of all subjective in-fluence   The world of the physicist consists (1) of places, the number of which is infinite, (2) of movements, the extent of which is unlimited, and (3) of moments, having a series without beginning or end. All other properties of things are referable to changes of place by the atoms.

The biologist, on the other hand, maintains that there are as many worlds as there are subjects, and that all these worlds are worlds of appearance, which are intelligible only in con-nection with the subjects.   The subjective world consists (1) of places, the number of which is finite, (2) of movements, the extent of which is limited, (3) of moments, in a series that has both a beginning and an end, and (4) of content-qualities, which are also fixed in number, and have laws which are likewise laws of Nature

For the biologist, the world of the physicist has only the value of a world created by thought ; such a world corre-sponds to no reality, but is to be considered as an indispensable aid to calculation, much as the logarithmic tables are, although logarithms admit of only a limited application.   To try to make use of logarithmic tables as an ethical law would seem as childish and absurd as Ostwald's attempt in Sunday sermons to exalt the laws of physics to the position of a moral ccde.

To the eye of the uninstructed man, all that is visible is his own world of appearances, enveloped in space and time, and filled with the things of sound and scent and colour. Scientific investigation attempts to influence this simple way of regarding the world, and from two opposite quarters. Physical theory tries to convince the plain man that the world he sees is full of subjective illusions, and that the only real world is much poorer, since it consists of one vast, perpetual whirl of atoms controlled by causality alone' On the other hand, the biologist tries to make the plain man realise that he sees far too little, and that the real world is much richer than he suspects, because around each living being an appearance-world of its own lies spread, which, in its main features, resembles his world, but nevertheless displays so much variation therefrom that he may dedicate his whole life to the study of these other worlds without ever seeing the end of his task

The laws connecting each subject with his appearance-world cannot be compassed by causality alone, but must be explained as conformity with plan. The distinguishing sign of this plan resident in every created thing, isolated within itself though it appears, finds expression in the saying, " All for each and each for all." Consequently, in considering a whole that is based on plan, it is immaterial where we begin. All things within it must react on one another. So we may begin either by studying subjects, or by investigating their appearance-worlds. The one could not exist without the other.

Now as soon as we have studied even a few animals long enough to show what is the world of appearance that surrounds them like a firm though invisible house of glass, we are enabled to fill the world around ourselves with a countless multitude of these iridescent worlds ; and this a thousandfold enriches our own, however full and varied it may be. And thus it is that biology can offer the plain man an unlimited enlargement of his world, whereas the physicist would reduce him to beggary.

THE FORM OF THE QUALITY-CIRCLES

A preliminary condition for the investigation of the appearance-worlds of others is an exact knowledge of our own. In the first chapter, which dealt with the spatial qualities, we succeeded in forming an idea of space that permitted us to describe around every animal a space like an invisible soap-bubble, within which all its activities were carried on. A number of fixed places give support for its sense-organs, and a definite number of direction-steps give the measurement of the magnitudes, and determine the movement of its limbs. The direction of movement is fixed, in many cases, by immutable direction-planes   The laws of the content-qualities of our mind are as changeless as the spatial laws of our appearance-world.

As has already been emphasised, by observing it in action, we can learn nothing as to the laws regulating our own mind. The activity of our qualities consists in constructing our appearance-world   Considered by themselves, all our qualities seem just a confused heap of building-materials, all more or less alike. The laws are revealed only when the work of construction is in progress.

When the content-qualities are fitted into the local signs, fixed places appear, having definite properties. And now the outline of a fundamental law is revealed. The " circles " of relationship, which were but faintly indicated in the original material, can be de-limited one from another. Each place, that is to say, can receive only one property from each quality-circle. A certain place may be blue-green, but never blue *and* green. It may be of medium hardness, but never both hard and soft ; it may be lukewarm, but never both hot and cold at the same time.

This circumstance (i.e. that at each place properties from all the relationship circles may be assembled, but never more than one single quality from each) shows that the qualities of each circle are connected together by law in such a way that the appearance of one quality excludes the simultaneous appearance of a related quality at the same place.

As soon as it enters into activity, the material of our mental qualities reveals a form governed by law, which form may enter into appearance along with space and time, or must especially be sought out for the content-qualities. Since only the form of the extensive quality-circles of the local signs and direction-signs is given by intuition, we must try to include within that extensive form the intensive quality-circles, in order to arrive at a clear idea of the laws governing them. To admit of comparison between the extensive qualities them-selves, we have already expressed in spatial terms the form of the moment-signs, which is not intuited ; and so we shall now attempt to represent in terms of space the other quality-circles likewise.

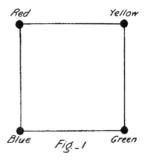

In looking for a spatial form for the laws obtaining in the quality-circle of colours, the best thing is to start with the spectrum of sunlight thrown by a prism. When we do this, four fixed points immediately strike our eye, at which certain colours emerge pure from the mixture. The point of pure yellow follows the red, then comes the green, and finally the pure blue. Between every two points of pure colour lie

the mixed colours formed from them. If we put down the
red point on paper, we can draw a straight line to the yellow
point, and on this line we put in the red-yellow tints. We
cannot carry the straight line from the red any further, for
here we are dealing no longer with red-yellow colours, but
with colours that are a mixture of yellow and green. To
express the difference, we must give the line a new direction.
So we shall place the green point below the yellow and connect
these two by means of a line representing the colours that
are a mixture of yellow and green. When we reach the green
point, we give the line another direction, towards the blue
point which is placed below the red. That is to say, it appears
that the colours of the spectrum following blue from violet
have obviously an admixture of red. So we may bring back
the line from the blue point straight to the red. In this way
we get a square, on which we may set equilateral pyramids,
one above and one below ; this gives a hexagon The apex
of the upper pyramid shall be white and that of the lower one
black. While all the angles of the hexagon carry pure colours,
on each of the edges will lie colours arising from a mixture of
two The faces of the hexagon, on the other hand, will
display colours formed by mixture of three colours, which
radiate outwards, in diminishing strength, from the three
angles surrounding each face. If we make a transverse section
through a face, we can always tell at what level the single
colours lie above one another, in order to produce in this
way all possible mixed colours

A colour hexagon of this kind reproduces in visible form,
even if imperfectly, the laws obtaining within the circle of the
qualities of colour

THE PRINCIPLE OF COMPARISON

If we ask how it was possible to transfer into the realm
of space the laws regulating a form of a relationship that is

not susceptible of intuition, we have only to remember that while our eye ran along the band of the spectrum, we noticed at certain points that a new colour-mixture appeared. This turning-point in the colour-sequence we transformed into the turning-point in a line in space

Our attention, at first focussed on the red-yellow colour-mixture, was suddenly compelled to turn to the mixture of yellow with green Even in ordinary speech we speak of our attention. "taking a new direction." By drawing a line which suddenly takes a new direction, we give a concrete form to the expression.

In both instances, a change occurs in the process of attention This yields us the common denominator that permits us to reproduce in the form of an event familiar to the eye one that is of quite another kind

We were employing the same method when we converted time-beats into a series of strokes set side by side, and thereby transformed time into space. Our attention was able to keep the change of content quite separate from the nature of the content, and to give this change a concrete expression by transference into spatial relations

It is therefore to the process of attention itself that we have recourse when we give a spatial shape to the forms of relationship of the central qualities. In order to reproduce in concrete form the relationship-form of musical sounds, we shall employ a seven-sided pillar, and on its edges we shall arrange all the sounds in a spiral, so that those that differ by an octave lie below one another. On the faces we shall place the transitional half-tones and quarter-tones.

As the relationship-form of the qualities of smell, Henning suggests a prism. For the other content-qualities, figures in one plane will suffice.

The particular procedure in every case depends on the same principle . the turning-points at which our attention

acquires a new direction are fixed concretely by the angles
or edges of a spatial figure.

By employing the method of determination of threshold,
and developing the same principle, we arrive at the concept of
the mark-sign. We divide up the whole colour-band between
two turning-points into tiny segments lying alongside one
another, and make them so small that at least two adjacent
parts, considered by themselves, are indistinguishable by the
eye. Now let us magnify the individual parts until every
two adjacent ones become just distinguishable from one
another   Then the number of individual parts gives the
number of mark-signs that the colour-band holds for us.
Interpreted in this way, the mark-sign means the alteration
in the content that is just perceptible to the attention.

The number of mark-signs for colour increases with the
skill of the individual observer in distinguishing colours ; it
gives us a clue to the amount of colour in his appearance-
world. From careful investigation, we know that the world
of the colour-blind is ever so much poorer than our own.
While the person with normal sight can make, by means of
certain artifices, some representation of the colourless world,
the colour-blind is quite incapable of imagining the coloured
world of the normal eye. Just as little can the unmusical
man conjure up the world of melody in which lives the man
who has a musical sense.

We can distinguish two kinds of mark-signs—those for
qualitative differences and those for differences of intensity.
The former are always associated with a definite quality.
They are represented by the angles in the spatial forms. The
majority of qualities, however, may appear in different grades
of intensity ; these are not bound to definite sensations of

intensity, but their number is fixed by the number of distinguishable sensations. I can easily determine how many degrees of intensity, or " thresholds ", I can distinguish in a red fluid, from complete saturation to complete colourlessness But I may choose quite arbitrarily any particular degree of intensity as the starting-point, and determine the thresholds either in the direction of saturation or of colourlessness.

THE INDICATIONS

In constructing the world, mental sensations become properties of things , or, in other words, the subjective qualities build up the objective world If we put the mark-sign in place of the sensation or subjective quality, we may say that the mark-signs of our attention become " indications " as to the world. Accordingly, the laws that are binding for the internal mark-signs must also hold good for the external indications. Immutable laws of this kind we call natural laws. All the dicta of physics relate to indications of the world, and are based on the laws that fall to their share as mark-signs of our attention. The fact that, like the moments in time, the places in space cannot be interchanged nor the intervals between them altered, is put beyond all question merely because such relations depend on the form of our attention which precedes all experience By means of this theory, Kant laid bare, for all to see, the very foundations of human knowledge.

This theory, however, must be applied in the same way to all the indication-circles. The number of indications, as well as their arrangement, precedes all experience. Even if this arrangement is not extensive, and so cannot be directly intuited, still the law of the regular increase in indications from threshold to threshold is immediately certain for each indication-circle. From the very beginning, with all the inevitability of Nature, the distance between the thresholds and the regularity of the increase in this distance are determined for colours and for sounds, for smells and for flavours, just as for temperature and for sensations of touch.

Just as the distance separating two places and the direction this separation takes, remain immutable, so also does the difference in colour between two impure tints and the direction of the·increase in its intensity. A degree of hardness differs from another degree of hardness or of softness according to the number of thresholds, as well as by the direction of increase, exactly in the same way that a certain low note in the scale remains always as far removed from a certain high note, and can never change places with it.

When indications make their appearance in the world, they are already in the grip of these laws, and this without any reference to the objects with which they are associated.

As soon as indications appear in the world, caught, so to speak, by the bull's-eye lantern of our attention, the process of apperception sets in, and creates from them new structures, i e. things, objects and implements. In the following chapter we shall deal fully with the nature of this process Here we shall merely point out that each new formation appears as a unity, and then, in its turn, becomes an indication. Our world is filled with these indications, which we usually describe as objects ; but we must not forget that, one and all, objects are built up from the indication-material of our qualities.

THE OBSERVER AND THE WORLDS OF OTHERS

If an observer has before him an animal whose world he wishes to investigate, he must first and foremost realise that the indications that make up the world of this other creature are his own, and do not originate from the mark-signs of the animal's subject, which he cannot know in the least. Consequently, these indications are, one and all,

beneath the sway of the laws of our attention ; and, as soon
as our attention is directed to them, we cannot free them from
these laws. I have tried to reproduce this in the accompanying figure, in which the indications A-K, which make up the
world of the animal, are connected by lines to the observer.
Since we are not in a position to investigate the appearance-
world of another subject, but only that part of our appearance-
world surrounding it, we had better
speak of the surrounding-world of
the animal. It is only for the observer himself that the surrounding-world and the appearance-world
are identical.

The material from which the surrounding-world of another is built
up, invariably consists of our own
objectivated quality, for no other
qualities are accessible to us. The
only difference from our own surrounding-world is that the qualities
are fewer in number. As soon, however, as qualities from the same
indication-circle are present, they
come under the laws of the forms

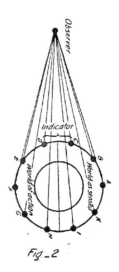

Fig. 2

of our attention. A place which for us lies more to the left
than does another, lies further to the left in the surrounding-
world of the other subject also, given that both the places
are present in that world as indications ; and this is true
even if the number of place-indications separating the two is
smaller than in our world. A moment which follows another
moment in our world can never become the earlier one in
the world of the other subject, if both are present in it as
indications. In like manner, the relation of two sounds in
our world can never be reversed in the surrounding-world

of the other subject, if both the sounds appear there as indications in it ; and so forth.

The observer's chief task consists in determining the number and the nature of his own qualities appearing in the surrounding-world of the other subject ; and he has to investigate also in what grouping they act as indications there.

We can divide up the surrounding-world of every other subject into two halves, as will be explained fully later on. The one contains those of the observer's indications that affect the animal as such ; on that account, I call it the world-as-sensed. The other contains those of the observer's indications to which the animal reacts ; this I call the world of action.

Now, since one and the same object, on the one hand, affects the animal with separate properties as indications, and, on the other, has properties affected by the animal, the boundary between the two worlds passes through the object.

Let us assume that indication C in the figure on the preceding page represents the scent of honey, and the indication D its fluidity, then it is obvious that, if the animal is a bee, the indication C, which acts on the animal, lies in the world-as-sensed, whereas the indication " fluidity," which makes it possible for the bee to drink, lies in the world of action.

It is only in our own surrounding-world that honey, as a sweet-scented fluid, is fused into one unified object ; in the surrounding-world of the bee this does not happen, for the indication fluidity does not act on the bee, but merely underlies the bee's behaviour.

In order that we may not sacrifice the indissoluble connection which, as observers, we perceive to exist between the two properties of the object honey, I propose that, when we are considering the surrounding-world of another subject, we employ the term " indicators " for such of our objects as play a part in that world. This will be used to mean that here certain indications are indissolubly associated, which, however, in the surrounding-world of the other subject, belong partly to the world-as-sensed and partly to the world of action.

THE OBSERVER AND THE ANIMAL

The properties of which the animal is composed are likewise indications for the observer   These, after careful study, he will divide into two halves—a receptor half, corresponding to the world-as-sensed, and an effector half, corresponding to the world of action.   The receptor half receives the actions of the surrounding-world, and the effector half reacts thereto.

There is an astonishingly close correspondence, on the one hand, between the animal's receptor organs and the world-as-sensed and, on the other, between its effector organs and the world of action.   This must strike every observer, and it gives the impression that the animal is merely an imprint of its surrounding-world.   On this impression are based all the theories that see in the living substance of which all animal bodies are made, merely a plastic element, passively moulded, which adjusts itself more or less exactly to external influences.'

These theories overlook one essential circumstance, namely, that the surrounding-world of an animal, if considered by itself, is not a unity   On the contrary, the properties of the surrounding-world become linked up into a unity only when they are in agreement with the properties of the animal ; without this bond, they merely flutter about disconnectedly.

The convincing proof that the animal body does not owe its form to external influences can only be given by our showing that it displays properties that could not have been imprinted on it from without.   And this proof can never be brought quite definitely.   In the arrangement of their receptive or sensory organs, all the higher animals show a distribution which has nothing to do with the arrangement

F

of the surrounding-world, but which, on the other hand, reproduces spatially the distribution of the circles of their indications.   In the eye are assembled all the nervous elements that are directed on the colour-indications of the surrounding-world   The same holds good for the ear, as regards the indications of sound.   In the mouth lie the receptors for taste, and in the nose those for smell.

As a rule people try to explain this remarkable anatomical separation of the quality-circles within the body by pointing to the uniformity of the method in which the related properties act in the surrounding-world.   The etheric vibrations require specific transformers if they are to be converted into nervous excitation ; so do the air-waves.   The same may be said of the substances soluble in water that yield the taste stimuli ; and the stimuli of the sense of smell are conveyed by air-currents

But this explanation will not hold for aquatic animals. Here the stimuli of smell as well as of taste are delivered by substances dissolved in water.   And nevertheless, fishes, like other vertebrates, have their olfactory and gustatory organs quite distinct from one another.

For the anatomical separation of the receptive organs into quite distinct unities, the chemical or physical connection with the surrounding-world cannot be held responsible. What are responsible are the attention-forms of the mark-signs, of which they are the spatial images.   And thus the representations we draw in space of the quality-circles acquire increased significance   When we study the sense-organs of animals, we see Nature herself at work, and in the very act of reproducing in extensive forms the laws of intensive magnitudes.

This makes our research very much easier, for, in investigating animals, we can never hope to attain to a knowledge of their sensations.   All we can determine by experiment is the number and the nature of the indications in the sensed world to which the animal reacts. Thus far, we have been able to group indications only according to the forms of our own attention. But by realising that the sense-organs of the higher animals correspond to this grouping, we are put in a position to go further ; by anatomical study of the lower animals, we can now undertake to group their indications also, and this even when we come across sense-organs that are quite unfamiliar to us.

The most important advance, however, lies in the following conclusion. If the laws manifested in the forms of our attention (which is the deciding factor for the appearance-world of our own subject) can be recognised not only in the shape of our own body, but also in the shape of the bodies of other subjects of whose attention-forms we know nothing, then this indicates that the work of fashioning by the mark-signs is not determined purely by our own subject, but is super-subjective. This means that we are on the track of a control by Nature pointing to a unity even higher than our own apperception, in which otherwise we must see the final unity.

The fact that the forms of our attention find expression in the conformation of our own frame is sufficient to suggest that there is a factor which uniformly determines the activity both of our consciousness and of our body. It is not enough to speak of a parallelism between mental and bodily processes ; an expression like this loses its sense when we are dealing with a comparison between intensive and extensive forms, for such forms are never parallel to one another. On the other hand, we may speak of identical laws, which express themselves both in intensive and extensive forms.

THE TEMPORAL BOUNDARY OF THE SURROUNDING-WORLDS

If we represent the surrounding-world of an animal at any given moment as a circle, we can add on to it the succeeding moments, each as a new circle of the same kind. In this way we get a tube, which would correspond to the length of the animal's life. On all sides the tube is formed of indications, which we can imagine to be built along and around the life-path of the animal. The life-path thus resembles a tunnel passing through the surrounding-world and closed at both ends. In this tunnel the nature of the indications that may appear is fixed from the beginning ; so we may say that its extent and the variety it displays are predestined. Moreover, the time-length of the tunnel has a prescribed measurement, which cannot be exceeded.

Proceeding from these immutable factors that determine all life in the world, we come to see that life itself is based on fixed laws, which are in conformity with plan : these laws do not become apparent, simply because the individual destinies are so numerous that we are unable to appreciate the influences they exert on one another. As a matter of fact, however, they are merely variations on a set theme, and a limit can be set to the possibilities they present.

SUMMARY

To space and time, the forms of our knowledge which are present before all experience, we have to add the forms of the content-qualities, which cannot be intuited directly. As we have seen, they can be brought nearer to intuition by trans-ference into spatial relations, as has already been done in the case of time, of which our extensive experience is direct

On this point, therefore, we must expand Kant's doctrine, and show that for all kinds of qualities there are forms which are present entirely a priori and precedent to all experience ; and these appoint to each quality, as soon as it appears, a fixed position in a system.

The neglect of the a priori forms of the content-qualities is partly referable to their having no names of their own, such as space and time have. The only familiar term has been the metaphorical " musical scale " for the form of sounds, and, using that as a basis, we also speak of a " scale of colour," a " scale of smell," etc. The use of the word " scale," or ladder, for the form of the content-qualities was the first attempt to make these forms accessible to intuition, and accordingly it deserves to be retained as the general designation.

In yet another point we are obliged to expand Kant's doctrine. Not only are there fixed forms for each quality-material, but the number of individual qualities within their form is also absolute, and precedent to all experience.

Even if the absolute number of qualities changes with each subject, and the determination of the number in individual cases is left to psychology—or shall we say, to biology ?— (it is not at all necessary that the particular subject should actually experience all the qualities present in its forms), nevertheless the law that the number of qualities present is absolute is a law of the pure theory of knowledge.

The second law of " increase in one direction " relates to the arrangement of the qualities within their particular form. This is likewise a law of the theory of knowledge.

The possibility of comparing with one another the different qualities and their forms, depends on the fact that each quality leaves behind it in our consciousness a sign—the " mark-sign."

In every instance where the qualities are known to us— i.e. strictly speaking, only in our own case—we may construct the world-picture directly from the objectivated sensations of the subject. Here the subject faces his appearance-world directly. Where we are denied a glimpse into the qualities of the subject, we should not speak of an appearance-world, but only of a surrounding-world built up from our own qualities. Since knowledge of the other subject's " mark-signs " is denied us also, we are confined to determining what properties of our appearance-world have value as " indications " in the surrounding-world of an animal. These indications (which must become mark-signs for us, if we are to experience anything of them at all), we shall treat like our own qualities, so far as possible, and arrange them in the forms given us a priori.

We see a justification for this proceeding in the fact that the anatomical structure of the sense-organs of animals brings together as a unity those indications that our attention also treats as a unified quality-circle.

Nevertheless, we should never forget that, so long as we are concerned with biology, we must not for an instant desert our posts as observers from the outside.

CHAPTER IV

OBJECT AND LIVING ORGANISM

THE BIOLOGICAL ELEMENTS

THE biological analysis is now finished. Through it we have
become acquainted with the ultimate biological elements, the
qualities! We have learnt to distinguish between order-
qualities and content-qualities. Further, we have seen how
the three order-qualities—moment-signs, local signs and direction-signs—as soon as they combine with any of the content-
qualities from any particular sense-circle, become converted
into moments, places and direction-steps , and these are the
organisers of the world.

The content-qualities, which we call content-sensations so
long as they are isolated, become content-properties through
their association with the organisers. Unfortunately, we do
not have for the content-qualities designations corresponding
to this transformation. Blue, warm, hard, bitter, etc —these
terms require the addition of " subjective " or " objective " to
show clearly whether we are dealing with sensations or with
properties.

Finally, we know that all qualities are the material of a
particular form. The form of the moments is time, the form
of the place is the extended, the form of the direction-step is
motion. Motion, by means of the planes of direction, becomes
space, which is enclosed on all sides by the extended.

As soon as a local sign links up with an optical content-
quality, it appears in space in the position determined for it by

the planes of direction.   Through the co-operation of objective
and subjective direction-signs, the place gets its fixed position
with regard to the direction-planes in objective space.

And in this way is constructed the actual scaffolding that
supports the world   As we have said, to make the world
complete it is necessary that the order-qualities be connected
with at least one content-sign, so that the scaffolding becomes
the bearer of matter.   The measurement of matter in space
and time is made possible only by means of the order-qualities.

The content-qualities of matter are, likewise, the material
of its specific form, and, in their relation towards this form,
they exhibit laws which are not susceptible of mathematical
calculation, or only very slightly so.   Sound goes furthest in
that direction, thanks to the repetition of the octaves in the
musical scale.   The colours in the colour-scale offer us much
more limited possibilities for calculation.   Smells in the smell-
scale are not calculable at all.   The taste-scale exhibits only
four qualities, the scale of temperature only three, and the
scale of touch has only two qualities, i e hard and soft.

The increase in intensity of the individual content-qualities
can be controlled in calculation by the introduction of " threshold."   The order-qualities show no such increase

Every substance contains in principle at least one content-
quality from each scale, though it may not be possible to test
this in every case.

We become aware of the content-qualities when we yield
ourselves passively to the influence of the outside world on our
sense-organs ; but in testing our muscular sensations, we have
to become active.   And therefore these qualities are, in
principle, separated from the other content-qualities, and are
ascribed to matter, as the effects of forces.

The atomic theory, even in its most modern form, does
not take sufficient account of the wealth of initial material
from which biology may work.   The atomic theory relies

solely on the organisers, and aims at suppressing the content-qualities. This is most striking when we consider the deliberate refusal of physics to consider the laws that prevail between the content-qualities and their specific forms or scales.

Moreover, physics chooses to ignore the fact that every substance can hold at every point at least one quality from every scale, for this is incompatible with the cherished hope of finding the primitive atom.

So long as we regard the atom as an actual object, and at the same time as the element from which objects are built up, we shall never get away from contradictions! If, on the other hand, we take it to be a local sign which can enter into association with every content-sign, we can meet all difficulties in a consistent way

It seems, then, that we must abandon our fond belief in an absolute, material world, with its eternal natural laws, and admit that it is the laws of our subject which make and maintain the world of human beings

THE CONTINUITY OF THE WORLD-PICTURE

The popular, physical way of looking at the world, which assumes the actual existence of objects, accepts unreflectingly certain axioms which assuredly cannot be arrived at from experience of objects, but are derived solely from the organisation of our mind, for that lies at the basis of every experience   Chief among these axioms is the theory of the continuity of the world, which contrasts so strikingly with the fragmentary character of our individual experiences.

The principle of the continuity of the world takes its origin, in part, from Kant's theory of the forms of experience. The forms space, time and motion are, in their very nature, continuous and quite independent of the individual experience, which is always discontinuous. It is interesting, however, to show how in single instances the gaps become closed up by the forms.

I have already drawn attention to the gap that must appear in the world-picture on account of the blind spot in our retina, but which gets filled in by the coloured surfaces of the environment immediately growing together

Still more obvious is the break in the series of our moment-signs which comes with sleep : it is filled in by the pure form of time.

Motion, the common form of the direction-signs, is also, in principle, quite continuous. It is here that the principle of the continuity of the world plays its chief part, for in this instance the gaps in the material of experience are most apparent Since all forces can be transformed into motion, the principle of the continuity of motion has become a fundamental axiom of physics, and, in the form of the law of inertia, for instance, has led to the discovery of consequences of the highest importance. The theories of the propagation of sound, light and heat are all based on it.

The Force of Gravity. But the attempt to deal with gravitation as motion has not yet succeeded, for propagation of gravity is not demonstrable. What Newton discovered under the apple-tree was not a definite property of bodies, which we call weight (that was known long before), but the invisible bond that connects all objects with the ground, a bond so tense that it bent down the apples on the branches, and sometimes tore them off. He saw this same bond stretching between the moon and the earth, and he realised that it drew up the tide towards the moon. He called this force a force acting from a distance, which was able to release motion without itself being motion.

The force of reciprocal attraction of masses undeniably exerted through space and, unlike all other natural forces, manifesting itself only at the objects and not in space, has given rise again and again to hypotheses which try to span this gap. But hitherto without success. This is the secret anxiety of all physicists, for naturally they do not wish to admit that an hiatus exists in their objective space.

What interests us most as biologists is that we are kept continually informed of the direction of this mysterious force. We have a special sense for detecting the position of the zenith   Unfortunately, we have no words to distinguish this special sense from the planes of direction   It is only when we are standing erect that the above-below of the zenith sense coincides with the above-below of the direction-planes   As soon as we bend our head, the two above-belows become distinct from one another, for that of the direction-planes alters its position with the position of the head, while that of the zenith sense does not

In the inner ear, tiny inorganic particles have been discovered, which balance on little hairs ; these are supposed to be the sense-organs of the zenith sense. Since the existence of such a sense, giving the direction of the force of gravity, decides the whole system of statics of the body, we speak of a static sense. Apart from this, gravity differs in no way from any other resistance, so far as our muscular sensations are concerned. For our muscles, it is all one whether we pull a nail out of the wall or lift up a weight.

The example of gravity shows that it is not possible to deduce the continuity of the world-picture from motion alone, as a form of experience, which is what the physicists often try to do. We see that this continuity arises from a more widely embracing law of our experience-activity, which, following Kant, we call the law of cause and effect, or " causality."

It is only this major premiss, valid for all human experience, that produces the ultimate continuity of the world-picture, by compelling us to inquire into the cause and effect of every phenomenon.

Space, time and causality guarantee the continuity of the world-picture, but they in no way guarantee its completeness. For the attainment of completeness, the forms of the content-qualities (the musical scale, the scale of smell, etc.) must first be taken into account

But even then, completeness is not attained. For an essential property of the world-picture, deliberately over-looked by the physicists, is still lacking—i e. grouping into unities. Separation into spatial atomic systems will not meet the case. Our world-picture is filled with unities. In order to appreciate unities, the mind requires the aid of a special expedient, the " schema " , and I shall now go on to deal with this.

THE SCHEMA

As soon as we proceed to deal with the things of the external world, there are three great questions that affect us as biologists—How ? Why ? and Wherefore ? As a rule, research sets to work at once on all these questions, while taking the world itself as given, and without taking into account the subjective factors to which the objective world owes its very existence.

It is through Kant that we have learnt sufficient self-knowledge to inquire into the subjective factors ; and this question, since we have become convinced of the subjective nature of the world, has come to seem the most important of all

We are now familiar with the content-signs and order-signs, but around these there lies a bond which is responsible for creating the clearly outlined things that we see all about us, and as to the unity of which no question arises in our mind. This bond is so deep-seated in the organisation of our subject, that a very special degree of attention is required to discover it at all

The order-signs and content-signs are easily brought to light, because, with every experience, they are directly given in our consciousness. But to throw the bond around them is an activity of our own, and we perform it quite unconsciously, for we are concerned only with the finished result, in which form alone do we deal with it consciously.

We can at any moment assure ourselves of the insufficiency of our knowledge even in relation to our conscious actions. We were surprised to find that the same command given to the left hand produced a different result from what we got with the right, when we wished to write the numeral 3. Familiar though the numeral 3 is to us when set down on paper, it is just as unfamiliar to us before it has become activated in a series of movement impulses, and died away in a series of impulse-signs

It is quite hopeless to learn anything about our mind before it gets into action. And even concerning this activity we learn nothing exact except through the agency of the direction-signs. If the movement goes so quickly that the signs cannot sound out one by one, then all we experience is the finished result ; and in the case of the left hand, this turns out quite differently from what we expected.

Analogous relations arise when we run our eye over contours, and the sequences of direction-signs determined thereby impress themselves on us as a melody would. The repetition of this melody takes place so quickly that we are not conscious of the individual direction-signs. Before it is played, the melody itself is quite unknown to us. Only the result is known to us, and it appears in such a form that we realise the presence of a something familiar.

In this process, the melody of the direction-signs does the shaping, but all we are conscious of is the " shape." Kant

called the form-giving melody a "schema," and the art of
shaping, which lies hidden in our mind, he called "schematisa-
tion."

Following Plato here, Kant compares the schema of
empirical things with a kind of monogram, which has stamped
itself on our mind, and forms the starting-point both for
shaping things and for drawing images in the imagination.

In order to convince ourselves of the correctness of this
theory, we must turn our attention to those instances in
which the schema separates itself from the sense-signs, for
here its efficacy becomes most obvious. I remember once
when I was at Naples how, along with two other biologists,
I looked for a microscope in vain, because one of us had said
that he had set it upright on the table. It was only when
the attendant, who in the meanwhile had tilted it, pointed
the microscope out to us, that we suddenly saw it there before
our eyes The sense-signs belonging to the microscope were
not hidden from us. but were concerned with other instruments
that were standing on the table. The melody of the direction-signs that should have formed the microscope could not
sound, because we were trying to proceed with the business
of shaping on the lines of the vertical microscope. Without
the subjective conditioning of the schema, no thing can exist
in the world

Those cases are commoner in which a wrong melody
sounds, with the result that we form a wrong object. To
this category belong the many mistakes we are so liable to
make in a half-light We usually find afterwards that the
contour of the wrongly formed object corresponds in some
essential points with the right one, and our mistake consisted
in our completing wrongly the first bars, which were the same
in both melodies In the twilight, we are very often uncertain
as to what melody ought to sound

In broad daylight, similar mistakes occur with moving

objects ; and it is worth while giving special attention to these confusions, for we can learn something very interesting from their study.   I remember once seeing quite distinctly a great toad hop across the road in front of me, and afterwards this resolved itself into a flat stone and a bumble-bee flying past.

The following experience made an especial impression on me.   I wanted to make sure that a boat, which I used every day for crossing a pond, was lying at its proper place, and I bent aside a branch of a bush that obstructed my view. There in the bright sunshine the boat lay before me, in its familiar colours , the oars, which had been shipped, threw their shadows on the seats just as usual   But as I came round the bush, the boat was gone !   Through the compelling force of the schema already in my mind, I had made use of the reflection in the water in such a way as to form the boat, down to every detail.

It is really surprising that these mistakes do not occur much more often, considering how swiftly the eye, when we come into a strange room, takes in a hundred different objects of all kinds ; and it is not possible for all the schemata to have died away completely while this happens.   No doubt the coloured content-signs make it easier to select the right schema.

That we do not make use of memory-pictures already existing, but of the process of image-creation itself, becomes especially clear if we give play to our imagination ; as, for example, when we see bizarre human faces in the pansy flowers, for which we have no preconceived image whatsoever. The man in the moon is another instance of the same kind.

It is very instructive to turn over the pages of a photograph-album, and study the impression produced on us by the sudden sounding of a schema   When, among all the strange faces, we unexpectedly come upon one that we know, something within us connects up, and we know that what we have before us is familiar, often we do not realise until later who the acquaintance is

The schemata are called forth in us, not only by spatial contours, but also by changes in time. We see a hundred strangers collected together in an open place ; suddenly one of them performs a movement, the rhythm of which makes a special impression on us, and we know for certain that this person is an acquaintance. Often, however, we remain in doubt as to who exactly it is.

From such instances it may be affirmed with certainty that what surges up in us is not a memory-picture, but that we are merely completing once more the restoration of a picture within ourselves ; the German word " erinnern " reproduces this very well. Sometimes we fail to restore the familiar picture with certainty, and the process is abortive. This gives us an anxious feeling, as though we were seeking something, and it lasts until the correct picture comes ; then we have a sensation of relief

We may conclude from all this that, in order to form things, we make use, voluntarily or involuntarily, of a mental process ; but of this process, although it is formed by ourselves, we know nothing. The process employs local signs as well as time-signs and content-signs, but depends in the main on the seriation of direction-signs Since it surges up from the complete unconscious, nothing more exact can be stated regarding it ; and we must agree that Kant was right when he said that it is " an art hidden in the depths of the human soul, the clue to which we occasionally and with difficulty wrest from Nature, and shall make manifest."

Perhaps we get nearest to the unknown process when we call the schema a certain kind of " line." Line, in this sense, is an expression taken from painting. Painting is very vitally concerned with the nature of schemata, for every artist must set on the canvas the content-signs corresponding to a clear-cut schema, if he is to achieve a convincing effect. Accordingly, he must pay close attention to the process within himself when he is drawing objects, so that this may dominate his representation of them as freely as possible.

In the line of the great masters we recognise this domination by their schemata ; and, at the same time, we get the conviction that the schemata are individual to the artist, and are markedly distinguishable from one another even when the commonest things are depicted.

Our whole memory is like the rigging-loft of a theatre with wings filled with schemata, which from time to time appear on the stage of our consciousness, not in their own character, but dressed up in the content-qualities of our mind.

It is most unfortunate that we can never behold the consciousness-stage of another living being ; nothing would be more instructive than to see the world through the schemata of another. But at least let us never forget, as we watch our fellow-men going to and fro around us, that they are treading the boards of our stage, and we theirs. The stages are never identical ; in most cases, indeed, they are fundamentally different. And we can never hope to play on the stage of others the rôle that we play on our own

THING AND OBJECT

Qualities and schemata together compose the things of the outer world, as we see them displayed before us. We say that things have such and such properties, and if everything remained in a state of repose, this would be a complete statement concerning the world But everything in the world is subject to movement and change, and all things react on one another reciprocally. In the course of their

G

activity, things display, in addition to the properties they have in repose, others which we name " capacities."

When we wish to embrace the sum-total of the properties and capacities of a thing, we speak of an object ` The possession of capacities characterises the object as contrasted with the thing. The distinction is important, because, through its capacities, an object reveals the whole of its reciprocal action with other objects.

Now a fixed subjective rule underlies this collective reciprocal interaction of objects ; this rule is the so-called law of cause and effect, or causality.

Without this rule, which embraces all change in the world, we should not be in a position to maintain the concept of the object, but should merely experience unwinding series of perpetually altered things. For, since we actually have the world isolated before us only from moment to moment, we see things cut off, as by a knife, from the moment that precedes and the moment that comes after.

The object as such is not visible, because it has extension in time. We may also call it a thing expanded by a moment-sign ; and, by the use of this expression, its capacities are revealed as new or altered properties. The fixed relations that altered properties bear to the same unity are created by the rule of causality, which makes the alteration appear as the necessary effect of external causes. So the object constitutes a higher unity than the thing, thanks to the law of causality, which likewise is an outward manifestation of our apperceptive process.

Causality compels us to seek for a cause for every change in the moment that has just gone, and for an effect in the moment that follows It is causality which, throughout the ages, throws a bond around all world phenomena

Beginning with any selected moment, we can follow the causal chain of change back into the past and forward into the future.   And, as we do this, we see how the various chains link up with one another to form a network which finally draws into its toils everything that happens in the world.

It is not surprising that physics should attempt to explain all associations in the world by causality alone, rejecting any other way of considering them   And yet physics is wrong, for causality is not the only rule at our disposal for systematising the world

MATTER

We call the content of objects, matter.   Like the object, ✓ matter has properties and capacities.   The science concerned with the investigation of matter is chemistry.   Matter is not freely exposed anywhere ;   in order to get matter, we must always first destroy an object.   This is most obvious when we wish to get matter from some implement that we have constructed ourselves   To do so, we must destroy not only the external form, but likewise its internal structure.

Let us assume, for instance, that we break up an old locomotive to get iron from it.   We then discover that, in addition to the conformation of the parts from which the locomotive is built, there is another which belongs, not to the locomotive, but to the iron itself.   In order to keep this distinction clear in words, we shall call the "*framework*" the disposition of the parts in space, in so far as that belongs to the locomotive ;   and the arrangement of the iron particles in space we shall call the " *structure.*"

The confusion of these two essentially different kinds of conformation has led to serious error ;   and still at the present day it misleads many scientists so far, that they even derive the framework of the living organism from the structure of matter.

Since structure really belongs to the field of physical

investigation, physics and chemistry assist one another in the study of matter.

But chemistry is also an ancient science, carefully nurtured through the Middle Ages by the astrologists, who have been most unjustly decried.

In comparing mediæval chemistry with that of the present day, we might easily suppose that we were dealing with two distinct sciences ; but the investigators of those times were trying, just like the modern chemists, to discover what are the properties and capacities belonging to the various forms of matter.

They studied not only the structure of matter, but also its other properties, and asked such questions as " What is its colour ? ", " What sort of a sound does it give ? ", " What does it taste like ? ", " What does it feel like to the touch ? ", and " How heavy is it ? "

For in principle we ascribe to every substance one quality from each of the sense-scales ; and if it cannot be demonstrated, we do not assume that the substance has not got the quality, but we say, for instance, " Smell or taste not perceptible "

In considering the sense-qualities in their relation to the local signs, we may, as has been explained, regard the latter as the smallest receptacles that have the sense-qualities as content. With the local signs we might therefore contrast the sense-qualities as content-signs. It is only when the two are in association that we have " matter."

The old chemistry and the new alike endeavour to separate the forms of matter from one another and investigate them (and consequently all the accessible content-signs of matter in all possible conditions), so as to get as exact a notion as possible of all the properties and capacities of each individual substance.

The mediæval chemist looked at a substance, touched it,

smelt it, tested its sound and tasted it.   Then he noted down
all the properties observed, and from these data he described
the substance as exactly as possible, in order to distinguish it
from others.

Very early the theory of the four elements was established
But the knowledge that every substance has three states
of aggregation controlled by heat was no more than a vague
presentiment lying at the basis of this theory.

The unreliability of the tests, and especially of those
for the intensities of the several qualities, led gradually to
the introduction of other properties admitting of more
certain determination.   Thus, in order to get away from
direct testing of heat, use was made of the expansion of
bodies, and the thermometer was invented.   To measure
weight, the movement of the balance was employed, and that
fixed the standard.

To test hardness, a series of special substances was chosen,
each of which would just scratch the others

In place of testing by smell and taste came later the study
of the relationships of those substances which either combined with one another or separated off from one another.

Thus by imperceptible degrees the whole study passed
from the domain of the other sense-organs to that of the eye.
All our apparatus has reference to the eye, and especially
since in chemistry the testing by sound has fallen more and
more into disuse

Small wonder if, in the course of time, the conception
of what a substance really is has become completely changed.
The study of the forms of crystals, which furnishes what is the
most reliable characteristic of substances, has been mainly
responsible for the present tendency to explain all the properties of matter on the basis of an invisible miniature structure.   It is in accordance with this that stereochemistry has
developed, a science which traces the affinities of substances to

one another from the arrangement of the atoms in space
And so, in place of chemistry, we have, in the last instance,
micro-physics. The ideal now is to refer all the qualities of
substances to the arrangement and movement of atoms or
groups of atoms. As a final outcome of this theory, the atom
loses every material character whatsoever, and becomes a
mathematical point in an eddy of a medium that is continuous and universally circulating, but not further defined.
And with that we get back again to pure local signs and
direction-signs.   ,

From the biological point of view nothing could be said
against this reduction, if physics recognised clearly that, in
the last instance, it builds its foundations upon purely subjective qualities, and that consequently all the structures
arising thereon are purely subjective appearances.

But this is by no means the case, for physics is all the
time under the delusion that, through its reduction of all properties and capacities of substances, it is continually getting
nearer to the true reality   When, for instance, in considering
the increase in warmth of a body, physics neglects the increasing intensity of the heat-quality, substituting for it the
growing extension of the body in space, and then uses this
alone for taking measurements, it has not discovered a reality
lying behind the heat-quality, but has merely chosen as the
sign thereof a parallel change in another sense-quality, because
that happens to be more accessible to calculation. And even
if it should become possible to substitute spatial characteristics for all the qualities, the subjective nature of the
spatial signs would not be altered in the least, and we should
not be one step nearer to the reality sought

The substitution of local signs and direction-signs for the
content-signs does not mean that these disappear from the
world   What one has done is to bring in a *common
denominator*, of general application, which alone permits of

working by calculation , and this has been the real aim in view throughout the whole development of chemistry.

OBJECT AND IMPLEMENT

If we are to put in the proper light the question at issue between physics and biology, we must use very clear-cut terms. Physics maintains that the things of Nature around us obey causality alone. We have called such causally ordered things, " objects " In contrast to this, biology declares that, in addition to causality, there is a second, subjective rule whereby we systematise objects : this is conformity with plan, and it is necessary if the world-picture is to be complete.

When the hammer strikes the string of a piano and a note sounds, that is a purely causal series   If this note belongs to a melody, it is interpolated in a sound-series, which also exhibits arrangement, but not of a causal kind.

When the carpenter's axe chops up the wood into planks and pegs, and when the drill bores through the planks and the hammer drives the pegs into the holes, these are all of them in causal succession. But the structure emerging from this process, the ladder, cannot be interpreted by causality ; it can be understood only from a knowledge of the designed arrangement of the rungs with relation to the main planks, and of all the parts to the whole

We shall call " implements " those objects the construction of which is not to be explained by mere causality, since in them the parts stand in the same relation to the whole as the individual sounds do to the melody.

Both objects and implements consist of matter ; but in the object there is no arrangement of the parts other than that which the structure of the substance brings with it. In the implement, there is, in addition, a framework which connects up the parts into a whole that expresses plan.

In outward appearance, objects and implements are indistinguishable from one another. The same local signs and content-signs, enclosed by the same schema, form them both ; just as the words of a language present the same optical appearance to the man who knows the language as they do to the foreigner. But the one knows the laws determining the juxtaposition of the letters in the word, while the other, not having this guide, stares uncomprehendingly at the words of the foreign tongue   The one sees before him only various assemblages of letters ; the other reads words.

Undoubtedly to the biologist of the present day many things around him appear to be objects pure and simple— such, for instance, as a heap of sand, or the water in a vessel. In both instances, the parts can be interchanged in every direction without the whole being in any way affected.   We shall admit, therefore, even from the biological standpoint, that there are objects without design, or mere heapings together of matter, in which at the present day we are unable to discover conformity with plan.   The whole of inorganic nature is usually looked on as consisting of objects governed by causality alone.   Inorganic objects are at present treated as substances held together by a schema, and forming designed implements only when they are used for the products of human beings.   The plan in such implements is exclusively a human one ;   matter is merely the medium employed in their construction.   Even the physicists cannot deny that there is a plan in human products, but they refuse to admit any other kind of conformity with plan in the things of the inorganic world.

Men did not always think in this way   According to the Greek view, nothing in the world was without design   The entire inorganic world seemed to them as much a work of art as the organic. Sun, moon, planets and the heaven of the fixed stars united in a vast work of art expressing plan, in which every substance occupied its appointed place   The water flowed on the earth and gave life to it, just as the blood does in the body.   There was no such thing as dead matter.

This must be obvious to any naturalist who passes through the museum at Athens, and looks critically at the ancient water-jars, which differ so essentially from our own water-vessels.   While our own, when they are good, reproduce in every detail of their form man's preoccupation with his own affairs, in the ancient jars these signs recede into the background, and the vessels come to represent as completely as possible a clothing of the water itself.

They are strikingly reminiscent of certain rhizopod shells, with which the fluid protoplasm of these wonderful organisms invests itself.   And thus we get the impression that, in those old Grecian jars, the water created for itself the only envelope that would exactly fit it, and that this was subsequently made use of by man.   In their perfection, these ancient vessels are true forms of Nature in art

In its claim of conformity with plan, the Greek view of the world far transcends the boldest dreams of biology.   The confidence and consistency of this way of looking at things, however, makes us wonder whether, by sacrificing the inorganic world to physics, we did not relinquish far too much ground to the enemy without showing fight—ground which occasionally we have to win back.

There are a number of facts that can be used in support of this view.   It is certainly no proof of the lack of plan in Nature that water is heaviest at 4° C., for this prevents the inland lakes from being frozen up, and so animal life is preserved.   Neither does the formation of snow-flakes suggest that there is no plan, for if in winter the water poured down on us in the form of icicles like so many winged arrows, the life of every creature would be imperilled

For the moment, however, it is not advisable to lead the attack in this direction, for the defence offers us more important strategic positions

The design expressed in our human products and tools is incontestable, and it is not denied even by the physicists that these are invariably to be reckoned as implements, for without knowledge of plan in them we could neither create nor use them.

An instance that I experienced myself brought the truth of this assertion home to me with peculiar force   A clever young negro, whom I took with me as my " boy " from the interior of Africa to the coast, was unable to climb up a short ladder placed before him, because he did not know what sort of a thing it was   " I see nothing but planks and holes," he said   After someone else had demonstrated ladder-climbing to him, he could at once imitate him, for he was a superb climber   The ladder was not shrouded in mist , it stood right there in front of him ; he could see it and touch it ; and yet for him it was not an implement, but an object without plan, of which he could make no use.

From this example, we recognise what it is that binds the parts into a whole.   The fixed rule of the action of climbing at once brought order into the confused medley of sticks and holes, and formed the ladder.   It is only the knowledge of the rule of action pertaining to its " function " that arranges the parts into the whole.   If we do not know the function, which establishes fixed relations, we cannot know the design, and we do not recognise the significance of the implement.
Accordingly, instead of the plan expressed by an implement, we may speak of its " functionality "

On closer consideration, it will be clear to everyone that by the word with which, for our mutual understanding, we

describe the implement, we make allusion to its " functionality "   A bench, for instance, may be called a " settle " ;
and in the word " steps " foi " stairs," the function is clearly
expressed.

Even the names given to objects originally imply a function   If you ask children what meaning they attribute to
the name of some familiar object, you will always meet with
a function, composed either from their own actions, or from
the action that they ascribe to the object. A stone, for
instance, always means something that can be thrown ; a
cloud, something that sails across the sky , and so on. It is
only grown-up people who define the object as the sum of
properties and capacities, and ignore the function around
which the properties have originally crystallised   From which
we may conclude that the child's world is still entirely built
up of implements, and that the object is a creation only of
later reflection

Accordingly, for the understanding of all things, it is of
fundamental importance to take exact account of the relations
of properties to functions   The most instructive examples in
this direction are those in which a new implement arises, or
an object is transformed into an implement.

When a boy collects " skipping-stones," which he wants
to send dancing across the surface of a lake, there arises out
of the general implement " stone " (whose function in general
is to be thrown) a particular implement, the properties of
which group themselves round the special function of " skip-
ping." The skipping-stone is hard, flat, circular and of a
certain weight. These are the properties required for this
special function ; the other properties it possesses, over and
above these,—such as colour, smell, taste and resonance,—
are " inessential," and are not determined by the function.
It follows from this that, by the much misused word " nature "
of an implement, we always mean its function.

I shall call *leading* properties those which are necessary and " essential " ; those others which depend only on the character of the substance, I shall call *accompanying* properties.

In every language, there occur words which have two meanings, according to the context in which they are found. Isolated, these words have no fixed meaning. In the same way, there are things which are susceptible of two different uses, and these, accordingly, when considered alone, have no fixed function Taken by themselves, they are not implements, but merely objects.

So long as I hold in my hand a circular, concave piece of glass, it is merely an object. If I set it in a window-frame, it becomes a window-pane ; if I put it on the table, it becomes a saucer, which I can fill with water. In both cases, the object has become an implement.

It must be borne in mind that the leading and accompanying properties change with the change of function. In the case of the window-pane, the transparency is the leading property, and the concavity the accompanying. In the case of the saucer, the reverse is true—the concavity is the chief property and transparency is the accompanying. Function acts like a magnet, which attracts towards it now some qualities and now others

Now it appears that the accompanying properties are frequently used by subsidiary functions, and so enter with them into a framework of the implement. Thus transparency becomes a subsidiary function of drinking-vessels, the contents of which we wish to test by the eye. In the same way, concavity becomes the subsidiary function of certain window-panes, which by reflections on the convex side ward off the gaze of the inquisitive.

The transformation of such subsidiary functions into main functions may easily take place under our very eyes ;

as an example, we have only to consider how a portable engine becomes transformed into a locomotive.

The great majority of our tools, machines and apparatus, show the following structure :—there is a " main function," to which a greater or less number of " subsidiary functions " are attached. However fully the framework be analysed, there is always some residue of accompanying properties that do not enter into it, but can be interchanged without damage to the implement. For the most part, they belong to an implement that has been destroyed in order to form a new one, or to the substance from which the implement was made

A boat, for instance, always shows certain properties of the tree from which the boards were procured, properties which are inessential to the boat as such. In like manner, all those of our implements which are prepared from metals or other substances are laden with properties which do not belong unconditionally to the framework of the implement, but are conditioned by the structure of the substance alone.

To all our implements something extraneous is attached, pertaining to the material only, and not entering into the framework of the functions and subsidiary functions.

The framework itself displays everywhere the same principle, i e. a main function, achieved often through the agency of a multitude of part-functions (one has only to think of how many functions must be exercised before an automobile gets going), and a large number of subsidiary functions (which are expressed in the " body " of the car).

In all cases, the properties of an implement can be analysed into the properties of the material and those of the functional framework, without anything being left over. There is never anything unexplainable attaching to our implements, such as makes the study of the living organism at once so difficult and so fascinating.

THE LIVING ORGANISM

The framework of our human implements is intelligible chiefly because they all refer to some very familiar human function. The actions of implements are never their own actions, but are merely counter-actions to our human doings, which in some way or other they support, refine or expand. And so we are never in any doubt about there being a main function ; we recognise quite clearly the part-functions and subsidiary functions, because throughout we recognise human action as the measure and basis constituting the cause of all the counter-actions, down to the smallest detail. The way in which the counter-actions express themselves in the framework is determined by the properties of the material from which we construct the implement.

Morphology. This certainty that a principal function forms the scaffolding around which the other functions group themselves, is lacking when we deal with living beings, and we very soon feel the effects. As a matter of fact, a new science, "morphology," has developed from the mere description of the framework of organisms, a science which, in contrast to the theory of function, is not applicable to our human implements.

The fundamental principles on which the classification of living things was undertaken sprang from this science. When we divide up animals into five-rayed, four-rayed and two-rayed (bilaterally symmetrical) and segmented animals, we are dealing with things from a point of view that has nothing to do with the functions of the animals

At a very early date the conviction forced itself on zoologists that a classification of animals must be carried out not according to functional, but according to morphological features ; not the "analogy" of the anatomical parts, but their "homology," is to be the standard for classification

And thus greater importance is ascribed to the position of the organs in the animal body than to their function

If we were to try to classify our tools in the same sort of way, the result would be sheer nonsense.

On this ground alone a mechanistic theory of living things should be rejected.

It should be noted that, of all our sciences, morphology has perhaps the most unsatisfactory theoretical basis, if indeed one can speak of a basis at all. It is certainly not admissible to speak of a theory of the structure of organisms that can be linked up with the theory of the structure of matter. It is understandable enough that, as a result of this confusion of quite different things, fresh attempts are perpetually being made to explain life as a further development of crystallisation.

It is not questioned that the rules of morphology relate to the framework, and never to the material We may say that *the framework of implements is judged from the point of view of function, but the framework of organisms both from the functional and from the morphological.* Of this, the recognition of the two principles of analogy and homology takes full account Moreover, homology refers only to the arrangement of the organs with regard to one another, but never to the framework within the cells, which is exclusively functional

Discovery of the morphological principles in the architectural plan of the animal is made possible by comparison. For if we consider the architectural plan of an individual animal taken by itself, all we shall be able to recognise at the first glance are functional principles.

This fact finds expression in our saying that morphology also means " comparative anatomy." Striking though the fact is, it was at one time taken quite as a matter of course, without anyone seeking for the explanation that lay so near at hand. It was reserved for Darwinism to assert that the morphological principles are referable to the physiological principles of earlier generations.

As a tangible proof of this very dubious theory, Darwinism discovered the "vestigial organs" said to be demonstrable in every individual now living as surviving remains of physiological requirements in past ages.

It is true that we sometimes see human tools, converted to other purposes, still retaining from the past certain useless parts that do not happen to be inconvenient. Thus when old railway-carriages are turned into workmen's dwellings, the wheels, now useless, are not removed, but are merely fixed so that they do not turn.

On the basis of such a superficial analogy, it has straightway been assumed that there might be vestigial organs with only a morphological, but no functional significance. Hitherto no single one of these organs has withstood careful testing; some function peculiar to it has always been revealed, and it is to be hoped that "vestigial organs" will soon disappear into oblivion. It is surely presumptuous to thrust on biology a theory according to which an absolutely useless tumour (which is what the vestigial organ represents, from the physiological standpoint) must be inherited for thousands of years throughout all generations

Apart, however, from this lapse in recent times, morphology has established very remarkable and stable rules, and to these we must unconditionally accord special importance. When, for instance, we find that the whale and the giraffe, which are both mammals, have the same number of cervical vertebræ, namely 7 (and this despite the extremely different length of their necks), but that the swan has more than 20, then morphology is completely justified in claiming to use its rules as indications for the determination of relationship. But the nature of the connection between relationship and homology, as regards the position as well as the number of organs, remains quite problematical.

We cannot say that morphology sought in Darwinism an explanation of her particular rules. They were forced on her by Darwinism, which had need of the stable rules of morphology for the support of its own very shaky edifice.

The association with Darwinism has not proved a blessing to morphology, for in place of critical examination of dry facts, the most fantastic genealogical trees have been drafted, and this kind of thing has greatly interfered with the workings of a science which has every right to be considered painstaking and cautious.

One thing, however, must be maintained   The existence of a morphological science of living organisms is not just a matter of course ; it is an exceedingly puzzling fact, which cannot be deduced from analogy with non-living implements.

Physiology   If by physiology we understand the study of the functions of living things, then its chief task consists in the functional analysis of the framework of organisms.   In making this analysis, it becomes evident that the structure of the substance of which living beings are composed passes over into the framework in such a way that we can never make certain just where the one begins and the other ends.

And here we find another reason for dissenting from the mechanistic theory of life   For with all implements of man's creating, as we break them up we always come upon properties of matter that do not enter into the framework, and this because we have only very imperfect control of the microscopic structure.

More thorough investigation of the microscopical structure ꞃ of the cells of all living organisms has brought to light the very significant fact that every cell consists of two parts—a part incorporated in the framework and a protoplasmic part. Only the framework part of the cell, which has arisen from

H

the protoplasmic part, undertakes the function of the cell, and therewith that of the organ. The protoplasmic part seems to serve merely for repair of possible injuries to the framework. Later on we shall have more to say about this remarkable " living " substance of the protoplasm.

If the protoplasm be left out of account, it can be said of the framework of the cell that it is an absolutely perfect machine (in contrast to our machines, which are always only approximately perfect), for no property of matter is present which does not enter completely into the framework ; moreover, the rules which hold good for the construction of this micro-machine are exclusively functional. This is in marked contrast to the arrangement of the organs, which is determined by morphological rules as well. Whether we consider muscle-cells, nerve-cells, bone-cells or sensory cells—in each and every instance we find the same perfection

In this respect, there is no such thing as evolution ; the lowest, just like the highest of living creatures, are, as regards their micromechanics and microchemistry, equally perfect In face of this fact, all attempt to explain living things as chance agglomerations of substances collapses utterly

We must also ruthlessly tear away the veil at another point where the evolution theory has shown itself misleading It is just as mistaken to say that whole organs are more perfect or less perfect, as it is to say this of individual cells. If an organ is differently constructed from another, that does not imply technical defectiveness ; it then has another function

An organ constructed for a narrowly restricted function is not, on that account, more perfect or less perfect than one that serves several functions   The foot of a fowl is neither better nor worse than the foot of a duck, although the duck's foot serves for progression in the water as well as on the dry land.

The inferiority of an organ in one individual when compared with the same organ in another of the same kind is a
matter for pathology, and has nothing to do with evolution.

In spite of our dissent from the doctrine of evolution,
it would be childish to deny that there are higher and lower
organisms. But we must confine ourselves to showing that
there are animals with more numerous, if not necessarily better
organs ; and these we call " higher " animals because they are
so rich in organs and in functions

If we wish to speak of an evolution from lower animals
to higher, we must in the first place get quite clear as to what
function the organ serves in the case selected, and what
position that occupies in the framework of the whole—whether
it is a subsidiary function, a part function, or a whole function.
For only then can we pass on to the essential questions, i.e.
whether indeed there is any such thing as a gradual passage
from one function to another, and whether a new function
can arise gradually.

When we examine our own functions or actions, which
have their faithful reflections in the counter-actions of our
implements, we come to the conclusion that every performance
of a function, whereby it becomes an action, consists of an
independent sequence of impulses, which forms throughout an
isolated unity   If I want to walk, run, or jump, I must
impart to myself a quite definite impulse-sequence, which puts
the organs into the corresponding degree of activity.   If I construct a staircase to climb up, or a chair on which to sit, the
implement so formed should also give the impression of being
an isolated unity.   There are, however, a great many different
kinds of chairs, which fulfil the same function in a more
or less perfect way.   And here we have yet a further illustration of the imperfection of our implements ; they cannot
bear comparison with perfect organs   For organs never show
this ambiguity ; they may, as in the case of our legs, serve

different functions, such as walking, running and leaping, and so are not concentrated on one function alone, as the leaping foot of the kangaroo is concentrated, down to the last detail. Considered superficially, they perhaps seem to be imperfect attempts to approximate to the function exercised at the moment , in reality, considering the changes that the subsidiary functions demand of the organism, perfection is always achieved.

Accordingly, we are not justified in comparing the various forms assumed by an organ with the gradual perfecting of our own implements, which are always merely approximately adequate to the counter-action.

But, by renouncing this comparison, we lose a very important piece of evidence, which has been adduced to prove the gradual evolution of organs, evidence that is especially convincing because the analogy seems so obvious.

The organs of animals are always the perfect expression of one function or of several, and consequently changes that take place in them point to a change of function. The functions themselves, however, are always unities, and not subject to change. One function, it is true, may more or less force another into the background or even cause it to disappear altogether , but functions themselves do not change.

For instance, I can take up a half-sitting, half-lying position, but it is as impossible for me to lie more or lie less, as to sit more or sit less.

SCHEMA AND FUNCTION

Again and again we can demonstrate that, when our eyes are shut and the order is given that the left hand is to write a certain letter quickly, it is very apt to lapse into mirror-writing ; and this does not happen if we guide the pen slowly. By closing the eyes and writing quickly, the control is removed which we otherwise exert over the direction the movement follows, and the sequence of the movement-impulse, thoroughly learnt for the right hand, produces mirror-writing in the left, which is its mirror-image. This experiment enables us to separate the impulse-sequence from the controlling schemata, which otherwise regulate our movement all the time

The separation becomes even more obvious in those cases where, as in the movements of our larynx, there is never any control by the eye.

In such instances, control by the outer and inner direction-signs disappears altogether, and is given over to the ear alone. For the movements of the laryngeal muscles do not reach us through inner direction-signs, but, along with vague muscular feelings, come to our consciousness indirectly only through the sounds produced.

From this it clearly follows that the impulse-sequence, ✓ although connected up into a compact unity, must not be confused with the sense-schema, which may be regarded as a space-monogram or a melody of direction-signs.

We make the schema of the alphabet our own through learning to read, a faculty originating from the direction-signs of the eye-muscles as our glance sweeps over the contours ; and it is not permissible to assume that this schema is transferred directly to the muscles moving the hand On the contrary, by performing the movements of the hands, we get another schema, coming from the direction-signs of the hand-muscles ; and it is this which, combined with the sight-schema of the eye-muscles, controls the movements in writing.

The schemata are undoubtedly acquired by movement of the muscles, because the direction-signs sound during the movement ; but they have nothing directly to do with the muscular innervation. The sense-schemata are aids to perception ; the impulse-sequences, on the other hand, are directors of our activity. When they come into action, the impulse-sequences, of which we never experience anything directly, create the functions   Our knowledge of the schemata may be extremely scanty, but we are still more in the dark when it is a question of the functions ; for concerning the exercise of the functions in every movement of the hand, in every inclination of the head, and so forth, we learn something only through the medium of the sense-schemata, and that thanks to the direction-signs connected with those movements.

We have no direct knowledge whatsoever of what we do quite as a matter of course   What we learn with regard to all our actions comes from the sense-signs alone, which serve to control our movement

This is why it is so extremely difficult to get deaf-mutes to speak, for they lack control by the ear, and the laryngeal musculature has no direction-signs   Only by calling in the assistance of the direction-signs of mouth and tongue do we succeed in impressing on deaf-mutes certain indications, which they can use in producing sounds. Learning to read and write, on the other hand, presents no greater difficulties to them than it does to normal people.

The case of deaf-mutes gives us a good idea of what our complete helplessness would be if we were deprived of the sense-control of our actions   We should actually be incapable of initiating even the least regulated sequence of movements.

In the case of animals it is not possible to make this statement. There are animals that execute quite definite movement-sequences, in which control by the sense-organs is lacking. Actions of this kind can come about through a special kind of nerve-linking ; they are called reflexes. When, on the other hand, regulated movement-sequences are performed by an animal that is without control by sense-organs, and such movements are not linked together and conditioned by any demonstrable structure, we speak of *instinctive actions.*

The concept of instinct covers, therefore, tacit recognition of function as an independent factor in addition to the animal's organisation

While the sense-schema brings rule and order into the perceptions, the impulse-sequence, as creator of function, brings rule and order into the actions.

The difference between animals that learn through experience, such as human beings, and instinctive animals like birds and insects, depends mainly on the latter having for their functions inborn impulse-sequences which proceed faultlessly without any further control. Intelligent animals require schemata in order to form the correct functions and maintain these by their control.

Before every single action, even in the case of a human being, the impulse-sequence for the function must be there ready and prepared   When this begins to come into play, the controlling schema strikes up along with it and at the same rate, and so brings the functioning to our consciousness   We are informed of every deviation from the normal function.

Since in ourselves the functions undoubtedly have to be learnt, we are apt to assume that they must somehow have fixed themselves in the framework of the nervous connections in the brain.   And this might be the reason why we are not conscious of them.

This is an open question.   It is of considerable importance, because the answer to it means neither more nor less than the recognition of non-physical natural factors in the working of the body

I may admit that the entire world is appearance, and that the things in it are composed of my sense-signs + schemata, and yet this does not force me to assume that the forms of movement observed in the world are directed by anything but causality and the conformity with plan that resides in the framework of implements   I am obliged, then, to assume also that the impulse-sequences are in some way or other laid down in the brain by nervous structure

This way of regarding the world reduces man to a machine, endowed by chance with consciousness, while all other animals are able to get along quite well without it

Instinct would find no place either, and, in spite of the non-demonstrable nervous organisation, would have to be interpreted as a highly complicated reflex action.

It all depends on whether we can explain the life of animals by the presence of a framework conformable with plan and analogous to that of a machine   We shall deal with this more fully later on.

THE FRAMEWORK

It is a remarkable fact that, while the assertion that a machine may be regarded as living organism excites general contradiction, the opposite assertion, i e that we may compare living beings with machines, finds many supporters. The contradiction in this becomes less obvious if we express the two statements in another way.   From the statement " machines have the properties of the living," we shall at once dissent ; on the other hand, the statement " living beings have mechanical properties " is certain to meet with general agreement.

It sounds positively ridiculous to maintain that a locomotive with an optical apparatus is a kind of horse ; but to compare a horse with a locomotive is very tempting.

As a matter of fact, it is impossible to get at animal action from the counter-actions of implements, even by very careful selection and the most delicate interweavings   All counter-actions, however complicated they are thought to be, have reference to a human action, and consequently remain dependent.   To unite them into an independent whole, we must always select as the starting-point a human being with his impulse-sequences.

On the other hand, it is quite reasonable to inquire whether we cannot resolve a living organism into a number of independent functions, which find their expression in the framework of the animal.

It has been shown that this method of analysis of an organism offers very considerable advantages   Indeed, comparative physiology maintains that we should consider every animal as a bundle of reflexes, work out each single reflex-arc thoroughly, and then study their common central connection.   Only by this method can we succeed in demonstrating completely the mechanical properties undoubtedly present in the organism ;   and this exceedingly important science we call physiology.

But every biologist must see that this does not complete the work of investigation, for a bundle of reflexes is not an animal, even if we bring into relation with its structure all the chemical actions of the body, organised, as they are, in full conformity with plan.

In addition to mechanical, a living being also possesses ⋎ super-mechanical capacities, giving it a character which would still be quite unlike that of a machine, even if the parts of the machine were constructed with the same perfection as are organs, and even if their counter-actions were real actions, i.e. were not referable to the action of a human being

The super-mechanical powers of all organisms consist in ⋎ this, that they include the activities exercised on machines by human beings   They make the machine of their own bodies themselves, they run it themselves, and they undertake all its repairs

All three of these super-mechanical powers—the construction, the running of the machine, and its repair—appear to be bound up with the existence of protoplasm, which machines do not possess. Every living thing proceeds from protoplasm ; traces of it remain in every cell, where it forms that part of the cell which does not pass over into the mechanical framework of the whole. And the protoplasm as a whole is kept in continuity throughout the body by means of fine connecting strands.

The anatomically demonstrable existence of protoplasm permits us to assume a fundamental division between the mechanical framework and the protoplasmic net that traverses the entire body, and to ascribe to the latter all the-super-mechanical powers

When this separation is made, we realise that an organism without its protoplasm represents an ideal machine   This skilfully interwoven bundle of reflex-arcs, with its perfectly constructed receptors and effectors, has become an independent machine, responding to the influences of the outer world by means of its own actions. But these actions are quite unalterable and automatic, and it is here that we see demonstrated the most essential contrast between what is living and what is dead. If, in virtue of its framework, a creature behaved physiologically like a living organism, but nevertheless was without protoplasm, we should be obliged to describe it as dead.

PROTOPLASM

Protoplasm, as it is found in all living cells from the germ-cell onwards, also possesses a mechanical framework, for it exhibits the fundamental mechanical actions of the living organism ; it is capable of movement, metabolism, ingestion of food and so on   One of the chief things it does, i e. cell-division, requires, indeed, a very complicated mechanism.

If this were all that we might expect of protoplasm, then we should have in it nothing more than another machine incorporated in the large one.

But fortunately, Nature, when she created the unicellular animals, such as amœbæ and infusorians, which consist, entirely or in main part, of protoplasm, has vouchsafed us a glimpse into its super-mechanical powers. Study of amœbæ has taught us two things—first, that in order to carry out a mechanical action, a mechanical apparatus must be present · and second, that protoplasm has the power to go on creating the mechanical apparatus anew and to break it up again.

Study of infusorians has shown that these creatures, whose animal activity is carried out by permanent apparatus, still depend for their vegetative apparatus on pure protoplasmic activity. Their interior still consists of fluid protoplasm, and this forms around each particle of ingested food a vacuole, which first becomes the mouth, then the stomach, then the intestine, and finally the anus

In this case we see that the impulse-sequence of the functions is present before the organs exercising the functions are in any way formed, and that the protoplasm has the power of shaping organs in correspondence with this impulse-sequence.

We see the organs appear one after the other in definite sequence , and each, when its work is finished, disappears again   In animals with a fixed framework the organs are permanently present, and in place of the sequence in time there is an anatomical connection.

There is, then, a non-material order which first gives √ to matter its framework—a rule of life   This rule appears only when it is creating the framework ; and this it forms on strictly individual lines, corresponding to the material properties of the protoplasmic animal concerned.

It is like a melody, which controls the sequence of sound and the rhythm in accordance with law, but becomes apparent only as it becomes operative, and then takes on the tone-colour which the properties of the particular instruments impose on it

These are simple and obvious facts, and in no way nebulous theories. And they give us the key to the three above-mentioned actions of protoplasm in the higher animals—construction, running of the machine, and repair   In all cases, something new is achieved ; but in accordance with an already existing rule, and always with special relation to the properties of the organs.   There is never evolution, but always epigenesis.

The concept of instinct having already shown us that we must recognise in the impulse-sequence a natural factor lying outside the anatomical framework of the animal, a factor which regulates the functioning, we shall now seek it in the protoplasm itself, which universally obeys it.   This factor does not seize upon the framework in any unregulated way, but with as great conformity to plan as do our impulse-rules in governing our own actions.

Such an analogy yields us the first hint as to the nature of this problematical factor, which resides in all protoplasm and in its very essence is a rule.

SUMMARY

In this chapter, devoted to synthesis, we have seen how, by the help of schemata, the things of space take on material form ; how, by the help of causality, objects, extended in time, are comprehended as unities ; and how, by the help of conformity with plan, implements arise. Furthermore, we have investigated conformity with plan, and we have found that it is always based upon a function.   By tracing back our own actions, we have referred function itself to the impulse-sequence, which comes to our consciousness indirectly through our own qualities.

Finally, we have been able to demonstrate that the impulse-sequence also controls the activity of protoplasm, and thus shows itself to be an independent natural force, producing organs with differentiated framework, and then causing them to disappear again. Once the framework is there, the activity can proceed automatically within its limits.

But since the framework is constructed by the impulse-sequence in conformity with plan, its action in the outer world is both in accordance with plan and also automatic.

The question concerning the conformity with plan is the business of biology ; the question concerning the mechanical running belongs to physiology.

CHAPTER V

THE WORLD OF LIVING ORGANISMS

Now that in a general way we have become clear as to the properties of living organisms, it must be our task to investigate the way in which these properties work.

Every animal is a subject, which, in virtue of the structure peculiar to it, selects stimuli from the general influences of the outer world, and to these it responds in a certain way. These responses, in their turn, consist of certain effects on the outer world, and these again influence the stimuli. In this way there arises a self-contained periodic cycle, which we may call the *function-circle* of the animal.

The function-circles of the various animals connect up with one another in the most various ways, and together form the function-world of living organisms, within which plants are included. For each individual animal, however, its function-circles constitute a world by themselves, within which it leads its existence in complete isolation

Let us now proceed to analyse this function-world into its parts The sum of the stimuli affecting an animal forms a world in itself. The stimuli, considered in connection with the function-circle as a whole, form certain indications, which enable the animal to guide its movements, much as the signs at sea enable the sailor to steer his ship. I call the sum of the indications the *world-as-sensed*.

The animal itself, by the very fact of exercising such direction, creates a world for itself, which I shall call the *inner world*.

The actions directed by the animal towards the outer world produce the third world, the *world of action*.

World of action and world-as-sensed together make a comprehensive whole, which I call the *surrounding-world*.

The entire function-circle formed from inner world and surrounding-world (the latter divisible into world of action and world-as-sensed) constitutes a whole which is built in conformity with plan, for each part belongs to the others, and nothing is left over to chance.

If this circle is interrupted at any point whatsoever, the existence of the animal is imperilled

It is not possible to write the biology of an animal unless one has first studied its function-circle from every side. However different they may be, all parts of it are equally important. When we go on to study the various parts in detail, this continuity of the complete whole must never be lost sight of.

THE FUNCTION-CIRCLES

Just as we broke up the function-circle into sectors, so we proceed to divide up the totality of function-circles into separate circles or circle-groups, which, biologically considered, are absolutely distinct from one another.

The first is the circle of the *medium*. This circle is characterised by the fact that the medium itself exerts no stimulus on the animal ; while on the other hand, if the animal forsakes the medium, a stimulus is immediately released, which results in the animal's being guided back into it. Accordingly, the medium is so constituted that in itself it possesses no indications on which the animal can seize ; the water does not influence the fish, but the air does as soon as the fish comes to the surface. Conversely, for the animal living in the air, the water is a stimulus, but the air is not   Animals are able to live only in water or in air ; even when they live underground, there must be some connection established with one or other of these media.

The ground and all fixed bodies always constitute obstructions in the medium, and consequently act as indications. So most animals are furnished with organs of locomotion for getting over these obstacles, while only a small proportion have organs serving for movement in the free media of air or water

In many cases, the medium is spatially restricted by special indications which fix the animal to a definite *habitat*. Thus for gastropods and crustaceans, and also for insects, dark and light surfaces give signs which influence them in their course   In addition, there is also in the bilateral animals an unequal development of the two sides, which favours movement in a circle.

In addition to the function-circle of the medium, we can distinguish the function-circles of *food* and of the *enemy*. In both cases, the animal receives a stimulus proceeding from the indications of the food (be it of animal or vegetable nature), or from those of the enemy, which latter is always, with almost negligible exceptions, an animal.   Following on the food stimulus, movement is turned in the direction of the food, and then, when contact is established, fresh indications, tactile or chemical, come in, which seem to guide the masticatory apparatus.   At this point a number of circles often appear, which belong to the food circle.   Following on the enemy stimulus, the organs of locomotion are directed to lead the animal away from the enemy, or else the organs of defence are directed to drive it away.   In both cases the enemy-indications disappear.

In many cases, as among the crustaceans, the function-circle of the enemy passes through the eyes, and the function-circle of food through the olfactory organs

As a fourth function-circle there is the *sexual*, which

in principle is like the food-circle, only that what is set in activity by the animal's "control" is not the feeding apparatus, but the apparatus of sex.

All the circles, however far they lie separated from one another in the world-as-sensed, intersect in the steering-apparatus of the inner world, and then separate from one another again in the world of action.

Biological treatment of the function-circles requires that we also consider from the point of view of conformity with plan that part of the circle which goes on outside the body in the surrounding-world We are accustomed to treat things lying outside the subject according to the rules of causality alone. But by so doing we are not taking account of the biological framework, which is co-extensive with the whole circle

Let us suppose that we wish to construct a complete mechanical function-circle Suppose, for instance, that we furnish an automatic locomotive with an optical apparatus capable of stimulation by the indications of red and green railway signals, and thus affecting the steering of the engine , we should be obliged to construct the surrounding-world— in this case the railway-track—in as exact conformity with plan as the engine itself.

Now animals are so much part and parcel of Nature that even the surrounding-world works within the whole like a part constructed in conformity with plan.

We may assume that where there is a foot, there is also a path ; where there is a mouth, there is also food ; where there is a weapon, there is also an enemy.

This last instance expresses a fact often misunderstood, namely, that struggle belongs to the universal plan. In opposition to what the Darwinian theory assumes, the struggle for existence is not merely one cause in the causal series, but an essential part of the general plan of life.

I

It is not only the creatures with weapons, but also the defenceless ones, that are involved in the struggle. Their protection lies either in their swiftness or in their numbers. The most striking instance of this is that many more eggs are laid than young are hatched, because the great proportion of eggs are always sacrificed to enemies Here we see clearly that a new sort of conformity with plan comes in, which hitherto we have not considered ; this is conformity with plan on the part of the species, of which we shall have more to say later on.

But first we must confine ourselves with conformity with plan on the part of the individual.

One thing has become evident from our treatment of the problem up to this point, i.e. that biology is concerned only with conformity with plan, and that the study of causality comes into the question only in so far as it contributes to that investigation.   All the things that play a part in the function-circle of an animal we consider only from the point of view of function.   This means that we have to do exclusively with implements, and never with objects.   The stone that a beetle climbs over is merely a beetle-path, and does not in any way belong to the science of mineralogy.   Its weight and its material properties, such as atomic weight or chemical valency, are for us matters of indifference.   These are all of them accompanying properties, which we may overlook, since we are interested only in the leading properties of the form and hardness of the stone.

In the body of the subject, physical and chemical causality plays a much more important part, because here the distinction between leading and accompanying properties disappears, since all the material properties are comprehended in the framework of the living organism   And so, when we are trying to grasp the chemistry or the physical properties of an animal, we are certain of meeting with a life-property ; but

it is the interpolation into the function-circle of the properties discovered that completes the physiological activity.
Even the numerous solutions of mechanical problems with
which the animal furnishes us from its world of action have
biological significance only as links in the chain of function.

As we traverse a function-circle, we are absolutely certain
that all the time we shall come upon fresh arrangements
expressing design ; but we have no confidence whatsoever
that we shall anywhere light on a mechanical arrangement.
We have already learnt that protoplasm is called on to play
a part that is not only conformable with plan, but also super-
mechanical.

Now since conformity with plan is the supreme law, not
only for material things but also for the processes of
the mind (of which apperception is the direct expression),
many investigators are inclined to transfer from physiology
to psychology, and from the body to the mind of the animal,
the guidance according to plan which constitutes the main
activity of the inner world.

There is one essential objection to this, and it is that we
are trying to treat the whole function-world of the animal
under investigation as our own experience, and not as the
experience of the animal   They are *our* indications which
are affecting the animal.   It is *we* who observe the guidance
given.   It is *our* apperception which recognises the plan.
If we tried to change the point of view suddenly and look
at things from the animal's mind, we should lose the inter-
connection of the appearances on which for us it primarily
depends   We should suddenly find ourselves surrounded
by the animal's appearances, which have no connection with
our own.   For the unity of appearances depends solely on
the unity of our own apperception.

It is another question whether the apperception of another
creature can express itself as an objective natural factor

in our appearance-world. Driesch has answered this question in the affirmative. As soon as it becomes a natural factor, he calls this other apperception a *psychoid*, in order to avoid the perpetual confusion of the other psyche with our own. According to Driesch, to whom we are indebted for the change of trend in modern biological theory, the psyche of the observer, when it investigates another subject, encounters the actions of the psychoid. And these then enter into the function-circles as super-mechanical factors.

THE WORLD-AS-SENSED

There are animals, such as the sponges, which are sedentary, and in virtue of their bodily constitution, unassailable ; and for these animals a single indication suffices. They cannot leave their medium, and they possess no movable weapons. They simply cast their sexual products adrift. Consequently they lack three of the function-circles which require a special guidance and special indications. The food-circle is the only one they have. But the food does not give rise to an indication, for it is whirled through the body with the sea-water, and carried off by the digesting-cells. Harmful substances all have the same indication, acids, for instance, exert a chemical stimulus, sand-grains, a mechanical ; these stimuli are not distinguished from one another by the animal, but all call forth the same reflex. That is to say, there is only one single indication in the sensed world of the sponge.

For the infusorian Paramecium, the same indication suffices for the circle of the medium and for that of the food, for all the stimuli that proceed from the various objects the animal may meet with as it swims ceaselessly to and fro, provoke it to shift the helm, as it were, and to hasten off again in another direction. The only things that do not produce stimulus are the bacteria of putrefaction, which form the creature's food. Beside these the restless infusorian takes anchor   When it touches these (second indication), even ever so slightly, it stops the movements of its locomotor cilia, and, by means of the cilia round the mouth, drives the food into its fluid interior.

The enemy-circle has a special indication, for the infusorian, when attacked by its enemy—i e *Didinium nasutum* —fires off a sort of gelatinous discharge. There is also an indication belonging to the sexual circle, which initiates copulation.

For further examples, I refer the reader to my book *Umwelt und Innenwelt der Tiere.* I shall mention only the mollusc, *Pecten jacobæus*, which has eyes that receive as indication the slow movement of all sorts of objects, but gives no active response to any of these pictorial impressions.

STIMULUS—INDICATION—QUALITY

From the examples quoted, it must be clear that stimulus and indication are not identical concepts, although they are applied to the same qualities.

Only if we bear in mind wherein the three modes of investigation—i e. the physiological, the biological, and the psychological—differ from one another, shall we understand how to apply these three elementary concepts correctly in each case.

In the process of investigation, the physiologist and the biologist take up the same attitude, for they consider themselves as observers external to what they observe. They have before them an object and an animal ; they both study the influence which the object exerts on the animal. But the physiologist investigates the causal connection, and the biologist its conformity with plan. As a consequence, the physiologist follows, on its path through space, the effect proceeding from the object.   In studying an animal, he will trace the air-waves to the ear, and there observe their transformation into nervous excitation ; in like manner, he will follow a light-ray as an etheric wave to the eye, investigate its refraction by the optical media, note the production of images on the retina, and discover the chemical transformation into nervous excitation that takes place in the rods and cones.   In the same way, he will follow the chemically active particles in the media of air and water as far as the smell-receptors, and their effect on the nerve-endings of the olfactory nerves. And so he will deal with the other sense impressions.

In the course of this study it becomes evident that, outside the animal under observation, numerous influences proceed from the object that are not taken up, because a certain intensity of the external influence is required if a nerve is to be excited.   Physical and chemical processes in the outer world must exceed a certain *threshold* if they are to act as *stimuli* affecting the nervous system of the animal.   This threshold can be raised or lowered by special means in the animal's nervous system   Moreover, by their anatomical structure, the receptors are obliged to admit only those stimuli that are *suitable* for them

By the structure of its receptors, every animal is cut off from a great number of physical and chemical influences coming from the outer world, and it is only through stimuli that the outer world gets in touch with the nervous system.

If we take the anatomical structure of the receptors as given, this whole process can be investigated by purely physical and chemical methods, and that is just what physiology has to do.

When an animal meets with different stimuli, the physiologist will be inclined to assume that these make different impressions on the animal, and provoke it to different responses. Likewise he will assume that the same stimulus makes the same impression on the animal, and calls forth the same response.

Neither of these assumptions is correct. As we have seen, different stimuli, proceeding from the most various objects, produce the same response in Paramecium. And the same stimulus—an air-wave, for instance—produces a different effect when it strikes the skin of a man from what it does when it reaches his ear : in the one case, we speak of vibration, in the other, of sound.

For the biological study of an animal, therefore, knowledge of the stimuli is not enough. Yet another factor must be sought in order to explain why the animal should give the same response. I shall call this factor an indication

The indication is not a physiological factor like the stimulus, but a biological factor which we deduce from the animal's response. It cannot, however, be constructed from the stimuli alone, because its formation depends on the animal itself, and because it cannot be understood at all without knowledge of the means that the animal employs for that formation.

As soon as we are dealing with the inner processes of the animal, the psychologist comes along all ready with his assertion that we must take account of the psychic qualities. Again we must insist that the biologist, like the physiologist and the physicist, cannot admit such a change of standpoint without deserting his science. This does not mean, however, that he should give up the critical judgment which should be his in virtue of his position as observer. In this sense, the biologist is also a psychologist, because any event that comes to his knowledge takes place in his world, and that world is built up of his subjective sensations.

It is not possible even for the biologist to transfer the

event observed by him (as in the case of an animal influenced by an external object) outside the frame created by his own subjectivity. He is always dealing with events that take place in *his* space and in *his* time and with *his* qualities.

Just as we referred physico-chemical processes to our own qualities, so we can never treat biological processes otherwise than on this basis.

If we consider the process, such as an implement influencing an animal in the direction its movement takes, we must first and foremost analyse the implement by breaking it up into its properties and looking for its rule of function, so as to decide which of the properties serves the animal as indication, or whether a function-rule belonging to the animal itself is employed in that way. Thus our research is everywhere limited by our own qualities and capacities.

We can indeed show that Paramecium does not use a function-rule as indication, and hence has no implements in its sensed-world. We can show that it does not use outlines as indications, and so has neither objects nor material things in its sensed-world. Further, we can show that the most diverse properties, which for us form very different qualities, fuse into one single indication : but what qualities this forms in the mind of Paramecium passes our comprehension. As biologists we can avoid these unanswerable questions, since our inquiry is not directed towards the content of the various qualities or mark-signs, but only towards their employment as indications.

This task devolving on the indications is clearly distinguishable from that of the stimuli and of the qualities, and thus assumes a central position in biology, which makes it necessary for us to discuss in detail the theory of indications.

The starting-point for an understanding of every theory of indications is the fact that every impression an animal experiences is both fundamentally like and fundamentally unlike all other impressions.

This seemingly very contradictory fact is based on the following arrangement, which is a fundamental one for all animals. Every stimulus meeting an animal is transformed everywhere in the body into the same nervous excitation : in thus far, all impressions received by an animal are essentially like one another   On the other hand, all the stimuli the point of entry of which is removed by so much as the diameter of one cell from the next point of entry, are taken up and led away by other nerve-fibrils : in so far, all the impressions that an animal receives are essentially different from one another.

By making use in various ways of these two contradictory possibilities, the organisation of the animal is, in principle, at liberty to convert every conceivable combination of impressions into indications   For instance, it may make all the receptor nerves run together to form a network, and then all the differences brought about by the presence of different nerves are lost. In such a case, all the impressions will deliver the same indication.

On the other hand, it is open to the organisation to preserve the individuality of the various nerve-persons, and to employ them in combination in accordance with plan ; then we get numerous and complicated indications produced.

From which we perceive that the number of indications and their composition are the business of the organisation of the animal subject.

It is important to make some sort of picture of this organisation, which, though only approximate, shall suffice for the chief requirements   It is characteristic of the animal's organisation as a whole that it consists of all the functional units which we call organs. These are divided up into sub-sidiary organs, on which devolve the exercise of part-functions, while collectively they carry out the function of the whole. Thus the receptor nerves (those which receive stimuli and conduct excitation) all form separate part-organs, which open into another organ, the nervous network for collecting stimulation. This network, on its part, sends out intra-central fibres to the motor organs of the nervous system.

The part-organs collectively form a closed organ, which, in virtue of its function, we may call a *mark-organ*, since its duty is to create the indications that are of importance to the animal.

If the mark-organ embraces the entire central network of all the receptor nerves, the animal has only one single indica-tion : this is the case with the lower animals.

In higher animals, where the mark-organ includes the receptor nerves in the most various combinations, the same receptor nerves can enter into connection with different nerve-networks. Then different indications in the outer world exhibit certain similar properties.

Finally the mark-organs may serve to unite into one indication, not merely simultaneous impressions, but impres-sions received at different times. And this is a super-mechanical faculty.

In animals that are little centralised, such as the sea-urchin, the mark-organs embrace without distinction the localised nerves lying alongside one another ; in such a case, the indications are separated from one another only by space In the higher animals, with highly developed sense-organs, the organs for the indications receive nerves, the local grouping of which retains its specific irritability In such cases, the indications differ from one another as regards content.

Even if we had very exact knowledge concerning the

mark-organs of an animal, and could determine the indications belonging to it, yet all we could say for certain would be,— " This animal fixes the limits between the qualities in the way we do, or in a different way from what we do." But as to the qualities themselves, we could state nothing further. An outside observer can never do so, for that would require his being able to get inside the mind of the animal itself.

Now in the great majority of cases we are in complete ignorance concerning the mark-organs of animals, and are compelled to deduce these from the indications to which the animals react. The indications that we study in this way are equipped with our human qualities, and there is nothing for us to do but to use them just as they are. But we shall fall into the crudest sort of error if we have not learnt to analyse the objects that we observe in their effect on animals so thoroughly that we are in a position to treat the qualities as independent factors. For it follows from what we have been saying, that every impression of every object is analysed down to its finest detail at the periphery of the animal, by being taken up into countless nerve-persons ; and it is only afterwards, in the mark-organ, that synthesis occurs. And for this synthesis there are various rules, which we can test only by comparing them with the rules known to us from the way in which our own implements are composed.

Now suddenly we see why it is that we cannot omit from biology the study of the theory of knowledge. For this alone teaches us to reduce our human indications to the simplest factors, and then to combine them once more.

All implements in the world are really nothing but human indications. If we want to study those of animals, we must know the fundamental factors of which the human ones are composed, and by what rules this composition takes place

Anything else is sheer amateurishness.

To ascertain correctly what are an animal's indications

requires considerable skill in observation and experiment ; but the most important thing is to formulate the question rightly, and this can come only from a sufficient knowledge of the basic problems

THE HIGHER GRADES OF THE WORLDS-AS-SENSED

As soon as outlines of bodies appear as indications, the picture presented by the world-as-sensed alters fundamentally, for now juxtaposition in space begins to become more and more important. It is true that in the lower animals, such as sea-urchins and molluscs, a stimulus coming from the left is responded to otherwise than one coming from the right, for, in the one instance, the effector organs of the right side of the body respond, and, in the other, those of the left side.

But the indication itself remains the same, and in its composition shows no sort of spatial differentiation. Only when spatial distinctions appear in the indication itself, can we speak of a higher grade of sensed-world. The eyes of insects have the power of transferring to the central nervous system in a schematic form definite spatial arrangements of the pictures appearing on their retina, to which we shall refer when dealing with the inner world of animals. For the study of the world-as-sensed it is sufficient to determine what sort of outlines, and in what degree of exactness, are employed as indications

It is worth noting that, in an insect, outlines are not swept by glancing movements of the eye, but by a stationary retina. It is very difficult for us to determine in how far our eye, when stationary, estimates outlines   In any case, when the retina is not moving, it deals only with surfaces, and not with solid bodies

It is very important, but very difficult, to set about these experiments with animals in a really critical spirit. We are brought to a standstill at the very outset It should be emphasised, however, that the Germans are the only investigators who have remained conscious of the difficulty of their task. The experiments by Americans are far too crude to be taken seriously. It is far from obvious why a triangle or a circle should serve as the basis of the first experiments to determine form-perception in an animal such as a bee, which has to distinguish the outlines of flowers ; and, as Fritsch has pointed out, this points to a complete misunderstanding of the biological problems.

Investigation of indications can be successful only when we have analysed the various responses of an animal within the setting of its normal life, for the difference in response affords us the most reliable clue to the differences between indications.

The circle and the triangle are symbols from plane geometry, which are constructed from our subjective direction-signs ; and they have nothing to do with the possibly recognisable outlines of the objects that are of importance for certain function-circles of certain animals, and there find application as indications.

If it is important for an insect to be able to recognise a certain enemy a long way off, it may be that the outline of this enemy alone serves as indication, and that no other outline in the world would so serve, although to us it might appear much simpler.

We must note, however, that the sureness with which flying insects avoid twigs and leaves does not at all imply that the outlines of these serve as indications. Whatever form they present, they one and all act merely as the same indication, namely, an obstacle.

If we want to get reliable information concerning form-perception, we must start from the form-signs and colour-signs of the objects that are the animal's prey or enemies, or from those signs in the males at the breeding-season. For only in such cases do we get an unequivocal response through the special reactions of the animal.

As has already been pointed out, it is not at all necessary that the indications of an animal should reach the same height in each of its function-circles.

As a rule, in the enemy-circle a mere movement will serve, whereas in the prey-circle even the outlines may have this value. The disputes between investigators hitherto depend on this difference, some maintaining that colours exist in the sensed-world of the lower animals, and others saying that they do not.

Among the Crustacea, the indications of the prey-circle seem to be of a purely chemical nature, while those of the enemy-circle are optical

The world-as-sensed undergoes an important enlargement when indications appear for the movements of the animal's own limbs. It is only among vertebrates that sensory nerves have been demonstrated with certainty in the muscles. And it is only when nerves of this kind appear that we can speak of a new function-circle, passing through the animal's own body.

From experiments on vertebrates in which the sensory roots of the spinal cord have been severed, we know something about this function-circle. There can be no doubt that it is only when the animal's own body in movement becomes an indication that a sharp line can be drawn in the world-as-sensed between the subject and the outside world. This separation of the two is quite lacking in the lower animals ; their own subject has no indications, for, as we shall see later on, in dealing with the lower animals even pain must be ruled out

The highest grade of world-as-sensed is reached when implements themselves become indications. Unfortunately, the American workers who have taken up this question have not thought things out on sufficiently theoretical lines ; and consequently the results they have achieved have no value at all. Who, having the slightest idea of what an implement is, would straightway proceed to the hardest problem of all, and confront an animal with one designed for man's own use ?

An implement is formed by a human function-rule, which combines the most various sense-qualities into a unity How can an animal in any way take up an implement as an indication, if the function-rule is not its own but the observer's ?

To presume the existence of implements in the sensed-world of an animal supposes that the animal has the power to form its own function-rules for what it does For this, firstly, its own movements must be turned to account as indications, and, secondly, they must be combined by rules into definite actions. Only then may one assume that this rule connects with other indications, and forms the implement.

If, for instance, we put a ladder in front of a monkey that knows its own movements very well, and whose movements have been compacted into actions, and the monkey climbs up the ladder, we may assume that for the monkey the ladder has become an implement for climbing on ; though even so, not a ladder in the human sense, for the climbing of monkeys is quite different from the climbing of men. But if the monkey is confronted with a door-bolt or a door-latch, how can it form this implement at all ? For it knows no concerted actions for door-opening, and so can have no rule for this action.

But even where there are unified actions, the connection of their function-rules with the indications remains an exceedingly difficult problem. The connection seems to be easiest between the function-rules and the medium, which has practically no indications. We can imagine that for a fish water, as what can be swum in, becomes the pure expression of the function-rule ; this rule connects with the indications thereby formed, only through the influence of the water-pressure on the lateral-line organs, and these indications correspond to our qualities of density. But it is quite uncertain whether a fish brings to its mark-organ in any sort of form the function-rule that governs its swimming movement.

This entire field awaits exploration. But it is extremely important that the road to true knowledge should not be blocked by arbitrary experiment and amateurish formulation of the problem.

Fortunately, Koehler has succeeded in showing that a chimpanzee which sees a banana lying on the far side of the bars of its cage and out of its reach, will use a stick lying at hand to pull the banana nearer. If the stick is taken away, the ape will use any movable object that it can push through the bars, in order to secure the fruit. The form, colour and consistency of the thing it uses is a matter of indifference ; the only consideration is the possibility of its efficacy in doing what is required of it So here also the function forms the object. Koehler speaks, in a descriptive way, of a "stick metamorphosis" of a bundle of straw, of an old shoe and of other things of the kind.

Later on, the optical image also comes in to form implements, when the ape pulls the leaves off a twig in order to make it look like a stick.

It is very interesting to find that at first the goal must be in view, if the stick is to be used. If the stick lies behind the monkey, it will not be used in the first set of experiments. As long as the monkey sees the banana, it does not see the stick ; and conversely, if it is looking at the stick, the banana disappears from his field of view, and with it goes the motive for making a stick. Later on, the indication of the banana outlasts the momentary impression, and the stick, wherever it be lying, is picked up and used.

Koehler lays special emphasis on the fact that every action is to be grasped as a unity, comprehensible as a whole only with reference to the aim.   He went on to alter and to multiply the part-actions which make up the action as a whole He made the monkey use a short stick to draw a long stick towards itself before it could get at the banana.   And here came in the limits of individual talent dependent on inherent differences.   To use my terminology, different monkeys had at their disposal different lengths of impulse-sequences.

The question of " intelligence " in monkeys, which Koehler raises, goes far beyond the scope of biology.

PAIN

Pain forms one of the most powerful indications   It is an indication of the subject's own body, and its chief duty is to prevent self-mutilation.   So it imposes a strong check which shall prevent, in all circumstances, the continuation of any initiated action that is hurtful to the body.

This is especially necessary in the case of carnivorous animals ; rats, for instance, will immediately devour their own legs, if the sensory nerves to these have been severed.

Now in many animals a tendency to self-mutilation is a fundamental arrangement in their organisation, serving to save the whole body by the sacrifice of imperilled limbs.   In such animals, the action of pain as a check to the reflex would merely be an inconvenience, and so we may assume that it is not there.

Moreover, in some cases where there is no tendency to self-mutilation, it can be shown directly that there is no pain, for even when the body is being injured there is no check set up.   You can put the hind end of the big brown dragon-fly between its own jaws, and see how it proceeds to chew up its own body.

K

Most of the lower animals are so constructed that they are never in danger of injuring their own bodies. When that does not occur, however, as in the sea-urchin, I have been able to show that there is a special arrangement, which I have called *autodermophily*, and this takes the place of pain. The skin of these animals secretes a substance that prevents the normal reflex of snapping by the pedicellariæ.

Amœbæ are able to distinguish the pseudopodia of their own body from those of other individuals. What this depends on we cannot determine. The conditions are reversed here from what they are in other animals. Since they have no framework which can be injured by their eating themselves, it is quite in order for them to be perpetually ingesting their own protoplasm. So that, in their case, pain would make their very existence problematical

Pain certainly does not play the absolutely senseless rôle usually ascribed to it, of transforming the whole living world into a vale of misery and fear. Pain is present only where there is a place for it in the plan of the organism, and where, consequently, it is necessary and useful.

THE INNER WORLD.—THE PHYSIOLOGICAL POINT OF VIEW

Whosoever turns from psychology or the theory of knowledge to the physiology of the central nervous system, will meet with very great disappointment. Here he might hope to find light thrown on many unsolved problems, for the organ that is generally supposed to serve as intermediary between the world of the flesh and the world of the spirit, ought surely to display, at any rate in its fundamental features, some resemblance to the spiritual organism which the psychologist and the student of the theory of knowledge thinks he can recognise in the mind. On this consideration the theory of psycho-physical parallelism was based, a theory which was

supported by many eminent men ; but the more the central
nervous system is investigated, the less are such hopes
realised. We might at least expect that the very marked
centralisation which is expressed in the apperceptive process
of our ego, should be discoverable in the central apparatus
of the body.

Instead of which, the investigator finds nothing but a
guiding apparatus, which serves to connect the two " fronts "
of the body—the one, the receptor, turned towards the world-
as-sensed, and the other, the effector, towards the world of
action.

In its main features, the guiding apparatus is the same
from the lowest animals to the highest   Wheresoever qualitatively different stimuli effect an entry, we find that their
specific peculiarity is taken from them. Whether an air-
wave strikes the ear, or an etheric wave the retina, the same
transformation is set going in both cases. A excitation is
around, which passes along the nerves in waves. The length
and speed of these waves may vary to a certain degree, but
fundamentally the process is always the same. The various
stimuli are not distinguished through different excitations in
the nervous system, but by the "person" of the nerves
through which they flow. We have already said something
about this fundamental law of the nervous system : it was
discovered by Johannes Muller, who made of it, along with
all its corollaries, the basis of comparative physiology of the
nervous system.

Nervous excitation itself is a process hitherto unexplained,
which reveals itself as electrical oscillatory waves on the
galvanometer, or as chemical waves of fibrillar staining.

The idea we get of it in these ways does not suffice to
give us a general survey of the way in which excitation
operates in the system as a whole ; so the physiologist must
make use of a current analogy, and treat the whole nervous

system as a system of tubes in which alterations of pressure and quantity are necessary.

This tube system is especially closely linked up with the muscles ; these are roused into activity by the waves of excitation in the nervous system, and the muscular excitation reacts again on the nervous. For this purpose, each muscle-fibre is connected with a motor-centre, which we may imagine as a self-working hydraulic apparatus, regulating both the pressure and the quantity, and throughout faithfully reflecting the condition of excitation of the muscle obeying it. I have called these centres *representatives*, because their duty is to represent the muscles in the nervous system.

We find the effector connections between nervous system and muscles already perfectly developed in the lowest animals, for even these, if they are to live, must have perfect control over the movements they perform, few and simple though these be.

In the lower animals we find the representatives grouped round a simple nerve network, which has so-called tone-centres ; these tone-centres are likewise automatic hydraulic apparatuses, controlling the state of excitation of the musculature as a whole.   Into this central network flow the excitations coming from the receptors.

If the central network is not subdivided, they all have the same effect on the representatives of the muscles, which, according to a very simple law, are set in vibration   The excitation always flows along in the direction of the extended muscle, and, since most muscles are constructed as pairs of opposites, which reciprocally extend one another, the contraction of the one muscle produces the extension of its opposite, and so opens, as it were, the gateway for the excitation to enter.   And thus a forward movement follows on every stimulus.

As we ascend the ladder of the animal kingdom, we notice that, first of all, differentiation sets in in the motor apparatus.

Portions of the central network are split off, along with their centres which control special groups of representatives and the muscles belonging to them, and these muscles constitute a definite locomotor apparatus controlling a leg, an arm, a wing, or a fin.

In cuttle-fishes it can be shown that in this way there arise higher and lower central motor apparatuses, of which the lower are arranged from the point of view of position, the higher from that of function   In insects the activities of the several limbs are completely governed by the centres directly coordinated with them ; and all that is effected by the sensory part of the network in the brain is the onset or cessation of the movement.

The sensory network is gradually moved further forward to where the main receptors lie, which, excited by the stimuli they receive, govern the activity of the animal as a whole.

Differentiation of the sensory network appears relatively late. In many cases, a division comes about simply by the regions which belong to the various sense-organs separating away from one another. In such animals, the function-circle of the enemy employs other receptors and parts of the sensory network than those used by the function-circle of food.

As soon as outlines serve the body as indications, differentiation of the sensory part of the nervous system speeds off. For now it is useful so to combine quite definite sensory nerves of the eye, that their common or successive excitations are linked up into a whole, which makes its way into the guiding mechanism as a new unity. I have called these nervous unities " anatomical schemata," because they do not give a complete reflection of the outline in the external world, but merely a summary combination of its most important parts, and this with a degree of exactness suitable for the particular animal

The appearance of such schemata in the brain is of twofold importance. Firstly, it enriches the world-as-sensed with the things of space ; and secondly, it permits the animal, as soon as the first spatial indications sound in the manner characteristic for the schema, to form the whole schema, and in this way to recognise the presence of, say, an enemy, when the enemy is only partially visible.

In the lower animals, the whole stimulus forming the indication must get going, whereas, when there are schemata, only the opening notes need sound for the whole schema to act as indication. In this way, the schemata acquire a high degree of independence in the steering mechanism. The animal no longer flees before the direct stimulus of the enemy ; it no longer is directly incited to seek its prey ; but it flees from and seeks for the schemata of these

Up to this point the guiding apparatus in the brain can now be traced with some certainty. All conclusions that go beyond this point leave the firm basis of fact   For instance, it is not yet possible to decide whether the law of the complementary effect of colours is referable to a special arrangement in the retina or to a special interlacing of the receptor nerves in the brain, or whether it does not elude a mechanical interpretation altogether   We have been able to establish only this much—that we are dealing with a law belonging to the subject alone, and completely independent of the reciprocal action of the stimuli in space.

In addition to the anatomical framework characterising the guiding apparatus of the brain, we must also take account of the brain's chemical framework.   We can compare the effects of the central nervous system on the muscles of the body with a typewriter, in which the striking of each key releases a certain letter.   We get the same thing on the chemical side, when we furnish the cells we want to affect with a specific chemical substance that will combine with only one other specific substance.

In this way, after the one specific substance has been formed at some part of the body, a certain cell at the other end of the body, can, through the agency of the circulatory system, be struck as precisely as the letters of the alphabet on the typewriter.

The part played in digestion by these substances cast into the blood-stream—the so-called " hormones "—has only quite recently been determined. But it has been known for a long time that the breathing movements of vertebrates are kept in full activity thanks to the stimulation of nerve-cells in the central nervous system by the chemical products of tissue-respiration.

Further, there can be no doubt that the completely different behaviour of animals in the states of hunger and of satiety, is referable to change in the irritability of the central organs belonging to the food-circle. For a newly-fed shark a dead sardine simply is not there, because in this condition the shark's " stimulus threshold " is too high. But hunger lowers the stimulus threshold, and then the sardine appears in the sensed-world of the shark.

Steinach's remarkable experiments have shown what an influence internal secretion exercises on the whole sexual life of the higher animals

The purpose of this chemical organisation is to regulate thoroughly the guidance of the central nervous apparatus vis-à-vis of the influence of the indications. In comparison with this, direct stimulation of the nervous system is relatively negligible. For the most part, only a kind of " chemical tone " is attained, which, in full conformity with plan, provides that, according to the needs of the body, one function-circle shall find acceptance rather than another, by the indications thereof being more powerful or alone operative. Thus at the breeding-season the prey-circle, and even the enemy-circle, yield to the sexual circle, the indications of which

are then more potent than all others This happens at the
time when many animals put on their bridal apparel, and
the colours and patterns of their dress act on direction as
decisive indications.

But there are many instances of reversal of the steering
gear, in which there is no proof that we are dealing with a
change of chemical tone. The best known example is that
of sleeping and waking Bohn was able to show that in sea-
anemones the ebb and flow persisted as internal change of
tone after the animals had been transferred to the still waters
of the aquarium The most remarkable example of one
single change of tone in the year is given by the palolo worm,
which, at the time of sexual maturity, and on one predictable
moonlight night, divides, and comes to the surface of the sea.

Both the anatomical part of the directing apparatus
(which we usually call the reflex apparatus, and which by
analogy we understand as a mechanism) and the chemical-
tone apparatus (which from the mechanical point of view
we are only just beginning to understand) are the expression
of a machine-like framework

THE BIOLOGICAL POINT OF VIEW

In contrast to physiology, biology considers the manifestations of the central nervous system, not as processes
going on inside of apparatus, but as processes within *organs*.

Physiology concerns itself only with the machinery inside
the framework, which undoubtedly constitutes the great part
of the central nervous system. Biology also includes in its
consideration the protoplasm not entering into the framework, which transforms apparatus into organs. Protoplasm
has the important task of continuously regulating the framework of the central nervous system, and of making good such
injuries as arise. This super-mechanical activity raises the

organ to a higher level than mere apparatus, and endows it
with the peculiar property of life.

The infallibility with which protoplasm, wherever it is
at work, is able to improve and repair the framework, shows
that its impulse-sequence corresponds to a definite rule,
which in this way governs the physico-chemical processes.
We can prove that the super-mechanical factor operative in
protoplasm must be a rule, bound indeed to a definite place in
space by the material with which it works, but in itself super-
spatial, since it disposes of the spatial arrangement of the
framework.

As we have learnt from protoplasmic animals that are as
yet without framework, the regulated impulse-sequence active
in protoplasm and creating the framework, is at the same
time a function-rule which compacts the separate movements
into an action. In order to perform this action, as, for
instance, in the action of digestion by Paramecium, framework
must be formed, which, in accordance with the function-rule,
comes into being and then disappears again, and which, still
in accordance with that same rule, kills the food, digests it,
and ejects the remains.

Where a permanent framework has arisen, as in the
majority of living creatures, the formative activity of the
rule persists, and is exhibited in the super-mechanical regulation and repair of injured parts.

From this it follows that an organ differs from an apparatus
in not being the product of a function-rule, at one time active
and then fixed, but in remaining continually under the influence of such a rule. Moreover, wherever there is unused
protoplasm, it is capable of an impulse-sequence, which, in
obedience to a rule of its own, produces new framework.

Now we can see that a difference in principle is involved,
when, on the one hand, the physiologist divides up the central /
nervous system into apparatus, and on the other, the biologist

divides it up into organs.   Where the physiologist analyses it
into sensory and motor apparatus, the biologist makes a corresponding division into mark-organs and action-organs.

The mark-organ includes the framework + protoplasm, in
so far as it serves for the creation of indications.   The action-
organ comprises framework + protoplasm, in so far as it serves
for the creation of a definite movement-sequence, which we
call an action.

Every time an indication appears, a function-rule lies
behind it, and comes to expression in the structure as well
as in the activity of the mark-organ.   In the same way, a
function-rule lies behind every action, and finds expression
in the structure and the activity of the action-organ   From
this it follows that the actions of an animal can be closed
within a definitive function-rule.   This may express itself
in an immutable framework, in which case an involuntary
action or *reflex* is created   Or the function-rule may make
the framework from time to time, as circumstances arise ,
then we get a protoplasmic *instinctive action*   Between
these two sorts of action come the so-called *plastic actions,*
among which *actions based on experience* are to be reckoned.
Finally, there are *controlled actions*, in which the function-rule
of the action-organ makes its determinative appearance even
in the mark-organ

The physiological analysis of a central nervous system is
finished, when the mark- and action-organs have been investigated.

The biological analysis is finished, when the function-rules
for perception and for action are laid clear

IMPORTANCE OF THE RULES OF FUNCTION
FOR THE FUNCTION-CIRCLE

It is impossible to understand the relation between mark-organs and action-organs, and the interdependence of their function-rules, unless we first separate from one another the individual function-circles of which these organs form the keystones.

We must note that each circle—for instance, the enemy-circle—is in principle always closed, however simple the indication that gives information of the enemy's presence, and even if it consists merely of a smell, or of a slight movement ; the act, whether of flight or of defence, that serves to ward off the enemy, will always be initiated with completeness. Consequently, the two organs may be of very different degrees of development. The indication may be highly complex, and the action may consist of a simple movement ; or, conversely, a very elaborate action may follow when the indication is quite simple.

To facilitate a general survey, I give below the simple diagram of a function-circle

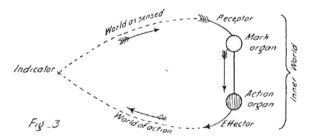

Fig. 3

As the diagram shows, the inner world is divided into two parts ; one, which receives the impressions, is turned towards the world-as-sensed, and the other, which distributes the effects, is turned towards the world of action. Between mark-organ and action-organ lies the watershed of the whole function-circle. The mark-organ and the action-organ are each of them controlled by a rule ; the one arranges the impressions in the mark-organ, and so creates the indications; the other arranges the effects produced by the action-organ, and so creates the actions   Both rules are focussed accurately on the indication in the external world, the appearance of which is the signal for the indications to arise, and which has then " to be dealt with." The circle forms a unified whole, for, just as in an organism, each part is dependent on the others. The design which connects each part becomes intelligible down to the last detail only when we see the circle as a whole. The receptors are focussed on the typical manifestations of the indicators, whether these be chemical, optical or of some other kind ; and, in virtue of their specific structure, the effectors deal with the indicator in the most effective way. The mark-organs and action-organs are just as nicely focussed on the indicator as are the receptors, and their rules embrace it with scrupulous exactness from the sides both of action and of reaction

The diagram given above serves to illustrate the whole of what is done by an animal's nervous system, in so far as this relates to reflexes, plastic actions, or instinctive actions. In the case of reflexes, however, we must assume that the framework of the action-organ is all ready and prepared beforehand ; while with instincts, the rule of the action-organ can still be built up and broken down again. We know a number of cases that are explicable only by super-mechanical regulation, and so prove the intervention of proto-plasm. In contradistinction to these, reflex actions, which are usually of a simple kind, unfold, as it were, automatically.

But it is characteristic both for reflex and for instinctive actions, that the action-rule reveals itself only in the actions, and in no way enters into the indications and the rules affecting these   In the highest animals, however, the creature's own action-rule penetrates further and further into the world-as-sensed, and there assumes direction and control.

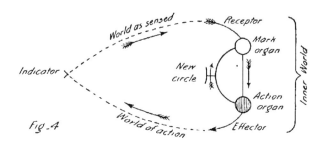

Fig. 4

A new circle is introduced within the animal's own central organ, for the support of the external function-circle, and this connects the action-organ with the mark-organ.   In this way, the animal's own action-rule fits in with the indications stimulated from without, and now serves the mark-rule as a skeleton to which it may attach the external indications.

Now for the first time there appear in the world-as-sensed actual implements, possessing a function-rule.   The world-as-sensed of the simpler animals contained nothing but objects. When the movements of the animal's own limbs enter the mark-organ, it becomes possible for it to control its own actions.   But so long as the action-rule taken over from the mark-organ is not used to form implements, there are nothing but objects in the world-as-sensed.

As we know, even objects are elaborate unities, extended in space and in time   But implements arise in the world-as-sensed only when the subject's own action-rule endows them with a function : this action-rule combines all the properties and capacities in such conformity with plan that they are obliged to obey an inner rule, which we call the function-rule of implements.   So we human beings transfer our own function-rule to implements, just as we transfer to them the indications we ourselves have formed.

These are general laws, depending on the structure of each individual subject. And so it is quite inadmissible to impose on the sensed-world of animals the human function-rules on which, as something taken quite for granted, we base all the implements that fill our sensed-world. We must first get to know the action-rules of animals, before we can proceed to the question of implement-forming in animals. As soon as an observer turns his back on an animal, his human implements disappear, and only these really belonging to the animal continue to surround it.

Moreover, we must learn to regard the function-rule as a real natural factor, and attempt to investigate its effects in all subjects

Even the " psychoid," introduced by Driesch into natural science, is to be understood in this sense The psychoid is an objectively active rule, which we must observe in operation. The word psychoid indicates that here we have to do with a creation by the psyche, for a super-spatial law comes in, not belonging to the body, but controlling it Can it be that in the function-rule we have come upon something that speaks for the existence of an animal psyche ? A something that justifies the psychologists in setting their science on an objective basis ?

I do not think that such an assumption is justified. There can be no doubt that there are super-spatial rules to which in the last instance the control of even the animal body is assigned. But knowledge of these rules, just as of those governing the animal body itself, must be referred to the laws of our own mind : and the term " psychoid " may easily mislead us into supposing that we have here the proof of an apperception by the animal subject. This is not the case. All we can make sure of is the operation of a rule controlling

the material of the central nervous system. We have
absolutely no knowledge as to whether that is apperceived
by the animal.

THE WORLD OF ACTION

When we considered the world-as-sensed and the inner
world of animals, we could not fail to recognise a certain
parallelism between the physiological and biological ways of
considering them, a parallelism which permitted of the two
sciences being mutually complementary and corroborative ;
but when we turn to consider the world of action, this parallelism completely disappears.

According to physiological notions, every animal imparts
to the universe the effect released by the movements of its
limbs or the secretion of its glands. And in the universe,
these manifestations of the animal body continue their effect
from atom to atom according to the law of causality. In
principle, the step of a beetle's foot or the stroke of a dragon-
fly's wing must carry their effect as far as the dog-star. For,
according to the causal conception, even the smallest component of natural phenomena is absolutely necessary, and
cannot be thought away from the general system of action
and reaction, without making the whole impossible.

It is perfectly obvious that this point of view does not
do justice to the marvellously constructed effector apparatus
of animals.

To appreciate rightly what the effector organs perform
in the function-circle, we must consider in more detail the
laws that govern our human implements   Hitherto we have
considered only our unified tools (such, for instance, as the
ladder), and shown that they have a framework constructed
in accordance with a function-rule, which fits them for a
counter-action in support of our human activities—in this case,
the act of climbing.

Now there are a whole number of tools, the framework of which does not express the entire counter-action ; and these always require the help of other implements in order actually to carry out a function   If, for instance, we take the nail of a box, there is required for its counter-action (which backs up our action of holding the box together) firstly, the hammer, for the blows of which the head of the nail is suitably shaped, and, secondly, the wood of which the box is made, the consistency of which permits the nail to penetrate, but prevents its coming out again easily.

The framework of the nail, then, unlike that of the ladder, is not in itself adequate for the exercise of a counter-action. In addition, a hammer and some wood are necessary, if the counter-action is to be achieved.   If we give a special name to the connection that exists, in strict conformity with plan, between different implements not having any lasting material association, we may speak of " *inter-adjustment.*"   In contrast to the framework, which word means a lasting functional connection according to a rule, " inter-adjustment " means a functional connection that appears only for a time ; it likewise is subject to a rule.

Graber has called the effectors of animals their tools. We might let this term pass, if the relations between tool and material were not really far too general to do justice to the extraordinarily close connection that is manifested in the function-rule.

In the function-circle, all the parts, even if not concrescent as in the organism, are nevertheless so perfectly fashioned with relation to one another, that they form temporarily an actual framework   Knowing this, we see that, in considering the world of action, the biologist must follow a completely different route from that taken by the physiologist.

To define briefly the very different attitudes of the two sciences, we may say that physiology regards the effectors of

an animal in their relation to the world as it regards human
tools, whereas biology regards them as human tools that
become effective in conformity with plan only when they are
fitted into the surrounding-world

INTER-ADJUSTMENT

In considering the inner world of animals, we have learnt
to distinguish between mark-rule and action-rule. These two
rules constitute only portions of the general plan that is
expressed in the whole structure and in all the actions of
animals. We have seen that organs are fitted into one
another like the parts of a machine, and so we have spoken
of framework. But there can be no doubt that this entire
framework is likewise subject to a rule. This rule is
manifested so clearly in the permanent anatomical framework that we need not discuss it further. On the other
hand, we must seek for the rule of inter-adjustment, when
the effectors, as they deal with the things of the external
world, create a temporary framework.

As a matter of fact, in the world of action we are dealing
with a temporary framework of this kind, which becomes
apparent only when the animal shows activity in one of its
function-circles. The most obvious inter-adjustment is that
which connects the effectors of animals with the medium.
Merely by looking at these, we can tell whether we have to
do with an animal belonging to the air, to the water, or to
the land   Fins, wings and feet bear the unmistakable imprint
of their vocation. The more closely the function is confined
to a narrowly circumscribed medium, the more clearly can we
recognise from the effectors to what it is they are adjusted.
We distinguish feet that act as suckers, feet for running, feet
for leaping, and feet for climbing, and these give us a secure
basis whence we may proceed to further classification of land

L

animals In parasites we find prehensile feet which are
exactly inter-adjusted with the tissues of the hosts furnishing
them with a medium.

There can be as little question about inter-adjustment in
the sex-circle. The mutual differentiations of the sexual
organs in both male and female, extending even to the finest
detail, is developed in butterflies to an especially instructive
degree. The study of the secondary sexual organs yields us
an inexhaustible supply of information regarding an inter-
adjustment that is positively marvellous. For here it is not
merely a question of an anatomical interlocking of effectors
constructed in pairs, but of an inter-adjustment which
connects the effectors of one sex with the receptors of the
other. There are female butterflies producing a substance
not yet demonstrable by chemical or physical means, the
existence of which Fabre could prove only by the fact that
the place where the female had settled attracted the males
towards it from miles around.

All conceivable effects, optic, acoustic and tactile, are
employed in the sexual life of animals in order to bring about
so-called sexual selection. That is to say, there is everywhere
an extraordinarily delicate inter-adjustment, which secures,
even if only for a short period, the association of the two sexes.

Another function-circle, which we have not yet mentioned,
connects parents and children among the higher animals.
We have only to remind ourselves of the familiar instance of
parental care, and we are at once convinced that here also
there is inter-adjustment.

We shall take only one example of this, which happens to
be especially instructive From studying Boldamus' vast
collection of eggs, I have convinced myself that the female
cuckoo always lays in the nest of other birds eggs that resemble theirs in colour. Which shows that the effector organs
of the cuckoo are harmonised with the mark-organs of other

birds in such a way as to secure that these shall take over the care of the young.

This is not a case of an effect on our human mark-organs ; these are not deceived in the least, for at the first glance we can pick out the cuckoo's egg.   But song-birds are completely taken in, and proceed to care for the changeling.   This gives us a really reliable means of defining the sensed-world of song-birds.

We may readily admit that inter-adjustment between the cuckoo and the song-bird is perfect in so far as it concerns the cuckoo ; but we shall the more strenuously deny that it spells perfection for the song-bird.

Here again we come upon a question that we have already touched ; and we must make up our minds about it before we proceed with our discussion of inter-adjustments

PERFECTION

We go on now to speak of a problem that is especially important in the function-circle of the enemy, when attacker and attacked come face to face.   We may assert that, in all such cases, perfection is not attained, at least by one of the antagonists, for the one that is defeated shows, by the very fact of its defeat, that it was imperfectly equipped for the fight.   Even when both appear quite remarkably well equipped for battle, and are perfectly fitted into the enemy-circle as regards their effectors, this inter-adjustment must be imperfect for one of the two parties, if that is worsted.

If even in such cases the inter-adjustment, though apparently in conformity with plan, is really imperfect, then the plan of Nature is not perfect ; and we have a right to be incredulous concerning the perfection of the framework of animals in general.   This seems to justify the view that Nature is full of imperfection.   The plan of Nature degenerates into a mere illusion, and what we admire as design might turn out to be a mere game of chance ; which is what Darwinism actually assumes.

It was not without good reason that Darwin made struggle the central point in his theory, for here there does seem to be a distinct hiatus in the perfection of design.

The limitations of the organism. This gap, however, is only apparent, and it arises from a false definition. *Perfection is not omnipotence, but merely means the correct and complete exercise of all the means available.* Even from the most perfect being conceivable we cannot look for the exercise of resources that it has not got. It must also be admitted that each animal, even if it employs perfectly all the means in its possession, cannot perform more than these permit it to do. By its resources, limits are set to the achievement of every animal. The sum of all the resources at an animal's disposal —such as the nature of its structure, the material of which it is made, its strength, its size, etc., i.e. the sum-total of all its properties and capacities—these make the organism. Every organism, accordingly, has fixed limits. It cannot be big and small at the same time, nor heavy and light, nor swift and sluggish. It cannot be built on a two-rayed system and on a four-rayed at the same time Its body cannot be both segmented and unsegmented ; its nervous system cannot simultaneously be coordinate and subordinate, centralised and decentralised A bee cannot be a lizard ; it cannot even be a wasp. Nor can it simultaneously belong to two species ; it can only be itself, within the limits set it by Nature.

Every organism can only be itself. But within itself it is perfect, because, unlike our human implements, which are composed of structure and framework, it consists of framework alone. Within it, all resources are exploited to the full. And so we may make the following statement :—*every living creature is, in principle, absolutely perfect.*

But every living creature may be worsted in conflict with an adversary, because that adversary has in its organisation other resources at its disposal.

In tropical countries there are two insects, the centipede and the bird-spider, which occasionally are very troublesome to man by reason of their poison. Once when I was at Dar-es-Salaam, a centipede appeared on our dining-table. I seized a knife and cut it through the middle. The result was that two centipedes ran away in opposite directions. A cut that divides a spider through the middle, finishes it at once. So here the centipede has an advantage. But if one puts both the animals in a glass, one can easily observe that the spider, beginning at the head end of the centipede, slowly devours it. The movement of the centipede, which snaps in every direction with its jaws, does not bother the spider in the least. As soon as the poison-jaw comes near the spider's hairy legs, the leg is lifted up and placed elsewhere. The animal built up of a number of similar segments is quite incapable of attacking its goal direct, and must succumb before the more highly centralised nervous system of its opponent.

But he who would conclude from such examples that superiority in the struggle is associated with higher differentiation, will reconsider his opinion when the life-history of the malaria parasite is put before him This minute uni-cellular animal has the power not only to adapt itself to the totally different tissue-juices of the mosquito and of man, but is able to find its way about in the anatomy of these two very unlike hosts.

In this case also, the animal that conquers has some kind of chemical resource, which extends beyond the limits set to the animal that is defeated.

Without making exact tests, it is impossible to say which animal will have the advantage over another. Sometimes

strength is victorious, sometimes poison, sometimes swiftness, sometimes inertia ; here the higher nervous system
wins, there the stouter armour, or sometimes the more subtle
chemistry ; and so forth.

But in each case we may assume that the animal is exploited up to the extreme limits set it by its organisation ;
not only does its framework employ all the resources available, but also its inter-adjustment within the function-circle
is perfect, an inter-adjustment which secures its food and
wards off its enemy.

It is as cheap as it is amateurish to sneer at the imperfection of Nature, without having regard to the limitations of
organisms. It is no sign of scientific insight. Unfortunately,
even Helmholtz did not a little to promote this view, through
his lack of caution in the comparisons he drew.

I think that I have now cleared up the misunderstanding,
and we can proceed with our consideration of inter-
adjustments

INTER-ADJUSTMENTS WITHIN THE ENEMY-
AND PREY-CIRCLES

Without some knowledge of what actually takes place in
Nature, it is impossible to make for oneself an adequate
picture of inter-adjustment ; just as with knowledge of the
framework, this can be got only through observation, and
never through logical discussion. I shall cite here two typical
examples, which illustrate the mutual relations of enemy and
prey, and give an impressive picture of inter-adjustment.

Sometimes it happens that prey and enemy are a match
for one another   Only when the weapons of the attacker are
parried by the adequate weapons of the attacked, can we
speak of a real struggle. Then the conditions at the moment,

which set the limit for each individual, decide whether attacker or attacked will emerge victorious from the fight.

We can watch a fight of this kind, when the star-fish Asterias attacks the sea-urchin Strongylocentrotus   The star-fish is provided with powerful tube-feet, which are covered with a poisonous mucus.   They are suited for gripping the firm shell of the sea-urchin and paralysing the muscles of the spines, while the five arms wind themselves round the spherical body of the opponent.   Then the membranous stomach bulges forth from the mouth, presses itself against the surface of the prey, and begins its digestive activity outside the assailant's own body

The behaviour of the sea-urchin is very remarkable. For general purposes, a close-set rampart of spines is sufficient to ward off hostile approach.   But the short spines cannot keep off the long tube-feet of this foe.   For this quite a different sort of defensive apparatus comes to the rescue. As soon as the tube-feet of the star-fish approach the sea-urchin, the spines lie down, and three-bladed pincers, swollen with poison, rise up, which hitherto have been hanging down flaccid.   The pincers grip into the tube-feet of Asterias, and, in so doing, break away from their base, so that, permanently lodged in the enemy, they can transfer to it their full load of poison.

If the sea-urchin is in good form and has not lost too many of its poison-pincers, it succeeds in driving off the star-fish   But if not, the star-fish is the victor.

The adjustment is as undeniable in the case of the sea-urchin as in that of the star-fish, and the limits set to both organisms are such that no one can say beforehand which will conquer.   The limit is determined by the condition of the animal's health at the moment.   The sea-urchin that is in bad condition will be conquered ; while the strong and healthy one, in full possession of its weapons, can count on victory, especially if the star-fish has recently fed well, and so follows up the attack feebly.

For another typical example we are indebted to the remarkable investigations of J. Fabre   I am thinking of the fight between the ichneumon-fly and the larva of the rose-beetle. The ichneumon-fly seizes the larva with her jaws on the dorsal side of the thorax, and bends her body round the larva, while her sting carefully feels over the ventral side until it comes to the place under which the ganglion-knot lies. (We do not know what indication guides the sting.) Then with her hollow lancet she makes one thrust, and smears the ganglion-knot with a weak poison, which paralyses the prey without killing it.   The defensive movements of the larva are completely unable to shake off the enemy for any length of time.

In this case the adjustment of the ichneumon-fly within the prey-circle is very delicately worked out, and this is made possible by the fact that the insect is concerned with one particular kind of prey and no other.   We may compare this to the key of a safe, which is much more delicately wrought than a skeleton-key, which has to open all manner of locks.

The organisation of the larva of the rose-beetle is no match for this delicate adjustment apparatus of the ichneumon-fly. Its limits are too narrow.   This is really not a battle, but merely a conquest of the prey as soon as the predatory insect discovers it   Naturally, the larva possesses other means of defence, which favour its concealment from the enemy.

Protective means of this kind are possessed by the eggs of marine animals, which are cast defenceless into the sea. They are either of glassy transparency and therefore difficult to see, or else enveloped in jelly, or protected with armour, or buried deep in the sand

The vast number of eggs that can be laid is to be reckoned among the means at the disposal of the individual ; but as they must also be accounted among the resources of the species, they will be described in a later chapter.

SUBJECTIVE AND OBJECTIVE ANNIHILATION
OF THE INDICATIONS

If we combine what we learn concerning the actions in all the function-circles taken together, we may say that the outcome is the annihilation of the prevailing indication that led to the action, and this automatically brings the action to a conclusion.

Annihilation of the indications takes place in two kinds of ways, which differ from one another in principle   An example will help us to understand this better.

A bee which finds a small drop of honey sucks it up and then flies away.   In this case it is obvious that the indication for honey—i e. its scent—which gives rise to the action of sucking, must disappear as soon as the drop is finished   This is an objective annihilation of the indication.

Suppose, however, that there is a great quantity of honey. After a time the bee stops sucking and flies away, leaving the remainder untouched.   In this case the indication was not annihilated objectively.   Why then did the bee cease its action ?   It has been found that if, while a bee is feeding, its abdomen be carefully cut off, the insect will go on drinking with the honey flowing out of it again behind   In this case the action does not cease ; the bee goes on drinking like Baron Münchhausen's horse.   The check set up by satiety is lacking.

We do not know all the details concerning that check, but from what we have learnt about the inner world of animals, we have every reason to assume that either directly through reflex mechanism, or indirectly through the chemistry of the mark-organ, a threshold is reached, and thereby the indication is subjectively annihilated.

Subjective annihilation of the indication plays the chief

part in the sexual circle, and leads there to the ending of copulation. This is seen most strikingly in the case of the praying mantis. Here, as soon as the male has fecundated her, the female proceeds to devour him. Immediately after the male has disappeared as a sexual indication, the food-circle comes in, and he now presents merely an indication for prey. Many other insects behave in the same way ; the females of spiders and of staphylinid beetles devour the males when copulation is completed, and the males offer only a feeble resistance, for the females never serve them as prey-indication.

Interesting though subjective annihilation of indications is, we must omit it in dealing with the world of action, for in that world only objective events take place.

THE INDICATORS

In considering all the various indications that surround an animal, we perceive that the indicator towards which the animal's action is directed, is very differently constructed according to the particular inter-adjustment between it and the animal.

If in the enemy-circle a simple movement of flight follows on a certain indication, whether that be of chemical, acoustic or optical nature, the indicator is merely the bearer of the property that is employed as indication by the fleeing subject.

If, on the other hand, effectors come into action that serve for defence, the indicator has a counter-framework which fits in with the framework of these. Among such counter-frame-works we may reckon those of the enemy's organs which contribute towards his defeat. Thus, for instance, we may reckon in the counter-framework of the sea-urchin, not merely the external form of the star-fish's tube-feet, on which the poison-pincers can lay hold, but also the nervous tissue affected by the poison, and the muscles that contract as a result of that nervous excitation

Often indeed we must reckon in the counter-framework a great part of the central nervous system ; especially in the higher animals, where the pain produced by the defensive weapons is such as to check the attacking movement and make the attacker recoil.

As we have seen, the counter-framework of the prey has been very exactly described in a number of cases. It extends not merely to the form and position of the ganglion-knot in the beetle larva attacked by the ichneumon-fly, but also to the specific chemical properties of the larva's nervous substance, which is paralysed by the poison.

When the beetle larva is paralysed, the movement ceases which was the indication serving to initiate the attack. Then the motionless larva forms the indication for the action of egg-laying. In egg-laying, there is a subjective annihilation of the indication.

THE COUNTER-FRAMEWORK AS EXPRESSION
OF THE FUNCTION-RULE

The study of the counter-framework in the indicator forms an especially important chapter, for by this a connection is established between the world of action and the world-assensed , and the surrounding-world emerges as a self-contained unity, enveloping the subject on all sides.

The function-rule, consequently, relates not only to the framework of the subject that it governs, but also to the counter-framework of the animal serving the subject as enemy or as prey. It includes, however, only the counter-framework from which the indicator is constructed, and completely excludes such parts of it as come into consideration when that other organism is the subject.

Not until we have completely worked out all the function-circles of an animal, do we get some idea of the closed surrounding-world, which on all sides shuts off each individual subject from the rest of the world, and forms the only outer world it knows.

It is especially instructive to know the medium thoroughly.

If we place before us, as our indicator, some human tool, its counter-framework is built up from our indications connected together into a unity by our rule of use If we try to do the same thing for other animals, we find ourselves unable to set up any adequate rule of the kind. (Not even in the case of our domestic animals, trained as they are for our service.) Instead, we are always seeking rules of action by which we may connect up animals into living unities A dog, for instance, is not merely a tool that we use for hunting ; but—quite apart from its services to us—it embodies for us human beings a whole number of action-rules, when it barks, eats, runs, etc., and these combine together into one extremely complex action-rule for the whole.

In this way the indicator " dog " becomes for us the epitome of a rule assigned to it for the totality of its actions ; and this rule distinguishes it from all other indicators.

If now we confront one animal with another as indicator, it is obvious that the indicator must change according to the nature of the animal receiving the indication. If the latter has not the power to receive its own action-rules in its mark-organ, the former does not constitute a unity for it. It is only we, as observers, who are in a position to see the indicator as a unity, in virtue of our own action-rules, which we transfer to it.

Nevertheless, we know that the indicator may form a special unity in the senses of the receiver of the indication, as bearer of function-rules, even if not as bearer of action-rules.

If we take a star-fish as indicator for a sea-urchin, the

action-rule of the sea-urchin, which would call the star-fish
" something to be poisoned " does not suffice the latter as a
comprehensive rule ; and this quite apart from the fact that
the primitive organisation of the sea-urchin's nervous system
excludes the possibility of action-rules being received by the
mark-organ.

The action-rule is confined to the nipping by the pedicellariæ and the emission of poison. We cannot refer the
consequences to it, i.e. the specific effect of the poison on the
nervous system of the star-fish, and the movement of recoil
that follows in virtue of that animal's anatomical organisation.
And yet there is revealed here a framework in the star-fish
that functions in the interest of the sea-urchin, and which
we may speak of as the counter-framework of that animal.
This counter-framework by no means includes the whole
framework of the star-fish as we know it, nor does it form a
delimited portion of the star-fish's body, considered either
anatomically or physiologically. From the sea-urchin's point
of view it can be comprehended as a unity only if we consider
it as an extension of that animal's action-rule

Although the counter-framework of the indicator constitutes an integrating portion of the function-circle of the
receiver, and consequently comes under the function-rule,
yet it is not subject to control by that rule as is the framework
of the animal's own body, which, after injury, can be formed
anew by the function-rule.

The activity of the function-rule does not extend beyond
the body of the subject ; nevertheless it embraces the counter-
framework of the other animal, although it exercises no direct
effect thereon. Especially interesting are the relations of the
function-rule to the medium, from which it also, so to speak,
cuts out a counter-framework in order to form the indicator
subjectively If we take into consideration all the inter-
adjustments of the function-circles that connect the framework

of the animal with the counter-framework of the indicator, we recognise that every detail in the one derives its final meaning from its relation to the other. If we grasp this fact, we shall not regard the bizarre form, colour and pilosity of some of the lower animals as just so much " decoration " (which was the old naturalists' interpretation), and still less shall we dare to dismiss them as accidents or vestigial structures.

To do justice to the fact that, in the whole counter-framework, one part enters into relation with the receptors of the subject and another part with the effectors, it is advisable to separate from the counter-framework, as indicators in the strict sense, those properties serving for indication, and, as registers, those that receive the effect of action. The remainder of the counter-framework then serves merely to connect together the indication-bearing and the action-bearing properties. We may then make the following statement, as the basic principle of biology :—in all surrounding-worlds whatsoever, the indication-bearing and the action-bearing properties of a function-rule are held together by the counter-framework of the same object.

THE WISDOM OF ORGANISMS

When the small birds that prey on it come near the eyed hawk-moth, it spreads out its wings ; and this seems to scare the birds, because they have to be perpetually on their guard against small carnivores. The eyes on the moth's wings do not deceive us, but they do deceive birds

This case is extraordinarily instructive, because it reveals to us clearly the difference between " knowledge " and " wisdom " in animals. If we try to combine as " knowledge " the sum-total of the indications that unite in the mark-organ of the hawk-moth, we find this extremely meagre, for the

onlyindication formed in general outlines is that of the moving
bird   No indication from the eye-spots on its own wings
reaches the mark-organ, and the moth knows nothing of its
effect on the specific sensed-world of the birds

From human analogy we are far too ready to seek in the
subject's knowledge the source of the correspondence between
an action and its use to the agent, a knowledge that is present
as mark-rule in the mark-organ and is able to foresee consequences. This is why the unfortunate expression " purposefulness in organic Nature " is always used, and also why
so much value is attached to the psychology of animals.
Now the psychic processes assumed in animals can play but
a transient part in their lives. When we speak of what the
psyche does, we can only mean by that the rules in the mark-
organ as observed from within, and we shall not get far if
we try to build up the purposefulness of life upon such a
basis.

For in the actions of the lowest animals (I need only
remind you of the malaria parasite), there is revealed in the
inter-adjustment the same wise foresight as appears in those
of the highest organisms.

And what would become of man himself, if he depended
for direction merely on his own knowledge of his psyche ?
The ideas that most people have concerning what goes on in
their own bodies are exceedingly meagre, and, for the most
part, incorrect   Modern hygiene gives us a great deal of
information as to the marvellous wisdom of our tissues in
their fight against foreign poisons ; but of this we should
never have been conscious ourselves.

This force of Nature we have called conformity with
" plan," because we are able to follow it with our apperception only when that combines the manifold details into one
whole by means of rules. Higher rules, which unite things
separated even by time, are in general called plans, without

any reference to whether they depend on human purposes or not.

Instead of conformity with plan, we might just as well speak of conformity with function, or of harmony, or of wisdom. The name does not matter; what does matter is that we should recognise the existence of a natural force, which binds according to rules. Unless we do this, biology is sheer nonsense.

SUMMARY

From the foregoing, it is easy to select colours with which to paint the various function-circles for a single organism, when we are investigating its relations to its indicators. The picture we get throughout is of a world that seems created exclusively for this animal. And so we are justified in assuming that there are as many surrounding-worlds as there are animals.

When we go further, and try to understand the connection between different animals, we succeed in this also to a certain extent, if we restrict ourselves to those animals that live in a narrowly circumscribed medium. We can paint a picture of the chains formed from the function-circles enclosing the enemy and the prey, and, as we pass from one to the other, show that the prey of one enemy appears further on as the enemy of some other prey.

But knowledge of single individuals is not sufficient to give us an impression of the whole living tissue in the carpet of Nature In order to attain to this, we must rely on the higher unities, such as are represented by the species We cannot go into this until later on.

MODERN ANIMAL PSYCHOLOGY

In recent years, since the appearance of the talking horse of Elberfeld, animal psychology has struck out new lines, and these are so worthy of consideration that we cannot pass them by unnoticed.

The statement that the psyche of animals contains within it this sensation or that, does not concern biology. It is for the psychologists to picture the animal soul as they think fit. The biologist must concern himself solely with such manifestations by animals as are perceptible by the observer ; and from these he must draw conclusions as to the organisation.

But modern psychology affirms that all animals, or at least all the higher animals, have a human intelligence, which is not expressed simply because the bodily organisation sets limits to it. If we succeed in getting an animal to produce a suitable sign-language by means of its organs, we can converse with it as with human beings.

This view should undermine the opinions held hitherto in comparative psychology, which infer the nature of the psyche from that of the organisation.

Biology is not directly affected by these heated polemics ; as the science of the organisation itself, it can calmly await the outcome of the dispute.

M

CHAPTER VI

THE GENESIS OF LIVING ORGANISMS

EVOLUTION AND EPIGENESIS

WHOEVER witnesses the genesis of one of our human appliances —the manufacture, for instance, of a candle from paraffin and wick—and compares with that what is done by the finished-article (in the case of the candle, its burning), must straight-way realise that the designs governing the two processes are completely different. Undoubtedly both are guided by a rule, but the two rules cannot be identical.

Hitherto we have been concerned only with the rule of the finished object, which we called its function-rule. In living beings we also met with a function-rule, which governs their doings independently, whereas the corresponding rule of implements has reference to a human performance, and so is always dependent. Accordingly we speak of the counter-actions of implements, in contrast to the performances of subjects.

Apart from this difference, the function-rules of implements readily admit of comparison with those of organisms. In both we find a fixed framework, which forms the externally visible expression of a rule. The framework is responsible for carry-ing out the action that follows the function-rule. From what we know of the spatial rules of the framework, we may con-fidently deduce the function-rule. So we have been able to show that, among animals, in so far as concerns the activity of the framework, all those mechanical rules hold good which we know in our own machines.

Even the rule of inter-adjustment, which plays the chief part in the function-circles of animals, we found again in human implements ; these enter into a framework with one another, though only temporarily, and from this framework we can deduce the function-rule.

Indeed it is possible, up to a certain point, to imagine machines possessing a mark-rule and an action-rule, as though they were animals   But such rules are not susceptible of any change, for machines consist entirely of a fixed framework, and all the rules that can be deduced from their spatial structure and their functions are human rules ; these do not belong to the machines, but are introduced into them from without. Consequently they can be altered only from without, by human intervention. And that is why we say that the running of machines is conditioned.   When machines wear out or are injured, their function-rule cannot immediately come to the rescue, as would happen if they were organisms ; an organism has its function-rule within itself, and in protoplasm the material which the rule independently employs for repairing the damage

From the way organisms behave, we become convinced that it is the function-rule itself which is able to make the framework. We were confirmed in this opinion by the behaviour of the unicellular protoplasmic animals, which form for themselves the necessary framework, and destroy it again in accordance with the function-rule controlling the action. In this way, the rule of digestion of Paramecium caused mouth, stomach and anus to appear, and then to disappear again, one after the other.

We found that, in all these cases, it is the function-rule that governs the impulse-sequence in the protoplasm. And so we might easily assume that this rule guides the whole process of organogeny, from the germ onwards.

The study of the genesis of the living organism has shown

us that this assumption is erroneous.   Just as with the genesis
of our implements, another rule comes in here, which is not
identical with the function-rule ; accordingly, to distinguish
between them, this must be called the rule of genesis.

For two hundred years the dispute has raged as to whether
it is necessary to assume a special *rule of genesis* for living
things.   Natural science, elsewhere so ready to apply the
analogy with machines, has here, strange to say, made an
exception.   As soon as the spermatozoa were discovered, it
was thought perfectly obvious that here we had human
beings in miniature, which only had to grow to full size in
order to be completely developed.   This was the foundation
of the later doctrine of " evolution," which saw in the genesis
of the organism merely a process of increase in size.

The theory of spermatozoa-men was soon shown to be
wrong.   Biologists then seized on the idea of plant-buds,
which not only grow, but must unfold in order to produce
leaves.   And so arose the doctrine of unfolding or genesis or
" evolution."

This doctrine was opposed by Wolff, who, as a result of his
exact observations, became convinced that in the genesis of
the living organism there could be no question of a mere unfolding   For Wolff, genesis appeared as a perpetual creation
of something new, an *epigenesis.*

It is not necessary to follow into detail the dispute that
ensued, for in our own day Driesch has finally settled it in
favour of epigenesis

Epigenesis, being the more difficult doctrine to grasp, had
a hard battle to fight, but it conquered at last through the
overwhelming power of facts   Again and again the evolution-
ists attempted to maintain the dogma of an invisible framework present in the germ from the beginning, by assuming
hereditary particles, which, in some way or other, were
spatially connected together.   Finally there could no longer

be any question of evolution in the old sense ; a real revolution was necessary to bring all the minute parts of organs into reasonable arrangement.

Haeckel's so-called " biogenetic law " was mainly responsible for giving evolution its last foothold. This law consists in the assertion that in the course of its individual development, every single organism passes through the developmental history of its ancestors, in abbreviated form. Since the history of the ancestors is unknown, it was deduced from the development of the individual, and so was proved by a vicious circle. The vast amount of " literature " that has been written with this fallacy as basis, almost passes belief. And so we may consider it a real feat, when Driesch put an end to the business by demonstrating that in the germ there is no preformed framework for the complete animal.

The proof adduced by Driesch is just as simple as it is enlightening. The essence of a framework consists in its being made of parts fitted together ; and when one tears it asunder, it is a framework no longer. If there is an invisible framework present in the germ, then, when the germ is cut up, the framework must be cut up with it. Now, a halved germ, if it develops further, yields, not two half-animals, but two animals of half the normal size. This fundamental experiment of Driesch's has been performed with all possible variations, with every possible precaution, and on all suitable species of animals.

While an anatomical framework must be destroyed by an anatomical interference, since it is expanded in space, a rule, which in its very nature is non-spatial, cannot be severed by the knife. Either the possibility of embodiment is taken from it by destruction of the material, or, if that does not happen, still it must come to expression even with reduced material.

GENERAL PROLOGEMENA

With the final proof that, at the beginning of embryonic shaping, there is no framework in the germ, but that there is a *rule*, the modern doctrine of the genesis of the organism began What the nature of this rule is can be deduced only after the history of the genesis has been laid clear. The question " How does a rule affect the protoplasm of the germ ? ", we answered when we considered the super-mechanical powers of protoplasm, by saying that it arranges the impulse-sequence.

As intermediary between the non-spatial rules and protoplasm, which is arranged with relation to space, we have placed the impulse, and about that we must now say something briefly. The impulse sets going a process in the protoplasm. We may picture this by analogy with the effect of ferments or catalysers. But whereas the physicists and physiologists have developed purely material conceptions of these releasing factors, and arranged them in the causal series, we must ascribe to the impulses a semi-immaterial character, which permits them, on the one hand, to initiate new causal series, but, on the other, places their becoming effective under the control of a rule that is in conformity with plan. As an analogy, we may refer to the way sounds appear under compulsion of the melody.

To Karl Ernst von Baer, " the father of embryology," belongs the merit of having compared the laws of melody with those that shape the germ.

But the discoverer of the impulses was Mendel.

The story of this discovery will ever be worthy of remembrance.   In the sexual crossing of peas Mendel discovered the rule of interchange of the rudiments of characters, a rule which holds good for sexual crossings in all organisms.   But, as happens to great geniuses whose intellectual course lies far from the beaten paths, Mendel's contemporaries, strolling confidently along the comfortable high-road of Darwinism, did not understand in the least what his inquiry meant. And so this great discovery was quite lost, until, eighteen years after the master's death, it was rediscovered by three scientific men simultaneously

What Mendel discovered was an entirely new natural factor, which only to his peculiarly endowed spirit appeared self-evident. To Mendel it seemed so obvious indeed that he gave it no name, and was interested only in the law in which this factor expressed itself

It was Johannson who first recognised the necessity for naming the new factor, and he called it a " gene." This name tells us nothing about the nature of the factor. And those investigators who first tested the general applicability of Mendel's law were not concerned with the conceptual classification of the new natural factor. The new knowledge led to practical results of the first importance in the cultivation of plants and animals, which called for the undivided energy of these distinguished scientists

And so it happens that the theoretical importance of Mendel's discovery is not realised even at the present .day. In order to grasp it, we must enter on theoretical considerations seemingly remote from it.

THE GENESIS OF IMPLEMENTS

As already emphasised, all human appliances agree in that they are supposed to have a rule of genesis in addition to a rule of use. And this fact requires that we shall make the genesis of implements the basis of our consideration of the genesis of organisms If we wish to apply conscientiously the comparison between human appliances and organisms, we must make up our minds as to fundamental concepts, so that we may be in a position to determine exactly what are the agreements and the differences.

Let us take as an example a staircase built of bricks. It is quite permissible to call the separate steps organs consisting of a brick-tissue, made up of brick-cells. If throughout we had only to deal with implements made of a uniform material which, through various chemical and physical processes, took on all possible shapes, colours and properties, the comparison of organisms with implements would be striking. We should find everywhere the same morphological basal element, an element which we could compare with the cell, the elementary building-stone of the organism The same substances that we recognise in different implements might be regarded as the same fundamental tissue This would also allow of our regarding as organs the various parts of implements, even where they consist of different substances.

Now since there actually are different implements made of the same original material treated in various ways (i.e. all the things built up of bricks), if we are to institute a sound comparison between organisms and implements, we must not dismiss the attempt to imagine all implements reduced to the like elementary denominator, the cell. On the contrary, such an idea proves very valuable, because after eliminating everything unimportant, it fixes our attention on the really essential differences, and gives us an opportunity of making more comprehensible, by simple relations in implements familiar to us all, the complicated relations subsisting among organisms.

This is very striking as soon as we employ the concept of the organ in the case of implements. As an example, let us take a cane chair, the back legs of which are in one piece with the back, which is fitted on to the seat ; and let us put the following question to an anatomist and to a physiologist, " Is this piece, composed of leg and back, an organ or not ? "

The anatomist will say, "Yes," but the physiologist will say "No."

The anatomist and morphologist delimits organs by their form, the physiologist by what they perform. As the above example shows, the boundaries of the morphological need not coincide with the physiological. The physiologist will prefer to consider all the legs of the chair as one organ, without regard to the number of joins that separate them, or how many parts intervene. Conversely, he will think the suggestion simply absurd that parts which have different functions can be ascribed to one and the same organ, even supposing there is a morphological connection between them.

From this simple example, we perceive that we must analyse all implements down to their morphological and to their physiological building-stones, if we are to do justice to the facts. In the case of our own tools, these facts seem perfectly obvious, for we know that the man who uses such an implement is a different person from the man who manufactures it, and that each of them, in analysing it down to its organs, works from a totally different standpoint.

The joins that we observe in our implements are there because only in certain special cases can the manufacturer make the whole article out of one piece : he is obliged to make the parts separately, and to connect them together later on ; and so it is impossible to avoid having joins.

Joins, therefore, are to be regarded as "signs of genesis," ✓ which direct our attention to the method by which the object was prepared. And so the morphological building-stones that the joins delimit, are to be considered as "genetical building-stones" : that is their real significance.

Now in most implements there are joins which are necessitated by the particular function , and I need only remind you of those that separate the wheel from its axle and make possible its turning. Joins of this kind must be taken into

account by the constructor when he is making the implement.
On the completed article, they separate both the " functional "
and the " genetical " building-stones from one another.
When they occur, the division lines between morphological
and physiological organs coincide.

Let us consider an implement composed entirely of very
small and similar building-stones—a brick staircase, for
example—and let us inquire whether it could not have come
into existence of itself, through mere use, or whether any con-
structional process is demonstrable which is independent
thereof. We are obliged to look for such signs as are not of
a functional but of a genetic kind, i e for pure signs of genesis,
not coincident with the signs of function.

The joins are not necessarily the only pure signs of genesis.
On the contrary, every indispensable property of the implement that bears no relation to the functions, may be so classi-
fied. Think, for instance, of the rough rim on the under side
of every china plate, which is elsewhere covered all over with
smooth glaze   Here we are confronted with a pure sign of
genesis, reminding us that, when it was being fired, the plate
stood on a red-hot support, which prevented the glaze from
forming there

On the other hand, when we examine a willow wand that
is used as a bow, and find that the woody fibres on the one
side are permanently more stretched than those on the other,
we shall explain this as a sign of function, referable to use
alone

Even if all our implements were composed of a three-
dimensional mosaic of very minute elements, we might neglect
this investigation into signs of genesis and of function, for the
history of the genesis of these things of our own manufacture
rests with ourselves. We should know precisely which alterations of the elementary mosaic had been effected by construction, and which by function.

We should be able to say exactly which groups of elementary stones are to be accounted genetic, and which morphological, because we can control the actions of both builder and user. We know that the construction and the running of what is constructed are two totally different events, and so we do not need to seek for special signs of genesis and signs of function in order to prove the existence of two fundamentally different processes.

But when we turn to implements about the manufacture of which we know nothing, and especially when we consider prehistoric finds, we are forced to go seeking for signs of genesis, in order to acquire some idea of the way in which they were prepared   And that is truer still when we turn to living things.

MORPHOLOGY

We may briefly define morphology as the science of the ✓ signs of genesis, for its task is to analyse organisms, not into their functional, but into their genetic building-stones.   By homology is understood the interrelations of these genetic building-stones ; by analogy, the relations of the functional.

Much that has hitherto appeared mysterious in morphology will now become comprehensible.   There is no morphology of implements as there is of organisms ; this is partly explained by the fact that implements are not constructed, as organisms are, from similar primary elements, and consequently are not derivable from shiftings, in accordance with law, of the same primordial mosaic.   This, however, is only one reason for the seemingly mysterious fact.   The second reason lies deeper.   All implements are made by a constructor standing outside, whereas all organisms arise from a germ set in a fixed position in space, a germ which has an immovable place within the structures arising out of it.

All implements are made by external agencies ; all

organisms arise from out their own germ. Thereby a starting-
point is given in space for the genesis of all living things ; the
germ is the first building-stone, and, as soon as the later ones
are formed from it, they are obliged to take up a position in
relation to a spatial centre. If duplication follows, we get
the bilateral type If the repetition is four- to sixfold, there
appear four-, five-, and six-rayed types. If the germ divides
up into several building-stones set one behind the other, we
get the segmented type.

If we bear in mind that the germ of the children arises
from the germ-plasm of the parents, we shall understand that
the manifestations of like germs are similar   Hence the first
shapings of the germ which find expression in type-formation
yield the surest criterion of relationship. The morphologists
are justified, therefore, in ascribing fundamental importance
to the morphological type, when they attempt to mark off
from one another the circles of relationship in animals.

It happens not infrequently that animals inhabiting the
same medium and living on the same prey, or hunted by the
same enemies, show, in correspondence with their approximately similar function-circles, a similar kind of construction
in their effectors and receptors. But such animals are not
related to one another, if the morphological laws of their
structure are different. They are analogous to one another
but not homologous.

Inevitably we assume homologies between animals now
living and their ancestors, and up to this point it is justifiable
to employ the morphological laws of structure for the determination of lineage. But we must altogether abjure
the Darwinistic misuse of these laws.

Morphology is a science that concerns itself with the
centrifugal mode of structure of the cell-mosaic of which all
organisms are composed. Where the support of embryology
is lacking—in palæontology, for instance—morphology is con-

cerned solely with the search for signs of genesis. To avoid going astray through taking a sign of function for a sign of genesis, morphology must call in the help of comparison Only when we have shown that, in spite of change of function, the same anatomical characters persist in various genera and species, can we decide with any confidence as to which are signs of genesis. For instance, the fixed number of seven cervical vertebræ in all mammals, whether they have a long, flexible neck like the giraffe, or a short, rigid neck like the whale, is undoubtedly to be taken as a sign of genesis. On the other hand, the arrangement of the lamellæ in the bones of mammals, which changes according to the distribution of the weight of the body, is a sign of function

There are immutable laws, according to which the shiftings of the body-mosaic proceed, before the definitive form is reached ; and these laws we strive to discover with the aid of the signs of genesis, for it is these which tell us not only about the delimitation of the genetic building-stones, but also about the changes that take place in these.

From study of the animals now living, it appears that the higher animals display, as transitory stages, rudiments of structures that become organs in the lower forms ; in the former these do not reach complete development

This fact, however important it may be for the determination of relationship, is no more than an expression of the centrifugal architecture of animals. How else, indeed, should this centrifugal architecture express itself from the germ ? Surely it is just what we might expect that, when we compare various kinds of animals together, the first systematic arrangements in the mosaic should resemble one another, and then, after a certain time, become differentiated from one another. A continuous chain of shiftings and changes characterises the development of even the highest animals ; and so we get the impression that certain stages are to be explained only on the assumption that they belong to the organogeny of lower animals, which have branched off at an earlier date. It will never be possible to prove that the organs of the higher animals can be formed without these " détours." Who will undertake to show that the so-called rudiments of gill-slits in the Mammalia are not necessary for the development of the organs characteristic of those animals ?

It is simply grotesque to talk of remnants from past ages, of vestigial organs, or of embryonic degeneration (cœnogenesis).

All such ideas originate from making a quite uncritical assumption of an analogy with the centripetal architecture of human implements, and then applying it to the centrifugal architecture of organisms.

Yet one thing more. The child is never created from the mature organs of its parents. Rather, the child, since it comes from the same germ-plasm as its parents, travels the same path of genesis as they, in order to develop finally its individual form   This form is not based on a model all ready prepared, but represents the definitive conclusion of a life-process that never before ended up in this particular way. And so it follows that the definitive form of an organism can never harbour within it the vestigial remains of an organ that once upon a time was functional.

If we insist on looking for a science corresponding to morphology to meet the case of our implements, though their mode of genesis is the very contrary of that of organisms, the science of architectural style might be considered, because even centripetal architecture shows at certain periods certain similarities. Moreover, the science of style does not concern itself with the functions of implements, but only with their mode of genesis. Like morphology, it is based on comparison, and seeks accordingly for signs of genesis and not for signs of function   It investigates homology, not analogy. But however exact the historian of art may be, the science of style can never attain to the exactness of morphology ; for the arbitrariness of the human architect has to be taken into account, whereas morphology finds its support in the laws of Nature herself.

THE MOSAIC THEORY

Undoubtedly we are entitled to regard each organism as a cell-mosaic ; in so doing, we refer to the cell as the smallest stone in the mosaic, and from this all the genetic building-stones are composed. Now, if this body-mosaic arises from a germ-cell, we may ask, " In what form are its rudiments laid down in the germ ? "

If to help us in answering this question we select for comparison the genesis of a mass of crystals from the mother-liquor, we see that formation of these, beginning at separate points, gradually spreads through the whole. The sequence and arrangement in which this proceeds depends on the condition of the mother-liquor at the time, and mainly on the position of minute foreign bodies suspended in it, which serve as points of deposition of the crystallisation.

If we imagine the position of these freely movable points to be determined by a hidden structure, then from a chemically homogeneous liquid the same crystalline structure will always emerge, whenever the liquid contains within it the same system of points of crystallisation. , The presence of a hidden framework of this kind would be necessary, if the crystalline structure were to serve a definite mechanical use   And so we put a hidden framework even into the germ of the organism, because the germ always allows a mechanism to proceed from it.

The simplest way we can imagine this framework is to assume a micro-mosaic in the germ-cell itself, simpler perhaps than the macro-mosaic, but of necessity already containing the properties of the definitive mosaic, since that can emerge from it. The body-mosaic consists of cells which have very different material properties. It has been unanimously assumed that in the germ there must be as many separate rudiments as there are material differences in the macro-mosaic This seems to simplify things somewhat. For the cells that are similar in material in the body-mosaic we hold responsible a corresponding framework of rudiments of the various substances, and this represents the micro-mosaic.

This solution of the problem is open to objection. If we try to picture the micro-framework in even quite a simple case, such as the mosaic of a chess-board, we meet at once with insuperable difficulties. Let us assume that within the primordial stone there are only two separate rudiments for black stones and for white ; it is very difficult to know how to picture the rudiments of the 32 black and 32 white stones, as well as their alternating positions in a square field.

If we are seeking for a material rudiment of the number and arrangement of the stones, we are obliged to picture over and over again a micro-framework exactly corresponding to the final framework. It is not easy to see how this can really make things simpler.

The same holds good for all mosaics. Even the micro-mosaic of a brick staircase, which need contain only one rudi-ment for all the bricks, must reproduce their number and their arrangement as steps, if it is to serve as the starting-point for the finished structure.

As I have already pointed out, Driesch's experiments have dealt the final blow to all speculations concerning a micro-mosaic in the germ-cells, a mosaic which would have to be vastly more complicated in the case of organisms than in that of simple implements, such as the ones just cited. In the germ-cells there is no micro-mosaic which could gradually spread itself over the building-stones as they increased in number.

Why is it that, in spite of Driesch's discoveries, men of science still cling to this idea of the hidden framework or micro-mosaic in the germ-cell ?   Seemingly only because they are unable to imagine a life-process otherwise than as performed by a mechanism   So in the genesis of a new mechanism they are obliged to look for a hidden system of mechanics to explain what takes place.

THE CHEMICAL HYPOTHESIS

If we consider more closely the signs of genesis in our implements (even if they be merely joins delimiting the genetic building-stones, or other genetic characteristics, such as the rough rim on the china plate, or the brush-strokes on oil-paintings, and the like), they always tell us about a process that is over and done with, a process having no relation to the function of the finished article.   We learn from these signs that in the manufacture of an implement certain distinct processes were necessary, which were connected together in conformity with a plan.

The same is true of the signs of genesis in organisms.   The most striking, i.e. the navel of mammals, indicates an important event which took place during birth.   But in the same way, all the others,—from the repetition of the same number of cervical vertebræ in the Mammalia down to the microscopic delimitation of the cells one from another,—tell us of a long series of processes, interlocking in accordance with plan, be it the process of cell-division, or that of the division into germinal areas, which determines whether an animal is to be of the radiate or the bilateral type.

Direct observation of the genesis of each animal from the first division of the germ onwards, confirms this impres-

N

sion, for the genesis is a process in which new part-processes
continually appear in conjunction, or else release one another.
These processes are carried out in the living material exactly as
they are in the non-living, when our implements take origin.

But if we inquire whence comes the impetus for the various
processes, morphology tells us that it cannot come from an
agent placed outside the material in space, since the construction takes a centrifugal direction, and not a centripetal,
as is the case with implements.

Every process in the animal body is led up to by a
chemically demonstrable change, produced in many cases by
substances which we call ferments, present only in minute
quantities. All of which indicates that we must not reject
the hypothesis of there being impetus-giving ferments ready
prepared in the germ, which control the physical as well as
the chemical changes during the genesis of the animal, and
supply the cause of all the part-processes that go to make up
the process of development as a whole.

It is to be noted that during cell-division the ferments
pass from cell to cell, and a sorting takes place, so that finally
there are cells with only a few, isolated ferments. These final
ferments introduce the micro-chemical processes which transform the last resulting cells into the definitive framework.

Thus far one simple chemical hypothesis will suffice.
But a fundamental fact stands in the way : the finished
cell is not an independent structure, but, as soon as it has
reached complete development, it is connected, conformably
with plan, not only to its neighbours but to all the cells of the
body. This result could be achieved only if initiation of the
various part-processes during genesis went on in perfect
accordance with plan ; and this again presupposes a hidden
framework in the ferments that give the impetus

While cell-division goes on, the formation of the germinal
areas begins, which are to be considered as genetic building-

stones   These areas, which are so exactly fitted into one another, are not left to blind chance, but are formed strictly in accordance with law.   If we wish to make a chemical process responsible for the formation of the genetic building-stones, we must suppose that certain cells affect their neighbours chemotropically ; in this way we can imagine a hidden chemical framework, which might possibly be adequate for all that is required of it.

But a chemical framework of this kind, in so far as its expansion in space is concerned, differs in no way from a mechanical framework, and its working is just as automatic. If the germ were divided mechanically, the chemical framework would likewise fall into two halves, and, just like any mechanism, would lose, in so doing, the properties of a framework.

The conclusiveness of Driesch's experiments is as much against the hypothesis of a chemical as of a mechanical framework.   It is quite immaterial whether we have before us a mosaic held together by chemical or by mechanical agency—the objections to the mosaic theory remain the same.

THE THEORY OF FACTORS

If we may not assume that any mechanism or chemistry, however delicate and however fully in accord with plan, can explain the genesis of the animal from the germ, we must look about us for a third possibility.

We are obliged to turn once more to the mode of genesis of our implements, and to ask whether it is sufficient to know the mechanical and chemical processes displayed in the course of their manufacture.   Into the construction of any implement whatsoever there enter a number of processes, which are independent of one another, but which link together in conformity with plan.   Between the axe that cleaves

the wood, the plane that smooths it and the brush that var-
nishes it, is there any sort of chemical or mechanical connection enabling them to produce their effect in conformity
with plan ? In the external world is there anywhere, even
if it be in the brain of the several workmen, a chemical or
mechanical mosaic that would justify us in deducing by
analogy a similar mosaic in the germ of organisms ? Does
the manufacture of an implement take place according to a
materially existing pattern, or does it occur merely in accordance with a plan following a given rule ?

We can answer all these questions out of our own experience, because we ourselves are in a position to manufacture
implements. And we must acknowledge that the implements
we ourselves make are not mere creations of the mechanical
play of our muscles, but originate from actions, i.e. from the
mechanical performances of our limbs, guided by our impulse-
sequences, about which we ourselves know nothing. The
impulses, indeed, are factors about which we are quite
ignorant ; nevertheless, they are subject to definite rules.

When we consider the actions of our fellow-men (even if
we leave out of account the whole question of conscious
sensations) we are obliged to assume certain conditioning
impulse-rules, if the plan expressed in these actions is to be
comprehensible.

Let us now introduce into the germ of the nascent organism
the factors (which in the case of developing implements come
from outside), and let us recognise them as primary natural
factors ; the contradictions disappear which would otherwise be inexplicable. The whole process of genesis then
resolves itself into a series of independent actions held together
in equipoise by impulse-rules.

The theory of factors requires no invisible, hidden framework to make plausible the plan underlying the genesis of
the nascent organism. The theory of factors takes this plan

out of the framework, making of it the framework-forming agent, and tries to show how, by consistent invasion of the material by the impulses, it imprints itself thereon.

The material to be thus seized on by the impulses in the given sequence, must, of course, be formative. As this material basis we may suggest the ferments, which initiate the chemical processes. But it is only when the impulses enter into the ferments that these become factors and the chemical process a living action.

In our attempt to picture the genesis of an implement in a manner analogous to that of an organism, we shall transfer into the germ-brick of our brick staircase not merely the factors for the absolute properties of the individual bricks (properties such as form, colour and hardness), but also those for the relative properties, so as to get correctly the relations of the bricks to one another in the steps   To make possible the development of the properties from their factors, we shall introduce a definite number of impulses in a definite sequence, and these will enable the ferment-material to release the part-actions in accordance with plan

Before the action begins, the separate factors for these part-actions lie unconnected side by side, and this makes it possible to interchange them with other suitable factors.   If we wish to change the red colour of the bricks to blue, all we have to do is to exchange the factor producing the part-action for red coloration with a factor for blue coloration.   In the same way, if we wish to construct an easier staircase, we can replace the factor producing high steps for one producing shallow steps

The comparison between the mode of genesis of living organisms and of implements can be carried right through only when we have recognised that both are referable to a final common factor   Even though it be true that the genesis of implements has a centripetal direction, and that of organisms a centrifugal, yet in the last instance it is always an impulse that permits the new mechanism to emerge, for both modes of genesis are based on actions

Later on we shall have to inquire how it is that the impulses influence our actions in the manufacture of implements   For the moment we are concerned with their invasion of the germ of living organisms, and there we recognise the presence of a material basis consisting of ferments, which, through their relations to the impulses, become independent factors, and these Johannson has called " genes." As Mendel showed, the genes are interchangeable with other suitable genes. The possibility of this exchange depends on the fact, not proved until much later by Driesch, that in the germ there is no framework for genesis. Mendel's doctrine, when understood in its full significance, refutes any mechanical explanation of the developmental process   And that is why I have called Mendel the discoverer of the impulses.

MENDEL

If we wish to understand aright the course that Mendel followed in order to arrive at his discovery of the life-factors in the germ, we must first get quite a clear idea of the " character," which he made the basis of his considerations. By character we understand in a general way every property of an organism that distinguishes its bearer from others of the same kind. Every absolute or relative property of cells and organs may become a character ; to establish characters, there must *always* be comparison   Colours, hardness, the shape of the organs or their parts and their position relative to one another may be alike in two plants or animals that we investigate, or they may be different. Only in the latter case do we speak of characters.

There are individual characters, which distinguish the

individuals of the same race from one another   There are
racial characters, which distinguish the individuals of the same
species from one another   In the same way, there are specific,
generic and family characters.

Mendel's inquiry was concerned only with racial characters : firstly, because these can be transferred in amphimixis
from one race to another, and secondly, because racial characters normally remain pure, and pass unaltered from parents
to offspring, which we know is not the case with the characters
peculiar to the individual.

The questions lying at the basis of Mendel's investigation,
namely, whether the properties of organisms can be transferred as units from the parents to the children, could be
decided only by crossing races, for here there were characters
belonging quite certainly only to the father or to the mother.
In such a case it must appear whether the properties, in spite
of their close interweaving in the organism, are to be regarded
as units, or whether they mutually crowd one another out
and modify one another   Only here could it be proved beyond
all question whether the paternal characters mixed with
the maternal, or whether they suppressed one another, or
were interchangeable.

Mendel finally decided the question in favour of the
characters being unchangeable magnitudes, which mutually
exclude one another. Even if he had discovered only this
one fact, he would have done science an immortal service, for,
by demonstrating the constancy of characters, he gave proof
of the constancy of the properties of all living organisms
whatsoever. Biology was shown the uniform building-stone,
which Nature uses unchanged for the production of so much
diversity, a diversity actually based not on variation but on
combination. Here at last we had in our grasp a biological
element which we could regard as an unalterable stone of
the mosaic, offering us firm foundation for all our researches.

It remained only to disentangle the separate elements from their interlacings and interminglings, and, from their sum-total, we should be able to reproduce in the imagination the construction of organisms.

But Mendel's discovery went much further than this. In addition to knowledge of the fundamental biological elements, it also gave us the rules controlling their suppression and exchange in the germ   The properties of the fully-grown organism are, as we know, passed on by the male and female sex-cells, which possess these properties only in the form of rudiments. The competition between the paternal and maternal rudiments takes place as early as the fertilised ovum. Accordingly we are justified in regarding as processes in the germ the results of this competition, which reveal themselves in the offspring.

In his seven famous series of experiments, Mendel proved that in peas, form, colour, size and position of the organs are to be regarded as independent characters, which, even as rudiments in the germ, have become involved in a competition regulated by fixed laws. According to his doctrine, the properties can be divided into "dominant" and "recessive," irrespective of whether they come from the father or the mother. The dominant rudiments suppress the recessive, without exterminating them, i.e. if, in the germ of an animal, the dominant and recessive rudiments have been in competition, the full-grown animal displays in its development only dominant properties, but it remains capable of transmitting recessives as well as dominants to its successors. Thus the offspring of the first generation from the crossing of short and tall races of peas all grow to be tall, but they retain the power of producing short pea-plants

By establishing this, Mendel discovered the presence of a law of supplantation of the rudiments of properties, which affects these quite independently of whence they come

Only in exceptional cases are the recessive rudiments incompletely suppressed, and so produce a modification of the dominants. Thus the offspring of the black race of Andalusian fowls crossed with white are not black, but blue. Such modified properties can sustain competition with the rudiments in the full-grown organism ; but, as we shall see presently, they furnish no constant racial characters. They appear only when the recessive property shines through the dominant.

In the majority of cases, the dominance is absolute, and crowds out the recessive property altogether. This exclusion, however, refers only to the organism immediately proceeding from the germ. Part of the germ remains unaltered, and gives the sexual cells from which the next generation springs. This part of the germ, whether it gives rise to male or to female products, contains at first both recessive and dominant rudiments unaltered side by side. At maturation of the germ-cells, there ensues, according to Mendel, a separation of the competing rudiments, so that, before crossing, both male and female germ-cells contain only one rudiment for each character of the body.

For this reason, the properties emerging modified from the competition (like the blue of the Andalusian fowl) are not further inherited as independent properties, but always appear only when a fresh crossing unites the rival rudiments.

It follows from Mendel's demonstrations that all offspring of the first generation, which comes from different races, possess germ-cells, half of which show paternal, and the other half maternal rudiments   If these sex-cells are crossed haphazard, then, according to the rule of probability, one-fourth of the zygotes must contain only paternal, one-fourth only maternal rudiments, while half contains the competing rudiments from the two parents.

If we call the dominant property " A," the recessive " B," and the corresponding rudiments " a " and " b," the whole process can be reproduced diagrammatically as follows :—

This diagram gives a firm basis from which we may dispose in a consistent fashion of all questions concerning heredity. It will also meet those complicated relations which come about when two or more pairs of competing properties come into question.

It is invariably assumed that, in the germ, all the rudiments remain completely independent of one another, and that each is inherited by itself as an independent magnitude. And from the outset this disposes of the notion of a hidden framework present in the germ and connecting the rudiments together. Occasional exceptions cannot overthrow the principle that each rudiment of a property is to be regarded as an independent natural factor.

The nature of these factors also emerges from the Mendelian experiments, which relate not merely to the absolute properties of the individual cells, but also to the relative properties, i.e. to the number and position of the cells and the organs that bear them. It is not only the colour of the peas that is determined by a factor ; so also is their roundness, and this depends on the position of the cells with regard to the centre.

If we attempt to find a mechanical solution of the trans-

mission of shape from the germ to the body, we find ourselves
in the following dilemma.   On the one hand, the roundness,
which is to arise from the position of the future body-cells,
can only be referred to a corresponding hidden framework
affecting the rudiments ; on the other, there can be no such
framework if roundness itself is an independent factor interchangeable with angularity.

We are faced with a very remarkable fact.   The coherence
of the body framework is not resident in the germ, but arises
from a number of independent factors having no firm connection in space but merely set alongside one another.   This
fact seems no less mysterious, if we realise that every spatial
relation of the body is created by a special process (form-
process)   It is true that the factors in the germ are not to
be regarded as direct representatives of the spatial relations
of the body, relations such as roundness or angularity, but
rather as the agents of these processes which connect together
the relations in the body   We may speak of certain substances
as releasing the processes determining forms ; but these must
take up a definite position in space with relation to one
another, if they are to effect the spatial connections, for
we know of no substance that can furnish mechanical unions
from out of itself.   But the factors have the power to impart
to the material a mechanical framework by means of a form-
process, and there actually are factors for roundness,
angularity, jaggedness, and so on.

The only agency that possesses the same power to release
form-processes, without itself being bound to a definite form
in space, is the agency of our impulses.   They also are non-
spatial promoters of spatial processes.   As, in ourselves,
separate manipulations unite to form one action, so the
formative part-actions arrange themselves with relation to one
another until the act of genesis is complete.

I set out to show that logical analysis of the facts established by Mendel could alone lead us to recognise that the properties of organisms arise from "manipulations" or part-actions of the germ-plasm.

When Mendel published his discoveries, which were to set a standard for all time, biological ideas were still in the melting-pot. The new way of regarding the world introduced by Mendel compelled us to analyse every organism into part-actions (much as one might analyse an oil-painting into brush-strokes) ; and this gave biology the chance of defending itself victoriously against Darwinistic materialism, since it was now in a position to base its structure on elements that were its exclusive property. But Mendel's discovery was disregarded, and biology was wrecked.

When Mendel's discovery was rediscovered in 1900, eighteen years after the master's death, it was too late. The meaninglessness of the universe had become a guiding principle. The eyes of scientific men were blind to all natural factors that were not of a material kind. In the pre-Darwinian period, two scientists engaged in the study of living things might still argue as to which properties of animals were referable to independent part-actions of the germ-plasm. After Darwin, the assumption that Nature could institute actions was unconditionally contradicted ; there were nothing there but mechanical and chemical processes.

So long as men listened, without preconceived ideas, to what went on in living Nature, they could not close their ears to the peculiar rhythm that distinguishes all living phenomena, and constitutes its own peculiar laws. But after Darwin, that was all over and done with : life was without autonomy.

Let us make a comparison. Suppose that a very illegible sheet of music is entrusted to two investigators to decipher ; in the pre-materialistic period they might have disputed as to which of the signs were to be regarded as notes and which as chance ink-blots. In the materialistic period, which knows nothing of music, the dispute has lost all point, for there are no notes any longer ; there are nothing but ink-blots.

Undoubtedly it is true that every written note, materially considered, is an ink-blot, and, as certainly, every property of the organism has a material basis. But to find in the properties of living matter nothing more than the expression of a dance of atoms is not only to be hard of hearing but to be stone-deaf.

Matters being so, it is quite useless to try to convince scientists with an eye only for mechanical and chemical problems, that there are biological problems as well. But we may hope that the younger men, who are not yet committed by oath to the dogma of materialism, will let themselves be convinced of the existence of life-factors, the more especially as continued investigations have brought ever further confirmation of Mendel's doctrine. Jennings has shown the immutability of the properties in Paramecium right through thousands of generations, when all crossing was excluded   Driesch, in quite a different way, has proved that there is no framework present in the germ. Histological research has found that, at maturation of the ovum, half the chromosomes are cast out , and this is confirmatory of Mendel's doctrine, which states that in the sex-cells the genes are simplified every time. .

But that it is the nucleus with its chromosomes which alone has the power to hand on the genes, was proved through Boveri's classical experiment   Boveri succeeded in fertilising an enucleated sea-urchin egg with the sperm of a different species, and in this way he got offspring possessing only paternal characters.

From all sides confirmation and supplementary evidence were soon forthcoming, which ensured that the Mendelian theory was not merely called on to set the breeding of plants and animals on a secure basis, but, by creating a doctrine of heredity that was generally applicable, could also throw light on the essential nature of the whole problem of the genesis of organisms

THE THEORY OF THE GENESIS OF ORGANISMS

The morphological building-stone of all living beings is the cell. Every cell consists of a protoplasmic cell-body and a nucleus, which contains the chromosomes.

From the work of Butschli and Rhumbler we know that the protoplasm of the cell-body resembles a foam, i e. a structure consisting of fluid partitions enclosing cavities filled with another fluid. The fluids in the cavities differ from one another, and this gives occasion for very complicated interchange, which induces complex physical processes.

Wherever we find protoplasm, we find the power to respond to external effects by irritability and movement, and also the power to take up and assimilate foreign substances. But we know of no case where these activities go on without regulation. In all cells a rule connects them together into a common function. This rule converts the cell into an independent centre having an autonomous existence. Each cell has its own set of laws ; consequently it is a subject, for it is in the nature of the subject to be a law unto itself. Therein lies the difference from all machines. They also have a rule which converts their activity into a function, but this rule is never subjective , it always enters into the machine from without. Hence machines are never autonomous and never subjects.

The function of all cells is twofold   Firstly, it is *vegetative,* when the cell takes up substances from the external world and assimilates them   The assimilated substances furnish the fuel for the movements of the cell, or serve for the cell's growth. Secondly, the function is *animal,* when it transforms the influences of the outer world into excitation, which then liberates movements

With this twofold function, demonstrable in the germ-cell also, a third is now associated, which provides the germ-cell with new properties. The nucleus with its chromosomes subserves this function.

Employing a crude but very obvious comparison, we may picture the chromosomes in the nucleus of the germ-cell as washing-lines, on which the factors for the absolute and relative properties hang, side by side, like articles of clothing which the subject will put on, one by one

Such a comparison, which naturally is far too crude to do justice to the complicated processes during the genesis of the animal body, has this value, that it compels us to divide up the process of genesis into an active process and a passive.

This prevents us from making the easy mistake of looking on the factors as mere ferments that call forth the properties by their physico-chemical action   The comparison with the garments hung on the washing-line turns our attention to the subject, which, by the active process of dressing, first gives the factors the chance to unfold.

In the genesis of the animal body there is a unity present that controls the phenomenon according to an autonomous rule   In contrast to what happens with machines, the builder resides within the organism itself.   The comparison also indicates that the process of genesis is divided up into separate phases, for each property, as a self-contained unity, requires special treatment in effecting its attachment to the subject. These separate actions are implicit in the concept of the factor or gene, but can be thought of as apart from it ; they are then called impulses, and point to the higher unity of the subject, which sends them out according to its autonomous rule.

A gene or factor, then, is a ferment activated by an impulse.

THE ACTUAL COURSE OF THE GENESIS OF NEW PROPERTIES

Unicellular organisms offer the clearest example of the genesis of new properties. They represent subjects clothed with only the most essential properties. But even the simplest amœba, despite its poverty, has a sufficient number to form the function-circles. What is striking here is that certain of these properties appear only from time to time, and then vanish again.

But the strikingness of this phenomenon must not mislead us to overestimate the processes, and so imagine that all the properties of the amœba are thus perpetually coming into existence and then disappearing again. Even in the amœba the basal element of the properties subserving function is there all the time. The power of receiving stimuli and transforming them into excitation is always present, and suffers no change at all; but the effect-organs are formed anew as occasion requires. Before the amœba encounters a stimulus, its entire mark-apparatus is there complete, and so is its general power of movement. The only thing lacking is the development of special effectors to carry out regulated movements. The properties of shape, consistency and adhesiveness, which the body-plasm makes into a pseudopodium, must be aroused before the action of the animal can begin.

If we turn to the genesis of multicellular organisms for an explanation, we may assume that, from the chromosomes of the amœba nucleus, certain ferments are furnished, which, when they are released, call forth by means of chemical changes the necessary properties in the plasma-foam. It is possible that the nucleus is continually giving off to the plasma a limited number of such ferments, which lie latent within it. This would explain the restricted length of life of portions of the amœba that are deprived of the nucleus.

The liberation of the ferments is referable to an impulse of the subject.

There will always be scientific men who try to make an invisible framework responsible for these processes, so as to get away from the uncongenial notion of the subject with its impulses.

And our reply to them must be that a framework without an autonomous function-rule can work only like a machine, and is never able to repair itself. How could the repair take place if the rule governing that were lost through the breaking up of the structure?

In the subject, however, the rule remains alive, i e independent of the destruction of the framework which it has itself created.

It would embarrass the biological point of view most unjustifiably to assume that, while the genesis of properties proceeds automatically, their repair does not. Both phenomena take place according to law, but not automatically, by an ordered sequence of impulses from the subject, which itself is nothing more or less than " a law of incarnation."

If we assume that the properties of the pseudopodia arise through the release of certain genes, we may conclude that the vanishing of the pseudopodia and the disappearance of their properties is the effect of certain " anti-genes," which likewise are under the control of the impulses of the subject.

The activity of the subject, consisting in the regulated giving off of impulses, that and the presence of genes and anti-genes, are quite sufficient to explain the appearance and disappearance of the vegetative organs in the Infusoria.

The interlocking of function-rule and rule of genesis in unicellulars can best be understood if we realise that all the rule of genesis has to perform in this case is to close the function-circle every time by creating the transient pseudopodia afresh as occasion requires. It lies therefore completely under

o

the rule of function, and, as soon as the function begins, merely furnishes it with the framework it lacks.

MULTICELLULAR ANIMALS

This interlocking of the two rules, which is characteristic of unicellular animals, ceases altogether when we come to multicellulars, in so far as these consist of permanent organs.

The life of such animals falls into two distinct parts. In the first, the organs are formed ; in the second, they are used. In the first, the rule of genesis controls ; in the second, the rule of function. Accordingly it is possible in multicellular animals to observe the rule of genesis more clearly at a given time, since it proceeds quite independently of interference from function.

The first activity of the fertilised egg consists in dividing equally into two halves In the course of this process, there first appears, as at every later cell-division, a remarkable apparatus consisting of protoplasmic threads, which meet at two nodal points. These points seem, on the one hand, to be firmly anchored in the cytoplasmic network, and, on the other, to be connected with the nucleus. The protoplasmic threads running to the nucleus must be contractile, for, when the chromosomes split longitudinally, they draw them apart as far as the nodal points. In this way there arise two new nuclei The division of the protoplasm then follows.

The first divisions of the egg transform the germ into a number of cell-spherules, which are identical, for, if we separate them from one another, they have the power of producing two (or even more) independent animals, although of half the normal size

Driesch succeeded in showing in sea-urchin larvæ obtained in this way that the half-size depended on each larva having

the same-sized cells but only half the number.   It follows that,
on the one hand, the number of cells is normally fixed by a
set number of division-impulses, and that, on the other hand,
the shaping impulses which come in later are to a great extent
independent of the quantity of material furnished them by the
division.

The first divisions give a number of similar cells, and these
form a sphere which, by taking up water, becomes hollow.
As soon as this sphere has invaginated and become a hollow
two-walled sphere, remarkable changes appear in the cells.
Those in the outer wall, the so-called outer germ-layer, which
furnish the organs of the skin and the nervous system, lose
the power to form whole animals ; but each retains the power
to form the organs that come from the outer germ-layer.   In
the same way, the cells of the inner wall, or inner germ-layer,
which furnish the digestive system, lose the power of forming
the organs of the outer layer.   This also holds good for the
cells of the layer in between, the middle germ-layer, which
has meanwhile been split off from the others, a layer which
has the duty of forming the muscles and the bones.

As soon as a germ-layer has been laid down, its cells each
retain only a limited formative power.   It is natural to suppose that, in the nuclei of all the cells of each of the three
germ-layers, only one-third of the genes are present, while
two-thirds disappear by unequal division of the chromatin
or are dissolved (genolysis).

The same thing appears later on when the germinal areas
are mapped out within the germinal layers, areas which
are to produce certain organs.   As soon as a germinal area is
marked off, the cells that compose it forego the power to form
the organs of another germinal area.

It may be taken as a fundamental law of genesis that,
when a structure appears, this excludes the power to form
anything else.   And so, as development proceeds, it is accom-

panied by impoverishment in formative cells, and this we must refer to the loss of genes

Through the loss of genes, the effect of the impulses, which manifest themselves in the individual cells, becomes more and more restricted and specialised, so that finally the definitive cells of the full-grown organism retain in their reserve-plasm, which does not enter into the framework, nothing but the power to furnish that with special cell-framework in the event of injury.

An exception to this rule is offered by the sex-cells, which arise from the first divisions, and pass over into the sexual organs of the adult unchanged and with all their genes.

The phenomenon of the systematic loss of genes is as important to the course of development of the complete animal as is the release of the genes, which likewise takes place conformably with plan   Here also is to be seen an invasion by the impulses according to plan, an invasion belonging to the general melody which all the impulses obey.

In many of the lower animals the loss of genes is not so rigorously carried out as it is in the higher.   This permits of regeneration after extensive injury, to a much greater degree than is possible among the higher animals.   In the case of self-mutilation especially, the cells, at least at certain places in the body, must remain in possession of numerous genes in order to make good the loss.

POLAR SYSTEMS

Thanks to the remarkable work of Braus, we are able to get a clearer idea of the way in which the rule of genesis affects shaping in space

If we cut away part of the homogeneous cell-material from the germinal area that serves for the development of the acetabulum, a socket is formed which is quite complete but corresponds with the reduction in material, and into which the head of the normally developed thigh-bone does not fit.

From this we may conclude that the individual cells of the germinal area are not of necessity destined to form special parts of the bone, but that other cells, which in the ordinary course of things would occupy other positions, are able to take their place. Driesch, in his experiments on the whole germ, draws attention to this fact, and from it deduces the concept of the " harmonious and equipotential system," in which each part can take the place of every other part without disturbing the harmony of the whole.

Moreover this fact proves that each individual cell does not create its own special impulse directing it to a predestined place, but that all the cells within a germinal area are directed in common, behaving like iron-filings under the influence of a magnet.

To continue this analogy—a definite polar system of " directives " acting in space invades the germinal area, and, according to the amount of material present, produces a larger or a smaller bodily structure, and from this, by release of the bone-forming genes in the individual cells, there subsequently arises the complete bone   The existence of direction-points has recently been demonstrated by Spemann in his remarkable series of implantation experiments. But he calls them " organisers," because they have the power to impose their organisation upon the still undifferentiated cell-material surrounding them.

Since at a given time the same relations hold within each germinal area, we can break up the whole embryo into a number of independent polar systems of direction-points, each distributing its own directives. But as Braus' experiment proves, no system is able to exert an influence on the directives of another system, although the work of the directives proceeds everywhere at a uniform rate.

Before the germinal areas are clearly established, various changes in configuration have taken place, and these we can also refer to invasion by polar systems. We shall assume that, in the beginning, the polar systems were quite simple, as when they induced the formation of a hollow sphere. After they have established the fundamental type of the bilateral or many-rayed system, they become more and more complicated. The systems require to be very complicated that produce the great variety of bony structure.

The succession of the polar systems in time proceeds according to a rhythm belonging to the organism itself, a rhythm which changes from one type to another.

THE IMPULSES

The appearance, during genesis, of the polar systems with their directives seems to point to a new factor that escaped us when we were considering the genes. But that is not the case When we consider the Mendelian properties, the genes of which lie ready prepared in the germ, we find that they include not only chemical properties, but also properties relating to form. We may confidently assume that the components of the chromosomes represent the genes ; but in considering the material basis of the genes we must not forget their non-material aspect, and that lies in the impulse, which follows the rule of the subject.

As already explained, the material basis is probably a ferment, which in a latent form lies waiting in the chromosomes. But, in addition, the gene consists of the non-material impulse, and this it is which activates the ferment.

As regards the chemical differentiation of the cells and the formation of the micro-framework, we find no difficulty, but try to refer their genesis to a simple fermentation, through which the foamy framework gradually assumes the definitive structure of a nerve-cell, a muscle-cell, a bone-cell, and so forth

The difficulty we experience in understanding how the form-giving genes work, lies in this, that, although they are tied to a definite place in each individual cell, yet they must act according to a system which is not present anatomically, although it embraces a whole germinal area with many hundreds of cells.

But this difficulty disappears when we realise that it is only the material basis of the genes that is of necessity bound to a definite position in space, whereas their non-material portion, the impulse, is not bound in this way

The impulse always plays an active part, now stimulating a gene, and now an anti-gene. An impulse, which is not fixed to a definite position in space, may easily be connected up with other impulses into a system

An impulse-system can allow a whole series of cells to be simultaneously invaded by a fermentative action leading to a certain chemical change   In the same way this change can release in the same set of cells a fermentation which brings about a certain change in their position , this change in position presents no difficulty, in view of the mobile foam-structure of protoplasm.   If we admit this, the sudden advent of the polar systems ceases to be incomprehensible   The polar system of directing points is then just a system of impulses, in which each gives guidance in a different direction in space.

Simultaneous and equipotential impulses of this kind must produce in a mass of similar cells a differentiation with regard to position, by prescribing a definite direction for the movements of each, the result of which will be that even the most amorphous conglomeration must take shape. The number of cells within the mass is quite immaterial for the achievement of the final form , and this is in agreement. with the results derived from experiment

Only as inference from their effects can we say that
impulses producing order in space as well as in time invade
the protoplasm conformably with plan by operating at one
precise spot in the nucleus of the cell on that particular substance which alone is capable of reacting to them. We
may say that the genes are " impulsive," but by that term
we must not presume a physical energy, following the rule of
causality ; rather, we must understand the power to convert
an extra-spatial and extra-temporal plan into a physical
phenomenon.

This enables us to understand the point of view of Bunge,
who first made the statement that " in activity lies the riddle
of life."

On the other hand, Baer's theory, which compares to a
melody the laws regulating the genesis of an organism, assists
us greatly in our attempt to understand things. In place of
melody, we may also speak of rhythm or of symphony,
according to whether we have in mind the rules of the impulses
in their simultaneity or in their sequence.

I must refer once more to the rough comparison I
attempted to make when speaking of the way in which a
subject clothes itself with properties. With regard to its
functions, the subject in the germ-cell is still very simple.
But in the genes it possesses a very large number of un-
exploited possibilities which will enable it to expand in every
direction. As the possibilities are made use of, their number
becomes more and more restricted. What the subject gains
in shape it loses in fresh life-possibilities. Thus the framework slowly increases in complexity and solidity but it becomes more and more like a machine, and loses one super-
mechanical power after the other, until finally there is left
in each cell only a remnant of the protoplasm containing the
genes that serve for the necessary repairs. *The framework
restricts framework-formation*

With the completion of the framework, function sets in ; function which, on the one hand, seems an outcome of the finished machine, but, on the other, controls it, for its rule is now substituted for the rule of genesis, and, in accordance with plan, guides the course of what happens.

While in unicellular animals the rule of genesis and the rule of function simultaneously affect the course of the impulses, in multicellulars there is a critical point at which guidance of the impulses passes from the control of the rule of genesis to that of the rule of function.

THE FINAL STAGES OF GENESIS

Before we set about determining this critical point, we must consider briefly the further course of development, from the time when the germinal areas are laid down

We are indebted to Harrison and Braus for some fundamental discoveries made from these final stages. It has been shown that the nerves grow out from their germinal area exactly in the same way that amœbæ send forth their thread-like pseudopodia. It is important to show that the two processes may be regarded as identical. Moreover, by transplanting nervous germinal areas, it has been demonstrated that the genes furnishing the motor nerves are the same throughout the entire body ; and this considerably restricts the number of different genes.

If the nerve that arises from the germinal area of the facial has to take the place of the sciatic, it adapts itself to the utterly unfamiliar limb just as well as would the normally developing nerve. If the cells of the engrafted germinal area have the same genes as the normal area, it is all one to the impulse in producing its effect.

This shows us the complete independence of the impulse-system of an organ from the source of the material on which it exerts its influence   The impulse-system merely conforms to the position that it takes up in the system of impulses as a whole, and if in so doing it comes upon suitable material, containing the right sort of genes, all goes well.

What goes on in the adjacent system is a matter of complete indifference to the individual part-system   Thus, after complete removal of a nervous germinal area, perfectly developed limbs have successfully been produced, which were nevertheless entirely destitute of nerves.

The individual impulse-system is dependent on the material only in so far as that must yield the suitable genes if the system is to become manifest.   It is dependent on the adjacent systems only in so far as its fixed position is determined by its being set between them.   For the rest, development within each system proceeds quite independently, according to the general rhythm which is prescribed to the systems collectively ; it is all one whether the normal quantity of material is present, and there is no regard paid as to whether adjacent systems shape structures in a normal way, or produce only a reduced organ, or no organ at all

All of which proves to us the existence of an independent natural factor, representing a self-contained rule built up of part-rules, which, on their side, arrange the impulses both in space and in time.

Once the impulses are set free, it does not matter whether they achieve a material effect or not ; the rule of genesis proceeds calmly on its way, and sends forth its impulses according to its own law and rhythm.

The rule, although it breaks up into separate part-rules, is in itself quite independent of space and time. The impulses that obey the rule, are fixed in space and time, but in themselves are still completely non-material   But, since they are attached to the genes, they dominate the material, for that is set in motion by the fermentative action of the genes.   The genes themselves represent a union of a latent ferment with an activating impulse.

A gene has very different aspects according to whether we regard it from the standpoint of plan or of causality   In the former case, all we see are impulses which obey an extra-material rule ; in the latter, we see a ferment which produces certain physical and chemical effects in the protoplasmic foam.

The genes are connected together by Mendel's law.   In so far as this relates to the mixing of the genes, it is a law of probability, pure and simple ; in so far as it refers to the dominance of certain genes, it is a biological law   Those cases in which the dominance is not perfect and the recessive character also finds expression (as in the Andalusian fowl, where the blue feathers come from a crossing of white and black parents) indicate that both genes are set in activity, but, for the most part, the recessive ferment is blotted out by the dominant.

It helps us to understand this, if we imagine the genes to be keys of a piano, only waiting to be struck for all manner of tunes to sound forth. We may consider the notes of the score, which arrange for us the laws of a possible phenomenon ; or we may listen to the playing, when the keys give out the sound according to the law prescribed.

The aim of descriptive biology must be to set down, by means of a kind of musical notation, the laws according to which the genes in various animals sound together or in succession , this notation is imparted to us from the beginning by the laws controlling the sounds emitted by the genes in any animal, the genesis of which from the germ we are attempting to observe.

The description of the rule of genesis of some chosen organism would represent just such a musical notation—but nothing more. It would tell us nothing about the rule of function in the full-grown subject, and nothing about the

original subject itself   It would be merely the rule of a
phenomenon, giving us no information as to the origin of the
phenomenon and its sequel

The genesis of an organism, however, is not just a musical
phenomenon. In the process of shaping, the full-grown subject finally recovers in fuller degree those functions which it
had in a more primitive form in the beginning.

THE CRITICAL POINT

I call the critical point that moment when the subject, on
completion of its shaping process, suddenly finds itself in
possession of a framework fully developed and capable of
functioning.

In the majority of animals the critical point becomes
clearly apparent when the creature leaves the egg, or when
it is born.   In other animals, through interposition of a larval
period, the critical point is not so obvious.   This difference is
the result of external circumstances which govern the taking
up of food and the growth during the process of shaping.

The functional activity of the developing animal never
ceases altogether. The foamy framework of the protoplasm
is involved in a continual metabolism, and for this it requires
a steady food-supply in order to make good the energy ex-
pended   The need for food becomes very intense on account
of the growth that accompanies the shaping. Nutriment is
furnished by a reserve supply accumulated in the germ, or
it is brought by the maternal organism, or it has to be got
by the animal itself.   In the last case certain genes must
provide larval organs serving for food-capture ; then the
animal as a whole continues functionally active throughout
its development. When the food is furnished by reserve
substances or by the mother, provision is made by development of special food-routes for the supply of nourishment

to the individual cells, without the entire organ-system taking part in the digesting activity; for the system of organs is at that time busy with its own development

The provision of food is regulated according to the requirements of the shaping process, and so is under the control of the rule of genesis.

This state of things changes as soon as the framework is completed and the function of the fully-formed subject begins. The majority of animals at this stage are not yet full-grown, but need a longer or shorter time before they reach their definitive size. Indeed, there are animals, such as some kinds of fish, that are never full-grown, but go on increasing in size to the end of their lives.

As Wessely has shown, growth during this period no longer obeys the rule of genesis, but the rule of function. By operating in various ways on one of the lenses in young rabbits, Wessely succeeded in so influencing the regeneration of the lens that the new one was sometimes smaller and sometimes larger than that of the normal eye   And it appeared that the growth of all the tissues of the eye, and even of the skull-bones that form the orbit, directed itself with reference to this new lens   Consequently the full-grown rabbit had in the one case a larger eye than the normal, and in the other a smaller.

If we compare this result with what Braus found after reducing the germinal area for the acetabulum, the radical difference between the two must be obvious to every one. So long as function has not begun, the immediate environment is not in the least concerned as to the size of the developing member; but if the framework has come under the sway of the rule of function, the whole environing region must, in growing, adapt itself to the growth of the regenerating structure, and keep pace with it

Before the critical point has been reached, the impulses governing growth follow exclusively the general rhythm of the whole germ according to the rule of genesis. After the critical point, growth is governed by the rule of function.

Now the critical point is not passed by all organ-systems at the same moment ; in especial, the cerebrum of mammals shows an important retardation in its development. On the other hand, Nissl was able to show that the roof of the skull of a rabbit from which one cerebral hemisphere had been removed at a very early stage, does not ossify, but becomes a tough membrane. The skull-bone, the function of which consists in protecting the brain, is put out of function by the removal of its 'charge. Correspondingly, it is no longer governed by the rule of function, but, like every functionless tissue, is checked in its development or simply absorbed.

The rule of genesis proceeds on its appointed course as an independent natural factor as far as the critical point, but no further. Its routes can be recognised by morphologists through the signs of genesis, and these furnish points of support for determining the relationships of animals. The rule of function, however, acts like a new broom, which sweeps away all that is useless, and retains only what is necessary. It is also an independent natural factor, which, according to its own rule, absorbs what is useless, checks in their growth the organs of the subsidiary functions, even suppressing the development of their properties, but increases the organs of the chief functions and develops them down to their last details.

An organ that functions has passed the critical point, and it degenerates if, later on, it is put out of function. The most exact information we have about the degenerative processes concerns the nerves. Accordingly, it is very striking that, judging from Nissl's discoveries, the central nervous system of the higher animals forms an exception in this respect   The half cerebrum of a young rabbit which has been deprived of all its nervous connection both with receptors and effectors, does not degenerate, but goes on forming itself normally, if it continues to receive nourishment through intact blood-vessels. This proves that in the cerebrum there are still present impulses which are not subject to the rule of function but to that of construction.

SUBJECTS

We have already learnt what are the characteristic features distinguishing the fully-formed subject from every machine. Chiefly they depend on the subject being a law unto itself ; and this law of the subject carries out its own performances but no counter-performances. All subjects have a rule of function of their own, which expresses itself not only in the framework, given once and for all, and in the activity thereof, but which also is able to repair all framework within certain limits ; consequently, this rule represents a natural factor that is continually operative

Moreover, all subjects are perfect, because, in functioning, they exploit all the properties of their material substance ; they make no distinction between leading and accompanying properties as implements do, the accompanying properties of which spring from the dead material out of which they are fashioned.

All living beings are subjects ; therefore all life must be traced back to subjects, and the attempt to derive it from any mere conglomeration of fermenting matter must be given up once for all

So far as we can judge at present, to be alive and to be a subject mean the same thing. To be a subject means, namely, the continuous control of a framework by an ∨ autonomous rule, in contrast to a heteronomous rule that loses its efficacy as soon as the framework is disturbed.

Therefore living matter must behave quite differently

from dead matter, even when they both show the same framework. This can be proved very strikingly by division. If
a dead cell is cut in two, the framework is brought to naught,
and the material halved ; if a living cell divides, here likewise
the original framework is annihilated and the material is
halved, but nevertheless the subject is doubled, for now two
like rules are present, which regenerate the framework in
both halves of the material. Through division, this material,
like all other, is reduced ; but the rule cannot be reduced
because it is an absolute unity. But neither can it increase ;
it can only become duplicate.

The recognition of this gives us an insight into the remarkable organisation of the subject, which is built up not of parts
but of whole subjects.

For simplicity's sake, we have hitherto described the
cell from which all living beings are built up as a morphological
building-stone, the bodily and material properties of which
pass over completely into the framework of the whole, and
serve only the framework of the whole body.

This, however, is not quite accurate. Each living cell of
the body remains an independent subject, possessing an
autonomous rule of function. Each cell retains both its
vegetative and its animal functions, but these are now
devoted to the service of the whole. Like the free-living
amœba, every living cell has to capture food, and has to
carry on metabolism. But the food is brought to it in the
body already so well prepared that it is deprived of the function of digestion, and can straightway make the food a part
of itself. Like the free-living amœba, every cell of the body
possesses the power of transforming stimuli into excitation,
and has some limited power of movement. In every cell,
therefore, there is a modified reflex arc.

According to the position that the cell occupies in the
body, part of this reflex arc is hypertrophied and part de-

generates   In the case of sensory cells, almost the whole becomes receptor ; in the nerve-cells, almost everything is a path of conduction ; and in the muscle-cells, it is practically all effector.   The same law can be shown to hold good for the cells of the vegetative organs.

Thus each cell remains an autonomous subject, the framework of which, in contrast to free-living cells, insinuates itself into a surrounding-world which is itself a subject.

For the sake of simplicity, we have hitherto assumed that the subject of the germ itself is the same as that of the full-grown organism, and has merely invested itself with all the necessary properties, so as to exercise in .fuller degree fundamentally similar functions   But now we see that it cannot be the same subject, because thousands of generations, which have arisen by division of parent-cells into daughter-cells during the interval, lie between the two   And finally, the full-grown subject is not merely one of the thousandth generation, but embraces all the millions of offspring that have arisen through the thousandfold reproduction.

If we let an amœba divide as often as this, and then consider all its offspring together, these do not form a coherent subject, but are merely millions of similar cells.   In contrast to the thousandfold division of the amœba, which always proceeds in accordance with the same law, the division of the germ constitutes quite a different process   It is governed by two sets of laws, which direct the individual daughter-cells to definite places, and, when they have arrived there, compel them to take on a definite form.   We have seen that this process is controlled by a series of polar impulse-systems released rhythmically   The second set of laws affects the internal changes in the individual cell-subjects, which, as they shift towards their definitive position, slowly become poorer in genes, until at last, having reached their goal, they have but one left ; this gene assumes the work of their inner shaping

P

and makes the individual subjects become an enduring portion of a dominating whole.

In the amœbæ even the ultimate offspring remain free, if by the word " free " we mean that they are not incorporated into a framework.

Now we are faced with the following remarkable fact. The egg-cell is a subject ; every one of its offspring remains a subject ; and the perfect animal is also a subject. If we regard the possession of an autonomous rule of function as characteristic of the subject, the process, up to this point, appears quite free from objection. Now let us consider the first divisions more closely. From the egg-subject there emerge two subjects, namely the first blastomeres. These can be separated experimentally : then again we have two independent subjects. But the connection between the two blastomeres, the self-constructing germ or embryo, is not a subject, because it has no unified rule of function. We have here another kind of unity, formed, not by a rule of function, but by the rule of genesis alone.

From the first blastomeres until the completion of development, the embryo is a unity which arises from a subject, it is true, is made up of subjects, and becomes a subject, but itself is not a subject.

THE BIOLOGICAL AND THE PSYCHOLOGICAL SUBJECTS

The contradiction that seems to be involved in the definition of the subject indicates that we have not yet elaborated the idea of the subject sufficiently.

Psychology employs the concept subject for the " ego," and understands thereby the unity of the process of apperception ; at the same time it regards the ego as the source of the ordered impulses.

From the standpoint of biology, which considers the

subject from the outside, the first part of the definition is of no value. The subject of another is always merely a formation of our own apperception ; only the psychologist who has introduced himself into another subject can say something about its apperception

The second half of the definition, however, is biologically admissible, for here we are dealing with effects of the ego in the direction of the exterior.

Admittedly we know something definite concerning even our own impulses only when we, so to speak, clothe them with our direction-signs. The rule according to which the impulse-sequence proceeds is known to us only through the melody of the direction-signs.

We can, it is true, distinguish the reflex closing of the eyelid from that performed voluntarily, but only because the involuntary act takes us by surprise, while the voluntary does not.

The impulse introducing the voluntary action possesses no quality, and we know of it only from its existence. Everything that takes place during the action comes to our consciousness only through the indications of the direction-signs, local signs and content-signs

Through the impulses a change, which is also perceptible externally, appears as electrical waves in the nerves or as contraction in the muscles. On the other hand, the qualities that in our consciousness accompany this change call forth no externally visible changes   On this account, for an outside observer the impulse can be used as the objective indication, but the quality can not.

The impulse-sequence, just like a phenomenon in the external world, is perceived by an outside observer only through external indications ; and this permits of our making certain important comparisons.

In general, the physiological action that proceeds without

impulse, is called a reflex, whether it be perceived from the standpoint of the ego or from that of an outside observer. In both cases the reflex is regarded as a mechanical process that owes its existence to a prepared framework. The obvious consequence of this is that we try to refer to impulses every action that is not a reflex.

I have already indicated the different types of action that we can distinguish in the life of animals. These are the reflex, the plastic action, the instinctive action, the action based on experience and, finally, the controlled action—which last, however, plays a part only in the highest animals.

The plastic action has been thoroughly analysed by Pawlow. He succeeded in demonstrating that, in dogs, the secretion of saliva and of gastric juice (which are considered reflex actions because in human beings they proceed without an impulse of the will) are nevertheless regulatable or plàstic. Dogs whose salivary secretion appeared only when they smelt food, learnt to secrete it also in presence of optical, acoustic or thermal indications, where such invariably preceded feeding.

Accordingly it is possible in this case so to modify the fixed framework, which releases the secretion as a reflex only when the olfactory nerves are excited, that it becomes focussed on new indications. In this way the indicator is furnished with new indications, and this means a considerable invasion of the dogs' world-as-sensed.

We must assume that in the mark-organ a change takes place which converts the old reflex into a new one. This is called plastic faculty. In the instance quoted, it remains a reflex, which presupposes a prepared framework. But the framework itself can be altered by experiment. The alteration in the framework cannot be a reflex process, and accordingly requires impulses

Instinctive actions afford an analogous case. We are

indebted to Wasmann for intimate knowledge of an especially typical instance   A little weevil, the so-called "funnel-roller," after its first flight settles on a birch-leaf, in which it makes an incision along a line which we human beings could discover only with the help of higher mathematics.   Then the beetle works on the veins, and rolls the leaf together into a cone-shaped bag, which it closes by pushing in the tip.

The whole action develops with unfailing certainty and absolute control both of the anatomical and physiological pro-perties of the leaf.   As soon as the eggs are deposited and the little bag is sealed, the same thing is done with another leaf, when again the same act proceeds with the same rhythm.

These instinctive actions, repeated with the same rhythm, remind one vividly of the formation of highly complicated pseudopodia by certain amœbæ.   Apart from the fact that the outcome of these actions is obliterated again in the case of the amœba, while in the case of the beetle it persists, the resemblance is perfect   In both, the action proceeds rhythmically and in accordance with plan, without any mechanism being demonstrable.

In the case of the amœbæ we assumed that a certain impulse-sequence conditions the formation of the pseudopodia.   If we likewise assume in the action-organ of the beetle the coming and going of central pseudopodia in the protoplasm of the brain-substance, the phenomenon is not explained, it is true, but it is brought into line with familiar biological processes.

Plastic, instinctive and actions based on experience indicate that the invasion by the impulses expresses itself in the appear-ance of fresh framework, which then proceeds to condition the functional issue.

Here we are once more treading on firm ground.   Now we may conclude that everywhere there are genes, which are stimulated by a definite sequence of impulses to shape the protoplasm in a definite direction.

We know that the whole framework of all organisms arises in this way, and that, when it is finished, it begins everywhere to work mechanically until it suffers an injury, when the impulses set in again at the damaged place, and repair the framework

In this way it is possible to bring the desired unity into the concept of the subject. From the subject proceeds the rule which, like a melody, binds the genes together. In the genesis of organisms this is a melody of construction ; when the building is finished, it is a melody guiding the working of the organism, and it becomes apparent only if that is disturbed. Thus the subject reveals itself to us first as an architect, and then as a director of affairs. We ourselves experience our subject always through the medium of the qualities which accompany the impulse-sequences of our actions.

The material plan of the framework in the body of the organism is thus referred to a non-material plan, which, so long as it represents for us a closed unity, we call a subject.

GENERAL CONCLUSIONS

From this we may draw some conclusions of a general kind   There are material systems that work in accordance with plan ; in these, material processes go on strictly according to the rule of causality   The material systems are either dead or living   The dead systems have only a rule of working, which we read from them, but which is quite without effect on the framework   In the living systems run according to plan, there is a reciprocal action with a rule which we call a rule directing the working.   This is not a mere formula ; it is a natural factor.

The plan appearing in rules affects the material indirectly by means of the impulses   Causality, in contrast to plan, affects the material directly, and requires no impulses for the attainment of its object. Like all material factors, it is employed by the plan to form framework functioning in accordance with plan. Though we may have established the purely causal running of a process, yet conformity with plan is not thereby excluded, for, in what it does, the completed framework, working in accordance with plan, does not show the slightest departure from causality.

Only when the framework suffers injury, does it become apparent whether, in addition to causality, there is a plan at work.

Two fundamental questions now arise. In addition to the plan discovered by biological methods that works through the help of impulses and genes, is there another plan which is capable of affecting the material directly in the way that causality affects it ? If we are going to call " subjective " the plan that works through the impulses, the question will run thus, " Is there a plan in the world other than the ✓ biological, or does all conformity with plan arise from subjects ? "

I think that some such conformity with plan, independent of subjects, rises before the mental vision of many scientific men when they speak of a new, formative energy. An idea of the kind seems to lie at the basis even of Loeb's theory of tropisms. From this point of view, we might assume that the entire world consists of nothing but material properties. But, in addition to their chemical affinities, these properties would also have special biological affinities From this could be deduced a sort of biologico-chemical law of formation for all manner of frameworks constructed in accordance with plan. This law would then mean a direct working of plan upon material.

At the present day it is impossible to decide whether there is a shaping law of this kind But one thing is certain ;

biological frameworks do not arise on this basis, but *solely
through subjects, by means of impulses.*

The second question is, " How is the rule of the subject
affected by the material factors ? " That there is an influence
of the kind is certain from the inter-action we mentioned
between function and function-rule, when the framework is
injured.

There is also a reaction of the same nature in the case
of plastic actions. But it is quite unknown in all those
associations which we bring together under the name of
" wisdom of organisms." The popular doctrine of adaptation
is totally unable to reveal these marvellous inter-connections.

THE TOOLS OF ANIMALS

The little bag rolled up by the funnel-roller beetle exhibits
all the properties shown by a piece of human apparatus.
Its function is not autonomous, but a counter-action which
makes the performance of the beetle complete. Since the
birch-leaf represents dead material to the external constructor,
the bag has accompanying as well as leading properties. The
same may be said of the nests of birds, and of all the dwellings
of insects. The less foreign material is used, and the more
self-produced substances serve for the construction of the
house, the less obvious do the accompanying properties
become.

Let us at once get rid of the mistaken attempts to
compare with one another implements such as birds' nests,
and to set up an ascending series indicating the gradual
advance towards perfection. Each implement can be judged
only with regard to its counter-action for a particular animal,
and consequently the implements are as non-comparable
among themselves as are the animals that make them. The
nests of birds, as Herrik pointed out, form merely an external

basis for parental care, and can be judged only in connection with that.

All implements of animals that we know as yet, arise through instinctive actions, in which neither memory nor experience play the slightest part. A bird that has grown up in altered conditions and has never known the parental nest, makes one for itself on exactly the same plan as that which governed the nest of its parents.

It is worth emphasising that every part-action, such as the seizing of the straws which are used to build the nest, is invariably carried out with unfailing sureness ; there is no hesitation or choosing   We do not yet know what are the indications that guide the birds in this.

Fabre did pioneer experimental work on instinctive actions when he disturbed the burrow of the digger wasp and interfered with its care of its young. He showed that, however well the entrance to the burrow be masked, it is confidently rediscovered ; as soon as the burrow is found, the insect feeds its larvæ in the prescribed manner   On the other hand, if the upper wall of the burrow has been removed, and the insect is allowed to enter its dwelling, which is no longer shrouded in darkness, the indications are lacking that lead to the feeding of the young, and the wasp gives that up, even if she be treading on her own larvæ.

It also seems that, with bees and wasps, certain indications must appear in a certain order if the rhythmical course of these insects' very complicated instinctive actions is to proceed successfully, whether these have to do with the constructing of the dwelling itself or with the actual care of the young

Recently, too, we have had some more exact information about the making of the spider's web. But concerning the co-operation between the rhythmical impulse-sequence conditioning the action and the external indications which affect this rhythm, we remain quite in the dark.

In principle, it is quite unnecessary that the tools an animal has fashioned should appear as such in its sensed-world   As I explained, an implement appears in the world-as-sensed only when the rule governing the course of the activity in the action-organ affects the mark-organ in some way, and there forms the basis around which the indications arrange themselves

In us human beings it is the rule of the use-function that furnishes the basis for forming implements, and not the rule of our own activity in making them   Accordingly, during the formation of the organism, the autonomous rule of function acts through our apperception as the basis for the properties of the creature formed   It is through the rule of function, and not through the rule of genesis, that we judge whether we have a foreign subject before us. In this way are explained the contradictions referred to in the definition of the subject.

SUMMARY

Consideration of the function-world of organisms showed that the animal-subject is not to be sought in an ego localised in the brain, but that the subject governs the entire framework of the animal body

Study of the genesis of animals disclosed, to our surprise, a new rule, which forms the framework   Karl Ernst von Baer, it is true, recognised that in the development of the animal body from the germ onwards, a special natural force must be active ; and this he called " effort towards a goal," because the finished framework always forms the aim of the processes during genesis

But it was the pioneer discovery by Mendel that first made it possible to analyse this natural factor.

As function is bound to definite material organs, so is genesis bound to certain material particles in the nucleus of the germ-cell, which are called genes The newly discovered natural force works rhythmically according to a definite plan , therefore it must be called a rule. The agency through which it materialised itself we called the impulse, and we identified it with the impulse that precedes our own voluntary actions.

As soon as the framework is completed and the function sets in as a purely material process, the control over the impulses passes from the rule of genesis to that of function ; this comes to the rescue when there is any injury, and, also with the help of the genes, carries out the repairs ; in addition, it controls the growth of the formed but not yet full-grown animal

We learn from these facts that, in addition to the rule that we form with the aid of our apperception when we consider the working of some particular framework (be it a living being or a machine), there is also a natural factor that works after the manner of a rule ; this is not operative in implements, but only in organisms.

To describe two different things as " rule of function " may easily lead to confusion ; so we might speak of a function-rule kept in permanence by a function-regulator.

If we choose to use this term, then the subject is distinguished from an implement by possessing an autonomous function-regulator, and it also has an autonomous rule of genesis ; this, being likewise a natural factor, may be called genesis-regulator. Thus the subject, as the visible manifestation of the union of both these regulators, forms the most important natural factor in biology.

CHAPTER VII

THE SPECIES

THE species has its origin in the concept of similarity. We say that organisms are similar which are not quite alike but are just distinguishable from one another in a certain respect. If several organisms are to be studied with reference to their similarity, we choose out a special individual as a sample, and compare with it those nearest to it. Then we go on to determine everywhere the just perceptible differences, and in this way we unite together the whole group of organisms When that is done, the group appears to us as a continuity, which we call " species."

Within each species we shall always find an individual which lies midway in regard to the total of all the deviations. We call this the " typical case," while those individuals most remote from it in any direction are called " extreme cases."

It is not at once obvious whether a species is a product of Nature, or whether it is to be considered merely as a means of classifying. But after it had been shown that all living things can be combined into continuous groups or species, and that these are separated from one another by larger gaps, men believed that they were justified in interpreting species as special products of Creation, whereas the individual " variations " within the species could change in the course of ages.

It was natural to go on to suppose that, in the course of ages, individual variations might drop out, and, as a result, the originally coherent species would cease to appear continuous, but would produce the impression of being two species. It is the questionable merit of Darwinism to have followed out this idea to an extreme, with the result that all gaps within species are filled in with products of the imagination. Darwinism could not really shake the fact of the existence of species quite distinct from one another ; so it contented itself with ignoring the differences, on principle.

Things being so, there is no putting an end to the dispute as to whether the species is purely a means for classification necessary for the systematising of the vast number of animal forms, or whether it is the result of a systematising force of Nature

But there is no agreement even in the methods employed in defining species, quite apart of their position vis-à-vis of Nature. All naturalists highly gifted with intuition, and of these Goethe was the supreme instance, start from one single instance or " typical case," group similar animals into a species around it, and determine the various deviations with reference thereto. For such men the species embraces all the deviations that branch off from the type of the animal selected.

For less "intuitive" naturalists, the species forms merely a group of similar individuals united by a certain rule.

In both cases it is open to doubt whether the rule by means of which the species is held together is merely a conceptual rule, or whether we see in it the expression of a natural factor.

To the question " Is the species a natural factor ? ", Darwinism, with the naïve confidence so characteristic of the whole spirit of that time, unhesitatingly replied in the affirmative. Since Darwinism was extraordinarily little gifted with intuition, it saw in the species merely a mixture of properties, such as one might find in any mass of fermenting matter. The species, like the individual, must be reduced to

a product of natural forces acting without regard to plan,
for the existence of such forces acting in accordance with
design was denied.

As the chance product of the general chaos of Nature, the
species and its origin would have become exceedingly uninteresting, were it not that the personal interest which everyone feels in the origin of the species " man " invested this
doctrine with immense popularity.

Darwinism referred everything to matter and the structure
of matter, and had no eyes for the living continuity ; then
Mendelism came, and swept the whole theory away.

Johannsen is responsible for introducing the distinction
between the appearance-type, or *phenotype*, of an organism,
and its rudiment-type, or *genotype*. By this means, certain
variants were referred to the effects of the environment
during genesis, and others to climatic and local influences,
while yet others were based on differences in the genes, present
from the very beginning.

Through the method of culture of " pure lines " (i.e of offspring from parents having the same genes) and through the
culture-experiments made on Paramecium by Jennings, who
raised thousands of generations by the division of a single
individual of this species of infusorian, it has been proved
beyond all question that the genotype of the animal is not
subject to any change The phenotype is exposed to all
manner of external influences, whereas the genotype is stable ;
this means that the genes present in the germ are inherited
unchanged, so long as there is no crossing with other genes

It is especially satisfactory that this result should have
been reached by Jennings, for he had to depend on it entirely
in order to apply to the origin of species his law of " trial

and error," a law, that is, of aimless testing in every direction
and of a " selection of the fit " depending on external circumstances.

As we already know, there lies ready in every germ a
definite number of quite definite genes, which together represent the genotype. They themselves have as yet no framework, but, through the ordered advent of impulses, they are
enabled to produce it.

Through the crossing of different individuals of the same
species, these genes are reciprocally exchanged, in accordance
with Mendel's rule.

If we consider the crossing, within a species, of individuals
that vary very much from one another (as in the fly
Drosophila ampelophila, which we know from the fine work of
Morgan and his pupils), we see that, compared with the sample
animal, the species possesses a much greater number of genes,
many of the properties of which absolutely contradict one
another. As well as genes for all conceivable kinds of eye-
colour, we also find genes for eyelessness. Likewise there are
genes for certain shapes of wings, and others for wingless-
ness , and so forth.

In spite of the extraordinary wealth in genes, yet from
every crossing that yields a living germ there arises an individual capable of functioning, which we call a *Drosophila
ampelophila*.

The same thing appears within every species. Even
Paramecium forms species, the individuals of which diverge
from one another in every direction, and nevertheless all
belong to one unity, which we call species.

Starting from this fact, the species has been defined as
that number of different individuals which, crossed with one
another, continue to produce offspring capable of living and
of reproducing themselves.

If we accept this definition, then the species consists of

a number of individuals, each one of which has a definite supply of genes Consequently, each species, as the sum of all the individual organisms, has a definite treasure-store of genes, which transcends in a greater or less degree that harboured by each individual.

Now undoubtedly the number and the nature of the genes in the individual is not left to chance, but is governed by a fixed rule, to which we give the name of genotype.

The question arises whether the species likewise has a genotype, or whether the boundary of one species with regard to others is decided by the possibility that, when too large a number of deviating genes meet one another, an individual capable of living can no longer be produced through crossing, for external, physiological reasons. Have we here a perpetual process of " trial and error " going on, which sometimes succeeds and sometimes fails ?   Or is the species a whole which works in accordance with plan, and is held together by a fixed rule ?   If so, what is the nature of this rule ?

WHAT THE SPECIES DOES

Merely from the circumstance that the process of genesis in the organism produces, as though confident of its goal, a functioning framework, we become convinced that we are faced with control by a natural factor working to plan.   If the development stopped prematurely, or if an inefficient embryo resulted, we would not be justified in coming to this conclusion. A whole that is incapable of performance is merely an object, it is not even an implement, and still less is it an organism.

This criterion may be applied to the idea of the subject that we must make for ourselves The species, and Mendelism confirms this, is not a mere classificatory formula created by us in order that we may get a better view of the whole : it is a real natural product, characterised by the fact that the individuals composing it are not in a condition to cross with those of another species. But is the species also a natural product arranged by some plan, or is it merely an object produced by mechanical causes ?

We must bring forward proof that the species as a whole expresses life in a unified way, and that in this expression somehow the parts determine the whole and the whole the parts ; and this can be shown only if they work in common.

It is not sufficient to show that there are functioning unities, consisting of a number of individuals, as in the case of the family or the animal community. Such instances merely prove that a whole which will function can be organised from a number of animals. On the other hand, it is no proof to the contrary that we as yet do not know anything about what the species performs, for so far no one has gone into the question.

Strange to say, there is only one species of which we assume as obvious that it has a common task or performance, and that is the species " man."

In especial, the existence of dark-coloured races of men in the hot zones and of light-coloured in the cold zones indicates that to them all is set the common task of " dominating " the globe Since the individual human being cannot simultaneously have a white skin and a black, it seems obvious to us that, to attain the common aim, there must be separate beings with different properties.

This simple instance suggests to us that the diversity of individuals within a species cannot be referred merely to a whim of chance, but may be conditioned by a higher plan.

If we could build up together the function-circles of all the individuals of one species, we should get the common surrounding-world of the whole species, and, in correspondence with the deviations of the individuals, this would be larger

Q

and fuller than that of any one of them. Within this surrounding-world the fate of many thousands of individuals
would have to run its course ; and thus we should get a glimpse
into the relations between surrounding-world and species, as
well as an understanding of the meaning of the differences
between the properties of the individual creatures. Although
each organism is perfect, in the sense that it exploits to the
full the means at its disposal, yet the perfection of the species
is higher, because the limits that are imposed on the individual
are shifted much further back. An individual cannot be black
and white at the same time, nor swift and sluggish, nor large
and small. But a species can possess and bring to realisa-
tion contradictory properties simultaneously, because it is
not bound to the function of one single framework.

Accordingly, the species and the individual are differently
armed vis-à-vis of all the vicissitudes of the external world.
And that, along with the increase in the surrounding-world,
is the chief reason for the existence of the species.

Let us assume that there were no species, but merely a
large number of individuals constructed in exactly the same
way ; a very insignificant circumstance might suffice to cause
all these organisms to perish ; while others furnished with
different properties would easily escape destruction. On
account of the presence within it of many different animals,
the species is not annihilated even if certain individuals,
built all alike, be lost. For the animals that survive are
able to replace those that have perished, since each may
contain, in addition to the genes for its own properties, as
many genes for recessive properties. So the species will
not find it difficult to make good the loss by crossing.

Sexual reproduction serves not merely for the continual
renewal of the same individual ; for that, simple division
would suffice, as we see it in the unicellulars, which split in
two and then regenerate once more. As Jennings has shown,

this dividing is useful for the individual and not for the species, if the offspring continue alike throughout. On the other hand, sexual reproduction is there essentially in the interests of the species, because it ensures the crossing of the genes

Moreover, the extravagant production of young is solely in the interests of the species, this perpetually gives the species the chance to make use to the full of all favourable opportunities, and to come through bad times without essential loss. If the genotype of the species is preserved by a few survivors, that is sufficient to secure its continued existence.

The difficulty of picturing the species as consisting of numerous individual organisms and yet being an entire organism itself, depends only on the fact that the separate creatures do not perform their actions at the same rate or at the same place Let us imagine the species as, for instance, a large shoal of fishes hunting a great quantity of pteropods, and followed in their turn by a number of sharks. We at once get the impression of a huge organism, pursuing and pursued, which now spreads out, now draws together, here becomes larger, there becomes smaller, but fundamentally remains the same throughout At one point speed, at another slowness, at one point dark coloration, at another light, here sharp sight, and there a keen sense of smell, act for the preservation of the whole. So long as the whole retains all these properties, it will continue its existence unchanged, although that essentially consists of perpetual flight and pursuit.

I think there can be no doubt that every species represents really an independent organism with a character of its own but endowed with tremendous longevity

THE PICTURE OF THE SPECIES

If some consider insufficient the picture of the species that I have briefly sketched above, let them try the following method, in order to get it clearer. The cinematograph enables us to consider an animal as a continuous series, and thus to pay special attention to each one of its actions.

Such serial pictures of animals assist our concrete view of things very greatly. We can use them to make a picture of the species. Let us take a very common animal, familiar to us, and one whose habits we know very well : a cabbage-white butterfly will serve. Imagine that all the eggs, which diverge from one another in their genotype, are collected together on a circular surface. They all begin to develop at the same time. Pile up the developmental stages one on top of the other like a rouleau of coins, so that together they form an upwardly growing stem. As soon as the phenotype is ready and the caterpillars hatch out, let them all crawl away from one another in every direction. Now note the fate of the various caterpillars with reference to their different properties. Some find the food that suits them on the cabbage leaves, with which they are very closely inter-adjusted. Some of the others succumb before their numerous enemies in the shape of mites, ichneumon-flies or birds. The inter-adjustment of the caterpillars vis-à-vis of these enemies is more or less adequate according to their properties. Consequently many perish. Finally all the survivors pupate at the same time, and hang in a circle around the original stem, like regularly arranged berries. Again the stages in the metamorphosis are noted in an upward direction, until the butterflies rise like a white cloud and pass in towards the centre, where they unite in pairs and lay their eggs on a circular surface, after which they fall down like withered leaves. From the eggs grows up the new stem.

In this way it is possible to reduce to a form that can be visualised the series of recurrent changes in the species. This form resembles a plant, the stem of which, by rhythmical repetition, gives off shoots ; of these a great portion come to naught, but the remainder unite again to form a new stem.

The greater our powers of visualisation, the better able shall we be to make this picture richer in detail and more true to Nature.

We can also think of this coming into being and then dying away as though it took place cinematographically ; then we participate in the rhythm, and so get the right impression of the species as a rhythmical sequence of acts The process of shaping, which follows on plan, and the forms it produces, which likewise operate to plan, mutually release one another.

Framework and action are always restricted to the individual organism, and only at one stage, that of sexual union, is there an inter-adjustment that does not belong to the plan of the individual, but to that of the species.

What shows us clearly that here the species itself comes in and determines the shaping is not the renewal through offspring, but the mixing of the properties.

The creation of new subjects from the rich material of the genes affords the species the possibility of shaping itself anew with each generation. Without this, there would be eternal repetition ; and so new variations on the same theme continually make their appearance

Were it not for the perpetually repeated union, the species would break up into long, uniform chains of individuals ; whereas, the union of all the chains in pairs continually revives the unity of the chains considered collectively.

Moreover the picture of the species enables us to visualise how species live together and affect one another, and so we get a glimpse into the living tissue of Nature ; this was quite impossible so long as we were merely considering the individuals separately.

The framework and the inter-adjustments of the individual organism are in themselves so manifold that it is impossible to take them in at a glance. The species is a thousand times richer than the individual, and consequently impossible to grasp in its entirety, if we consider it merely as the sum of its members. We can arrive at an intelligent notion of the truth only by grasping the species as a unity and confining ourselves to the ultimate inter-connections that bind it into a whole. Then every species appears to us as an ingenious structure formed by Nature, the several parts of which, as they separate from one another, are perpetually reunited and renewed by the sexual process and the inter-adjustment of the sexual organs.

RACE—PEOPLE—FAMILY

The large species readily fall into groups, which are arranged around a typical sample animal.

Among these sample animals, one can always be found that serves as such for the whole group.

Such groups, which usually display a marked tendency to avoid mixing with one another, are called races. We see in them the starting-point for the formation of new species.

Races are divisible into peoples, held together, as a rule, by geographical circumstances, which afford them special conditions essential for their life.

The ultimate member of the species is the family. Races and peoples may be described as subdivisions of the species, but the family is the true building-stone of this elusive natural unit. In the family occurs the mixing of the genes that makes of the species something other than the mere renewer of the same individual.

The family forms the visible expression of the species ;

in it we see the effect of the continually recurring tendency to union which prevents the species from falling asunder. The family provides that the perpetually renewed reciprocal action of the treasure-store of genes continues vital and unified It is through the family that the fullest conceivable reciprocal exchange of properties is ensured.

If we develop further the picture of the species as I have sketched it, we get a chain that stretches away back into the past and forward into the future, beyond the eye's reach.

To get an idea of the relations of the separate families to one another, independent of the phenotype of the individual organisms, we must set, one behind one another, copies of the familiar picture of the bifurcating genealogical tree, and, by means of common ancestors, run connecting lines from one tree to the next. We get in this way a pillar-like, ascending, three-dimensional network, the meshes of which cross one another in the most various ways

If we wish to add the distribution of the different genes, we can imagine that the separate strands forming the meshes are made of various coloured threads twisted together, which continually separate from one another and come together again. To each species we must apportion a definite number of coloured threads, which give to the whole its characteristic colour. In this way we get a picture of the stable genotype of the species

All such pictures are merely aids to our restricted powers of visualisation , but they are very important, because they admit of our imagining, on the lines of an actual model, people, race and species as separate and yet belonging to one another

However this model be constructed, and however the threads interweave, the family, which forms the knots of the meshes, is throughout the true building-stone of the whole. People, race and species are merely links between families

Through Mendel we have learnt about the distribution of the parental genes to the offspring. But the laws according to which the parents find one another in order to effect this distribution have as yet been little studied. It is here that sexual selection, so-called, plays its important part. As Darwin showed, the breeder can step in in place of natural selection, and produce new races and peoples within a species. These artificial races play the determining rôle in the case of our domestic animals and plants. We may still expect great results from work in this direction.

Artificial races enter our human surrounding-world in a way that is conformable with plan. We are as yet without the fundamental clue as to the rôle which natural selection plays in the life of the individual species ; but we can be certain that some day, when we have learnt to look more closely into the surrounding-world of the species, our eyes will be opened to plan here also.

THE GENUS

The genus does not represent a connection between families. Nevertheless, it is not considered as a mere human means to classification, but as a true product of Nature. We assume that the genus depends on the relationship of species one with another. Now relationship can be based only on the family. √ Therefore we assume that, countless years ago, separate offspring arose from one family, which so differed from one another that they no longer crossed, and in this way they established new species. As an analogy, the formation of races is cited, although all that we can as yet establish is that certain groups belonging to a common genotype within the species display a tendency to separate. But, so far, absolutely nothing has been discovered concerning a common derivation of the species from one pair of sample animals.

The assumption of one pair of ancestors meets with such ✓ difficulties that, even in the case of races, it comes up against contradictions For even in the race the treasure-store of genes is much too large to be united in one single pair. How much the less can a single pair of parents contain all the genes of all the species belonging to one genus !

But this very real difficulty, obvious though it must be to everyone, was cheerfully ignored by the Darwinians, in a manner ill-befitting the seriousness of the problem.

THE SPECIES AS A MEANS TO CLASSIFICATION

As soon as we regard the species merely as a means to classification, we take up a totally different position In such a case, we are no longer concerned with bringing into line the whole wealth of species, but merely seek for a group of characteristics that are displayed by all the individuals of one species, and at the same time are typical of this species alone

This is made possible by the fact that all the interchangeable properties of the individual organisms within one species are built up on a stable basis of properties common to them all. The species belonging to one genus have, in addition, a smaller stock of properties, which, after removal of the group of characters typical of each separate species, remains over for the genus.

If we continue on these lines, proceeding to larger and larger animal groups, we gradually demolish the stock of properties, until we come down to the first germinal rudiments that determine the radiate or the bilateral type.

When we start from the species, and ascend to the genus and type as natural phenomena, the number of forms and of properties increases with the size of the circle enclosing the individuals ; but when we consider the species, genus and type as a means to classification, the number of common properties present in each group diminishes. This must be so, for, the more unlike the individuals, the fewer properties they have in common.

Through confusing these fundamentally different things, which unfortunately bear the same names (for species, genus and type mean both the logical concept and the visible phenomenon) it became possible to construct animals with properties acquired in purely abstract ways, and these impossible hybrids were called ancestors.

In this there lies a fundamental misconception. An animal, even though it be the most remote ancestor, always remains an individual, which must have individual properties exchangeable with others of the kind in crossing. But it is just these properties that admit of inter-adjustments in the various function-circles.

How is it possible to imagine an animal having only the properties of the species, if, for instance, the individuals composing the species are some of them winged and some of them wingless? In a case like this it is quite possible for the stock of properties characteristic of the species to contain both winged-ness and wingless-ness together. But, in its structure, a living individual cannot simply ignore the question as to the existence of wings. Either it has wings, or it has not. There is no third alternative.

The wider the circle, and the more the tension increases between wealth in different properties on the one hand and poverty in common properties on the other, the more obvious becomes the impossibility of making a living individual out of those that, as a means to classification, characterise the animal group. How, for instance, am I to imagine an animal that is merely five-rayed, and has no other properties whatsoever?

It is perfectly justifiable to read the relationships of animals from the stock of their common properties, as we might read them off a measuring-rod ; but by this means we learn absolutely nothing about the methods Nature has employed in creating relationships.

THE COLONY

Hitherto we have considered only such organisms as came from an egg, and by means of eggs gave rise to independent offspring. There are also, however, organisms that do not arise from independent eggs, but from germs that remain connected with the mother organism We call such germs " buds," and the organism arising from a number of buds is no longer an individual, but a colony composed of persons The most striking instances of this kind are given by certain siphonophores These multiform colonial medusæ are composed of a series of individual persons, each of which has its own organs for food-capture, for feeding and for sexual purposes , but all the persons are connected together by a common alimentary canal.

Colonies composed of a number of similar persons give the impression of being a unified animal, possessing, however, many mouths, many arms, and so forth The function-circles resemble those of an individual animal in all particulars. They have arisen through a definite rule, and have a definite rule of function. Accordingly, there is no reason why animal colonies should not be called subjects.

ANIMAL COMMUNITIES

Animal colonies such as we have described are distinguished by the fact that the individual persons together form a fixed framework It is easy to imagine that there are other colonies in which the individual persons are not connected in this way, but by an inter-adjustment that expresses a plan. Colonies of this kind we call communities.

In addition, animal communities are characterised by a marked differentiation of the various persons, a differentiation which also sometimes occurs in colonies. The persons, especially in the familiar bee and ant communities, fall into groups according to their special vocation ; and these groups differ widely from one another in their bodily conformation. Each group serves some one function-circle more particularly : there are soldiers for driving off enemies, workers for collecting the food, and queens serving for reproduction. It is impossible not to see in the community as a whole a modified organism, which has its own function-circles in addition to those of the several persons.

Nevertheless, the individual persons arise from independent eggs, which are laid by the queen. Already in the ovary the genes are distributed in these eggs in different groups according to the vocation, or, as in the bees, a suppression or an accentuation of certain gene-groups is effected by means of different methods of breeding.

The result is always an independently functioning unit, the parts of which are represented by the several independent persons. Whereas the organs of the free-living single animal are equally developed in every direction of the function-circles, the individual animals of the community, as the result of the common life which robs them of certain parts of these, are in a position to develop themselves with special reference to one function. The queen-bee can devote herself exclusively to the work of reproduction, for she is provided with food and protected from enemies by the workers. Conversely, the workers, relieved of the business of producing young, can develop with reference to fighting and food-capture.

This separation of the function-circles goes furthest in the case of the traveller ants. The long procession of these insects, containing various kinds of workers and queens, is covered by a thin veil consisting entirely of soldiers, which support and carry one another and threateningly turn their gaping jaws, swollen with poison, towards every enemy that appears

Such a community resembles a very long worm with a thick, stinging skin, and having the stream of food in its interior distributed by individual animals instead of by cells. In place of its organs there are large numbers of separate creatures, which move forward on their own legs at the same rate as the whole animal.

By this "army" worm of the traveller ant, Nature has saved us the trouble of constructing a picture of the community, with all the individual animals moving at the same place and at the same rate—a picture such as we had to make for ourselves in the case of the cabbage-white butterfly. Here we have before us in a tangible form the whole community as a unified organism.

COMMUNITY AND SPECIES

Now we are in a position to compare the community and species as concrete phenomena On the one hand we have the picture of the species as I presented it in the case of the cabbage-white butterfly ; and, on the other, the picture of the community as Nature gives it us in the traveller ant. It is obvious that both structures are built in accordance with plan, i.e all the separate creatures are connected together, with all their function-circles and their surrounding-world, by means of a great organisation. In all of them a rule has become incarnate. This incarnation is everywhere effected by impulses, which are obliged to subject themselves to the rules.

We have already learnt that the impulses may obey two

rules , for the rule of genesis controls the impulses in the embryo, and the rule of function those in the full-grown organism.

I have already pointed out the relations between rule of genesis and rule of function, and I have shown that in the amœbæ both rules together control the formation of the pseudopodia. In animals with a framework, on the contrary, the rule of genesis holds sway only during the first portion of the life.

Now Roux, the pioneer founder of experimental embryology, showed that the goal (namely the finished framework capable of functioning) is more certain than the route followed (i e the normal course of development). From this we may deduce an influence of the function-rule on the rule of genesis, an influence not yet investigated.

If we find it difficult to admit the influence of the one rule on the other, let us remember that, in their very nature, the rules are active factors, and so may also be called regulators. Now the analogies for these regulators are to be sought, not in the domain of mechanics, but in that of music. And so we may say that the melody of function influences the melody of genesis

It is very difficult to visualise even this much in the required degree ; and in considering the origin of species and community it is at first utterly confusing, since we have to keep before our eyes the influence of three melodies on the melody of genesis The melody of function, the melody of the species and the melody of the community come to expression in the arrangement and seriation of the polar systems of impulses The individual organism formed during development in such a way that it becomes a structure capable of functioning, becomes at the same time a member of the community, and, by the mere fact of its existence, forms a part cf the species

So every individual being, when it is completed, is a
product of three rules—the rule of the species, the rule of ✓
the community and the individual's rule of function. All
three rules, therefore, must together have been determining
the rule of genesis, which imposes their arrangement on the
impulses.

Reference of the phenotype of the individual organism to
its genotype permits us to separate off the rule of the species,
and reduce the species to a rule of mixing of the genes—a
rule which I put into concrete form in the image of the
columnar network. This rule of mixing, which supposedly
forms the family, produces individuals exploiting all the given
possibilities according to the number and quality of the
properties present, and creates a wide-embracing surrounding-
world, within which the species as a whole continues to live
and move.

The picture of the species as phenotype, such as I gave it
in the case of the cabbage-white, may be pictured as stationary
or in action, according to whether we project it in space only,
or in space and time. One thing remains characteristic of
this picture throughout, and it is that while the individual
organisms considered show a collective organisation, they are
not connected together by a function.

By their individual actions the individuals do not participate in the collective action of the species in such a way that
one part-action conditions the other in space and time ; but
the sum of all the part-actions of the individuals forms in
each association the collective action of the species.

As soon as the organism is completely developed, the phenotype of which was determined through the genotype given by
the rule of the species, the influence of that rule ceases, and
the collective action of all the individuals forms that of the
species, without further functional binding together of their
actions as individuals.

And so we may say that, though without functional framework, the species acts in conformity with plan

It is only by seeing the species as a living thing that we are enabled to understand there being unities which have arisen in accordance with plan and yet can do without functional connection ; for here the action by the whole, which is in full conformity with plan, arises quite of itself from the rudiment so laid down.

In the species there is no vocational organisation, but the performance by the whole expresses itself directly in the activities of the individuals.

In this respect the community is essentially different from the species. The community is distinguished by a pervading inter-adjustment. In it the unified action arises through a unified rule of function, and the function-circles are sharply defined from one another, at least in so far as they relate to the world of action For in fully developed communities we find builder-persons, who arrange the medium to form a dwelling, soldiers who fight the enemy, and workers who see to the commissariat ; finally, there are the sexual persons, whose business is reproduction. There is a functional division according to vocation. Organisation through vocation is characteristic of the framework of the community. ·The various vocations are expressed by the different development of the effectors in different individuals. Occasionally also there are vocational groups in respect of receptors : swans, for instance, set as outposts those individuals possessing especially keen sight.

According to the type of the animal community as a whole, the inter-adjustments within it are very variously specialised. If there are vocational groups of workers that never leave the dwelling, their receptors, in correspondence with the restriction of the function-circle, are reduced so as to deal only with those indications that have importance within the organism of the community : among the termites, there are totally blind workers. The analogy here is very striking with the different development of the cells within the framework of an individual creature. We find this familiar process within the organism repeated in the case of the individual cell-subjects, of which the function-circles are some of them suppressed and some of them intensified.

The unified behaviour of the entire community is conditioned, as a rule, by the interlocking of the various vocational groups in conformity with plan, without there being demonstrable any unified centre which, notified by its receptors, would set in action now one group of agents and now another.

Animal communities are constructed, as a rule, purely on ✓ the principle of coordination, and not on that of subordination.

There are, however, certain exceptions : in the bee-community the queen is sometimes described as the leader, for she has not only to look after the production of young, but also has to show the swarming community the direction its flight must take and the place on which the new colony shall settle ; this place, it would seem, is reconnoitred by certain workers, whose vocation, in this case, is that of spies.

We find this distinction even among individual animals. For instance, I have called sea-urchins " reflex-republics," because, in these animals, many organs, such as spines and pedicellariæ, have become independent reflex-persons, whose actions are inter-coordinated, and not subordinated to the central nervous system.

In the framework of the individual creature, as well as in the inter-adjustment within the community-being, there is a coordinate type of structure as well as a subordinate. Thus the laws of function of the community approximate closely to those of the individual creature, whereas the corresponding laws of the species are of a different kind

R

THE WEB OF LIFE

Starting from the shaping process of the individual organism, we perceive that we have before us a product of several formative factors.

We can rightly appreciate the movements of a drop of water on the rippled surface of a lake, only when we have studied the direction as well as the force of the intersecting lines of ripples : in the same way, the form of each living creature can be brought nearer our comprehension, only when we have analysed the action of the formative impetuses that cross one another within it.

We may prelude the attempt by picturing the formative tendency of each impetus as dominating freely. In so doing, we become aware of the restrictions imposed on it by the others.

If we concentrate our attention solely on one formative impetus, we cannot fail to perceive that, from the standpoint of the individual organism, both community and species impose on it restrictions that are antagonistic to it as an individual In the same way also, from the standpoint of the species-impetus, we feel the embarrassing restriction that the demands of the individual and of the community lay upon that. The same is true of the interest of the community, which finds itself hemmed in by the interests of the individual and of the species.

These mutual restrictions give us proof that we have before us a coarse-meshed tissue, which can be comprehended only from a standpoint higher than those afforded us by individual, community or species. This all-embracing inter-weaving cannot be referred to any particular formative impetus. Here at last we see the action of life as such, working in conformity with plan.

As a rule, the attempt is made to place the interest of the

individual foremost, and to demonstrate its interest in the formation of species and community. Actually, there can be neither species nor community without the individual ; on the other hand, it is possible to conceive of individuals without species or community.

Beginning with the unicellulars, we must admit the possibility of there being among them individuals entirely lacking the function-circle of sex, reproducing themselves by fission only, and in this way perpetually starting afresh and multiplying Of such individuals we might admit that they were, in a sense, immortal ; but their immutability, though certainly to the benefit of the individual, is obviously not in the interests of life. Consequently, each one of them is furnished with a special inter-adjustment urging it to conjugation and the creation of new and modified individuals, which take its place. Through the introduction of the sexual function-circle, the individual organism becomes a member of the species

When individuals are merged in the species, their immortality and immutability are sacrificed in the interests of life, and this shows that the two interests are not identical Moreover, each organism is obliged to take on a new function-circle, which it can perfectly well get on without. The sexual circle requires special effector apparatus and a special steering bearing on special indications. This imposes an extremely heavy burden on the framework of the individual, and means a great increase in the dangers it has to run, for at the breeding-time the other function-circles are forced into the background. And thus, in the interests of the preservation of the species, that of the preservation of the individual is thrust into a second place

The stamp set on the individual by the community-impetus is different No new function-circle is required ; on the other hand, the individual's function-circles are

markedly altered, and that of sex is often completely suppressed, as in the case of sexless workers and soldiers among
the bees and ants. Which demonstrates, in a very striking
way, that not only is the individual organism able to live
without the sex circle, but that it even displays an increase
in its other functions. When the community selects only
certain individuals for reproduction, the species-impetus
becomes suppressed in the other members of the community.

It is impossible not to recognise here that three rules
interlock in conformity with plan.

In the majority of animals, it is only the rules of the
individual and of the species that take part in shaping the
organism ; in all communities a third rule is added to these.
In spite of this incredibly heavy handicap, the result is always
a perfect conformity with plan.

And there is spread out before our eyes a multiform
wealth of transitional forms, which we can only describe as
countless variations on the theme of life.

Only through complete misapprehension have these
transitions been regarded as links between the more perfect
and the less. The central power, to which we give the name
of " life," is, by its very nature, in accord with plan, and quite
incapable of producing anything void of plan and imperfect.

THE EVOLUTION OF SPECIES

It is remarkable, to say the least of it, that the Darwinians
always speak of the evolution of the individual, but never
of the evolution of species, although they distinguish between
highly evolved animals and primitive animals.

Indeed the entire genealogical tree of animals, which
we see depicted in zoological text-books, is supposed to
represent an evolutionary sequence from the simple to the
complex And Darwinians love to place the evolutionary

idea in the forefront of their expositions. Why then this inconsistent avoidance of an evolution of the species ?

It is because the whole sequence of the various species which palæontology reveals to us from the Cambrian up to the present day, is regarded by them, not as a life-process, but as explicable by chemical, physical or mechanical causes.

Variation, according to them, is a chemical process which, without any plan, creates organisms, from among which the struggle for existence exterminates the unfit, i e. those incapable of life, so that a selection of the fit is effected.

The genealogical tree is not meant to give a picture of an inner growth, but merely the result of the influence of external factors. The shape given to the animal kingdom at the present day is the outcome of the action of physical factors on a chemistry that displays no conformity with plan.

I simply cannot understand how, holding such views, men can talk of an evolutionary idea. For the external factors can at any moment become such that, by extermination of the complex, they make the simple animals the only ones capable of living, and thus bring about a return to the primitive.

In contrast to the Darwinians, the Lamarckians see at work an internal shaping force, which, in accordance with plan, creates beings that express that plan. The Lamarckians, therefore, may speak of an evolutionary idea. But the significance they attach to the shaping force is psychological, and so is not controllable by an outside observer. Biology must insist, without qualification, that it shall be so controlled

Before examining the scanty facts at our disposal for the comprehension of the evolution of species, I must state the reasons that incline biology to speak of an evolution of species and not of an evolution of individuals

I have given detailed reasons for the opinion that, in the

genesis of the individual organism from the germ, we are not dealing with an unfolding — " evolutio " — since in the germ there is no framework lying ready prepared, and only requiring to open out in order to give the finished animal On the contrary, the germ and the embryo are unfinished structures, which are transformed into completed frameworks only through invasion by impulse after impulse, working in accordance with plan. By the formation of new folds, the simple becomes complex. Thus we have to do with a folding up, and not with an unfolding ; with a " *com*-plication," and not with an " *ex*plication "

With species it is quite otherwise. There is no such thing as an unfinished species (in the way that there are unfinished single organisms), and there never has been.

If by " species " we understand an association of different individuals according to a plan, then such associations exist both among organisms with complex and among organisms with simple framework. The association, i.e. the method by which the connection is effected, is the same in all cases. When we consider together simultaneously the family organisations of animals as they succeed one another, it is always a chain ; when we separate them from one another, it is always a network.

The more numerous the different genotypes within a species, the more readily do they seem to split off into different races, which may then form new species.

That is the only thing we can say with much probability concerning the evolution of new species. All the rest is the work of imagination.

It does really mean something, then, when we speak of the evolution of one species from another We are then picturing the races as having been wrapped up within the species Or the species unfolds into different species when its races separate from one another.

One association splits up into several. The first, it is true, included a greater number of differences within it ; but it was no more firmly knit together than those which arose from it ; if it had been, it would have been able to hold together the greater wealth of variety.

If we try to represent graphically this splitting off of new species, we get the familiar picture of the genealogical tree. Since the species-associations are constructed in conformity with plan, we may see in the genealogical tree the representation of a living phenomenon.

It is obvious that, by mere splitting off, no higher complexity can be created. Higher complexity in no way owes its origin to the appearance of new species, but to that of new individuals. When the complexity of the individuals within a species increases, there comes a moment, it would seem, when the bond no longer suffices, and races begin to branch off, which ultimately become independent.

The inquiry as to increase in complexity, therefore, must be directed, not to the species, but to the individual organism.

THE IDEA OF EVOLUTION

The enthusiasm with which Darwinians advocate the idea of evolution has something absurd in it ; and this is not merely because their view of the world, essentially based as it is on physics and chemistry; cannot create the idea of evolution out of these sciences, which are fundamentally opposed to any evolution whatsoever. It is also, and chiefly, because the word " evolution " expresses just the opposite of what it is intended to mean

" Evolutio," or unfolding, clearly means that the forming of folds becomes less and less. But " evolution " is used to express the increase in complexity observed in the realm of living things, beginning with the simple amœba and going up to the mammals. It is obvious that here we are dealing with a complication; for no one will deny that in mammals the relations of the parts to one another and to the whole are far more involved than in the amœbæ. Thinking of this transition from the simple to the complex organism, how can we speak of an evolution, an *un*folding?

It will at once be admitted that evolution is perhaps a badly chosen terminus technicus; for it is customary to speak of more highly evolved animals, when what is meant is that there is an increase in complexity.

But this is not correct; for when Darwinism speaks of the evolution of the individual, it means quite rightly the decrease in the number of its folds. In the Darwinistic sense, evolution means that within the germ the finished animal already lies concealed, just as the folded bud contains the perfect flower, and in addition to growing, has merely to unfold and evolve in order to produce it. That this idea is false does not affect the present argument; it merely proves that Darwinism, here using the word in its right sense, sees in the genesis of the individual a decrease in the folding, and, accordingly, a simplification.

It cannot be denied that, in the same breath, Darwinism uses one word in two opposite senses. When it speaks of the evolution of the individual, it means simplification; when it speaks of evolution in the animal kingdom, it means complication.

It is not surprising that the hopeless confusion obtaining at present (and not only among laymen) with regard to fundamental questions in natural science, should be the outcome of this unconscious juggling on the part of Darwinism.

Darwinism, the logical consistency of which leaves as much to be desired as does the accuracy of the facts on which it is based, is a religion rather than a science. Consequently all arguments levelled against it rebound without effect ; it is nothing but the embodiment of the impulse by the human will to get rid, by every possible means, of plan in Nature. The idea of evolution has thus become the sacred conviction of thousands, but has ceased to have anything to do with unprejudiced investigation of natural phenomena

INCREASE IN COMPLEXITY

We turn again to the question, " On what is based the increase in the complexity of animal forms, which in the course of ages has come about upon the earth ? "

As has been shown, this increase cannot be explained by the splitting up of species   So far as we can judge at present, this splitting up is merely the consequence of growth in complexity within the confines of a species, to such an extent that it becomes incapable of holding together any longer.

The next question is whether this growth in the complexity of the completed form of the phenotype within the species can be adequately explained by increase in the mixing of genes in its fixed genotype.

There is no doubt that the variational extent of the phenotype, given by combining the genes in every way possible, is very great indeed : and indeed, it may be that this enrichment of the phenotype without change of the genotype may lead to the formation of races and to the splitting off of new species   What is certain is that every new species arising in this way must be poorer in genes than was the mother-species.   The result of each splitting off is an increase in specialisation, combined with a decrease in the variational range, and this conditions a greater stability in form production.

In the splitting of species we seem to have a division in which there is unequal distribution of the heritable properties,

while in the genesis of individuals we may also assume a progressive genolysis   Both lead to similar results by methods
that are wholly in accord with plan.   Just as the final products
of the germ, the completed somatic cells, are at once more
differentiated and poorer in potentialities than are the germ-
cells, so are the species that have arisen by splitting off
more differentiated and less rich than is the mother-species

✓   All of this concerns merely the increase of complexity in
the phenotype, but tells us nothing about its increase in the
genotype   The genotype can become richer only through
new genes arising ; and as to this we know nothing.
Kammerer's experiments, which are intended to prove that
new genes do arise, certainly give interesting preliminaries
for elucidating this problem, but are far from containing
sufficient evidence for the settling of anything so far-reaching.

    It is also possible to take up another attitude, and suppose
that new genes do not arise at all, and that it is only the
melody of the impulse-sequence that changes.   If we compare
the genes to the keys of a piano, it is obvious that all tunes
can be played with relatively little material substance   If
we assume that in the germ of the first living organism were
present all the ferments necessary to effect all the changes
in form and substance that we observe in the development,
we might maintain that the difference between the forms
of animals from that time until now depends merely on the
fact that only a limited number of ferments were used by the
primitive impulse-sequence of the first organism.   In course
of time, the impulse-melodies became richer and more in
tricate, so as to create at last the symphony of the Mammalia.

    At the same time, perhaps, in consequence of the splitting
off of species, the originally complete keyboard lost more
and more of its notes, so that in animals at the present day
the possibility of shaping new melodies diminishes as the
melodies are developed.

This theory rules out the possibility of the forming of new genes—which has certainly not been proved ; but just on that account it is remarkably simple and clear. It transfers the centre of gravity from the material into the plan of Nature, and thereby pushes the limits of the investigable as far back as possible, to the limits, namely, of what human knowledge can reach. Knowledge of conformity with plan belongs to the capacities of our apperception ; and beyond the limits set by that it is impossible to know anything

The special advantage of this theory, I consider, lies in its putting aside the utterly impossible idea of each species or genus having sprung from one pair of ancestors ; for it is quite out of the question that one pair should contain all the genes forming the genotype of the species or of the genus.

To assume that the shaping of animals advances in accordance with plan certainly gives a more solid foundation from which to consider Nature than does the so-called evolutionary idea, which is really just a misconception And we can put the more confidence in the idea, since, by amplifying the melody " man," it leads us forward towards ages far richer in possibilities than those offered by the physical forces, which at any moment may induce a degeneration of the creature that has been formed.

Lastly, through the idea of shaping melodies that progress step by step, we come to understand why it is, for instance, that mammals still show rudiments of gill-arches In fishes these structures become gills, whereas in mammals quite different organs are produced, for the development of which the rudiment of the gill-arches seems to us a " détour "

The melody " mammal " did not arise all by itself, but at a certain point branched off from the melody " fish." This certainly proves that mammals are related to fishes, but not that mammals ever bore gills. If we ask whether we ought to regard fishes as the ancestors of mammals, we must get quite clear as to whether by the word " ancestor " we mean only the material basis from which the new melody derived its building-material, or whether we mean the new melody itself. In the first case, fishes are obviously our ancestors ; in the second, they are merely our relatives, in so far as their melody of genesis coincides with our own.

If we regard the increase in complexity that we see in the development of each living organism, as the reflection of the increase in complexity of organisms in general, we arrive at an idea that is contradictory to Haeckel's biogenetic principle (which requires that we have sprung from function-ing, full-grown ancestors) ; we arrive at the idea that the melody of genesis that forms fishes, at a certain period in certain germs ended differently, and that when this new melody or rule of shaping set in, the new forms arose.

Accordingly, we introduce an inner cause as determina-tive, a cause which we do not know, and which we can do no more than recognise, a sort of " further composition " accord-ing to plan ; and plan we have recognised as being the creator of life in general.

In order to carry on a melody, it is not necessary to introduce new notes : in the same way, it is not necessary that new impulses and new genes should come in. The same impulses can reach back and seize on the genes that are already present, and in this way develop the melody further. We may assume the impulses to be all alike, since they all display the same activity, namely that of mobilising the genes ; it is the genes which they affect that produce the difference. It is also reasonable to suppose that the same genes arranged in different sequence may give completely different results, and produce new kinds of organisms.

Admittedly, the foregoing are mere conjectures, for we are without any reliable evidence. But they move in the same direction as the laws with which our study of the genesis of the individual organism has made us familiar. They are therefore analogies, and in the present state of our knowledge we cannot look for more. These analogies have the further advantage that they do not lead us into speculations concerning the existence of impossible ancestors, but simply indicate the given relations. There can be no doubt that the melody of genesis in mammals repeats in its opening measures that of fishes, and diverges therefrom at a certain point. This is the material that we have before us ; we have nothing further. From it I conclude merely that, at the time before there were any mammals, the mammalian melody had not struck up.

It is quite possible that the introduction of new melodies coincides with changes in the medium ; but of this we have no proof One thing only I assume as certain—that when the new melody struck up for the first time, it did so in the way that we can still observe at the present day, when we compare together the shaping process in two related animal forms. That is all one can affirm.

But it is a good deal, for the idea of an invasion by new melodies according to plan gets us out of the difficulty of appealing to chance to explain the genealogy of animals. The genealogical tree becomes a living structure developed in accordance with plan, and, under compulsion from within, perpetually forms new growths of the same kind.

I consider that to compare this inner urge with a psychic affect is merely a sign of the inertia of the powers of our human imagination, which is unable to free itself from a highly deceptive tendency to anthropomorphose natural processes If Lamarckism would but throw off its psychological wrappings, it would pass over straightway into the biological doctrine of conformity with plan.

CHAPTER VIII

CONFORMITY WITH PLAN

INTRODUCTION

IF by biology we understand the doctrine of conformity
with plan in the world of living things, we shall realise that
one of the fundamental inquiries of the science must be
into the nature of this conformity. Is the conformity with
plan that we can demonstrate in all organisms, inseparably
associated with their being? Or is it merely a creation
by uncritical analogy with our human life, perhaps incapable
of sustaining objective consideration, which sees nothing
but causality in all natural phenomena? There has been
much in favour of the second view, and more especially
the name given to conformity with plan. Instead of seeing
in it merely a rule stretching across time and space, men
have spoken of "purpose" and "purposefulness" in Nature;
and this introduced the idea of Nature as a sort of human
being, foreseeing future events and acting accordingly.

But just where conformity with plan is easiest to detect,
we can find no trace of any such human-like being. It is
advisable therefore to dismiss from biology, for all time, expressions such as "purpose" and "purposefulness." What
remains uncontested is the presence of a rule in living Nature,
which reveals itself even in the mechanical processes of the
organism. The only debatable question that remains is
this—" Is there only a mechanical law in the world of living

things, or is there also a super-mechanical law, for which we wish to introduce the term ' conformity with plan ' ? " Are the processes in conformity with plan, which we study in the living world, connected solely with the rules of a mechanical working that has been there from the very beginning, or are they controlled by rules of function embracing not only the working but also its guidance ?

To advance as far as possible by means of the more simple assumption is entirely in accord with the scientific method of thought. But it is not scientific to make of the simpler assumption an article of faith that excludes other assumptions. Those investigators were right who demanded of the vitalists, " Show us the point at which a super-mechanical activity begins to supersede control by the mechanical. Until then, we must refuse to admit a super-mechanical factor."

In the case of the genesis of the living organism, this requirement has now been met, and as clearly as could be wished. We have demonstrated the coming into activity of a super-mechanical factor in the genes, which are lodged in the nuclear substance of the germ, and we have called this factor " impulse." It only remains now to investigate the effect of the impulses on the actions of the fully formed animal.

IMPULSES IN THE ACTIONS

From the genesis of animals we have learnt that the general, fundamental principle is this—where new framework is formed, there a super-mechanical factor is in action. Accordingly, all we have to do is to determine in what actions new framework originates ; and we are then in a position to say, " At this point an impulse must come in." The possibility of forming new framework is given in every organism everywhere and at all times, because in every cell part of the unincorporated germinal substance remains in the protoplasm of the nucleus, from which the framework portion of the cell proceeded, and may at any time again proceed.

Every organism, therefore, represents not merely a machine, which has nothing but a framework ; but it consists of framework + protoplasm, which itself has the power to form fresh framework. Whereas in a machine all wear and tear of its parts through use must be repaired from without by the director of the action, in the organism this is done by the framework-forming protoplasm, which, by means of this faculty, takes the place of the external direction.

Hitherto we might have written the formula for a reflex action R—MO—AO—E (Receptor—Mark - organ—Action - organ—Effector), because we were concerned only with the rule of working of the finished framework. If we wish to combine with this the power to direct the working, we must write the formula $\frac{R}{I} - \frac{MO}{I} - \frac{AO}{I} - \frac{E}{I}$, thereby indicating that every part of the framework occasionally comes under the influence of the super-mechanical factor active in the protoplasm. The formula R—MO—AO—E, accordingly, stands for the known rule, while I—I—I—I indicates the unknown rule of direction. It is only by taking the two together that we get reproduced the function-rule of the reflex action.

Now the reflex action is by no means the only action of which animals are capable ; but, in the reflex, all the parts of the framework are ready prepared from the beginning, and so it is only in reflexes that the action completely reproduces the rule of working. In all other actions, framework-forming comes in, and this necessitates the entry of the super-mechanical factor of direction. In this case, therefore, the " I " must be included along with the main formula. According to the points at which the " I " comes in, it is possible to institute a classification of actions which agrees in the main with the one that is in general use.

For the sake of clearness, I shall now give the formulæ for the various kinds of action, and I shall discuss these afterwards.

The reflex action $= \frac{R}{I} - \frac{MO}{I} - \frac{AO}{I} - \frac{E}{I}$

The form action $= \frac{R}{I} - \frac{MO}{I} - \frac{AO}{I} - EI$

The instinctive action $= \frac{R}{I} - \frac{MO}{I} - AOI - \frac{E}{I}$

The plastic action $= \frac{R}{I} - MOI - \frac{AO}{I} - \frac{E}{I}$

The action based on experience $= \frac{R}{I} - MOI - AOI - \frac{E}{I}$

THE REFLEX ACTION

Hitherto the reflex action $= \frac{R}{I} - \frac{MO}{I} - \frac{AO}{I} - \frac{E}{I}$ has been treated as a purely mechanical process, without taking into account the " direction," which, here also, is going on all the time. And again and again there have been attempts to interpret all other actions as reflexes This is justifiable in so far that, during every action, the course of excitation in an animal presupposes a flawless steering-mechanism, since the transmission of excitation and its reversal are purely mechanical problems In a number of works I have pointed out that, in excitation, we have to distinguish between amount and pressure, and that the nervous centres have a varying capacity for it. Furthermore, there are nervous arrangements that can best be compared with valves.

In spite of all this very finely elaborated detail in the steering-mechanism of animals, the machine of the body, like any other machine (even if its rule of working is elaborated very precisely) is never in a position to go on continuously without direction. Accordingly the mental image we made of the body-machine is necessarily incomplete if we leave out

S

the protoplasm and the impulses, which dominate it, and on which the direction devolves.

THE FORM ACTION

The form action $= \frac{R}{I} - \frac{MO}{I} - \frac{AO}{I} - EI$, which we observed in unicellulars, is remarkable in that here the effectors are formed anew each time under our very eyes, before the real action begins. Here, apparently, the forming of framework enters into the action, whether it be the forming of pseudopodia in amœbæ or of digestive apparatus in the Infusoria. In the course of this, the direction reveals itself as an independent process, having its own rhythm. This rhythm is especially obvious in the successive formation of mouth, stomach, etc. in the case of the Infusoria. The rhythm is affected, indeed, but not created, by the excitation proceeding from the receptors. The impulses bringing about the formation of framework must be connected together by a rule of their own into a unified imperative, in the same way that the handles which an engineer pulls in reversing the levers of some steam-engine must follow a fixed rule. But the directing of the organism does not lie in the hands of a being standing outside ; it is entrusted to the protoplasm from which the whole machine has proceeded, and which, from the initial constructing of thereof, reveals a rule of its own.

THE INSTINCTIVE ACTION $= \frac{R}{I} - \frac{MO}{I} - AOI - \frac{E}{I}$

The form action of unicellulars, characterised by alteration of the external or internal shape of the animal, is distinguished by the release of the action being reflex-like, while its performance follows laws of its own, influenced, but not created, by the process of excitation. Accordingly, the execution of the action is not conditioned, but plastic. And it may remain plastic, if the effectors have a fixed shape, and only the rule of their use is influenced from without by means of the excitation ; in this case, the framework cannot be lodged mechanically in the action-organ, but in its formation follows the rhythmic law of the impulses.

This is typical of the course of the processes described as instinctive actions in the steering-mechanism of animals. The extraordinary number of separate movements, which fit into one another in conformity with plan during the course of an instinctive action, makes it difficult, however, to assume a prepared framework in the steering-mechanism that would be adequate to these demands. The plasticity shown in the execution of the instinctive action makes such an assumption impossible.

If now we observe the actions of the funnel-roller beetle or the ichneumon-fly, we may note again and again that these are influenced by a number of external indications, and yet proceed according to laws of their own   The number and the nature of the indications is absolutely immutable, but they need not all become effective at each action.   Since the animal is quite incapable of receiving new indications, the taking up of indications remains strictly reflex and quite non-plastic.   The plasticity of the actions performed comes about only through the animal having at its disposal a larger number of indications, and this enables it to accommodate itself within a wide range to the external circumstances that offer, by altering the rhythm of its action-sequence according to the difference in the indications.

Again we see the two rules at work in order to give the actions their especial stamp,—the rule of working, controlling the mechanical course of the process in the steering-mechanism, and the rule of direction, which, by modifying the working, introduces plasticity into processes that otherwise would run automatically. We even call our own actions instinctive, when a series of movements in conformity with plan are performed by us according to a law of their own, which adapts itself to the external conditions without being automatic.

$$\text{THE PLASTIC ACTION} = \frac{R}{I} - MOI - \frac{AO}{I} - \frac{E}{I}$$

The plastic action, in the narrower sense, refers only to the plasticity of the mark-organ, while the course of the processes in the action-organ is reflex. I would remind you of the dogs in which Pawlow managed to connect the secretion of saliva with new indications of an optical or acoustic nature. In this case also there can be no doubt that new framework appears. The presumption, of course, is that the indications brought into fresh prominence were already there. But there is introduced a new kind of connection between these indications and effector processes not hitherto under their influence.

The plasticity in this case depends, not on a mere influencing of the rhythm of a given impulse-series, but on the introduction into this law of impulses hitherto unused. Not merely is the rule of working governed by a rule of direction, but a new one makes its appearance. In such a case, after formation of the new framework in the mark-organ, this rule may withdraw, leaving behind it merely a new reflex action as evidence of a plasticity that once was there.

$$\text{THE ACTION BASED ON EXPERIENCE} = \frac{R}{I} - MOI - AOI - \frac{E}{I}$$

When, by whistling to his bull-finch, a boy gets it to pipe a new tune by itself, that is an action of experience on the part of the bull-finch. It is characterised by there arising, not merely a new combination of indications in the mark-organ, but also a new rule in the action-organ that controls the muscles of the syrinx. Accordingly, formation of new framework has come in both in the mark-organ and in the action-organ , so we may assume an invasion by impulses.

The plasticity of the action based on experience bears on the direction itself, and not merely on the rule of working, as it is in the case of the instinctive action, which is subject to an unchanging direction As a result, the instinctive action appears from its very inception fully prepared, whereas the action of experience must be learnt gradually. Simple actions based on experience, if often repeated, may become reflexes.

$$\text{THE CONTROLLED ACTION} = \frac{R}{I} - MOI \underset{\leftarrow}{\overset{\rightarrow}{=}} AOI - \frac{E}{I}$$

The bull-finch that has learnt to pipe a new tune forgets it again if it is prevented from hearing its own voice This demonstrates the necessity of controlling the animal's own effectors by its own receptors The controlled action is an action based on experience that does not become a reflex and then run automatically. On the contrary, the new rule of direction in the action-organ requires to have its running continuously controlled by the mark-organ ; and, in order to develop into greater permanence, the rule of direction that has been newly formed in the mark-organ has need of the continued influence of the rule of working in the action-organ. To grasp these complicated combinations, it is useful to make a diagram of the steering-mechanism of a simple controlled action. is the diagram of the steering-mechanism as I gave it when describing the function-circle. is that of the steering-mechanism when we have to do with a controlled action, in which the influence of the effectors on the receptors occurs outside the body, as happens in the case of listening to one's own singing.

Much more frequently the control occurs inside the body. Here there are two cases to be distinguished : either the movement of the effector muscles is received by special sensory nerves, as the accompanying diagram indicates , or else the excitation conveyed to the effector nerves is partially taken up by special central receptors and conducted back to the mark-organ. . These receptors form the central sense-organ of Helmholtz, which, anatomically speaking, is still undiscovered.

In the human being all three kinds of receptor occur : he has the power of controlling his own movements, firstly, by the eye or the sense of touch ; secondly, by muscular sensations ; and thirdly, by direction-signs.

Our ignorance of the relations of the central receptors prevents any dealing with their relations to the organ for giving direction in space that lies in the semicircular canals.

I shall bring together all controlled actions under the common formula $\frac{R}{I} - MOI \underset{\leftarrow}{\overset{\rightarrow}{} } AOI - \frac{E}{I}$.

THE RECEPTOR ACTION

If I lay before a draughtsman an unfamiliar arabesque, and after it has been taken away, he is able to copy it, that is an action based on experience, essentially indistinguishable from the imitative piping of the bull-finch that has heard a new tune.

The draughtsman, however, must, in receiving, execute a movement, and this makes his action more difficult. In listening to a piece of music, the hearer does not have to make any movement, whereas the draughtsman, as he observes, moves his eye to and fro with his eye-muscles, so that his glance follows along the line of the arabesque ; and it is this directing of the sight that must be formed anew like a melody, if he is to be in a position to put the arabesque down on paper on his own account. Just as the melody is decomposable into separate notes, so the line may be broken up into separate direction-steps. Just as the notes connect up together into a melody, so the direction-steps connect up into a line. The direction-steps forming the line of an arabesque or the outline of some object are exactly as objective as the notes proceeding from some source of sound in space.

The receptor action which forms merely the introduction to an action based on experience or a controlled action, consists in furnishing melodies of direction-steps in the mark-organ, melodies which then influence the action-organ. The forming of the melody of direction-steps is of very great interest, because usually it is associated with the excitation coming from a receptor that itself is moved to and fro through the subject, as when the eye or the finger "feels." Here subjective and objective indications are bound together into a single unity.

There appears to be a contradiction here. I have just been emphasising that the direction-steps of which the line is made up are indications as objective as are the notes composing the melody. In like manner, the optical stimulus proceeding from the black colour of the arabesque is undoubtedly also an objective indication; but now the line appears to be a subjective indication, because it arises through the movement of the eye-muscles of the subject

If the eye were mechanically connected with the arabesque, and if the movement of the eye automatically followed along it, then each step that the eye made along the line would undoubtedly be an objective indication, as soon as it became transformed into excitation by a corresponding effector. The eye, however, follows the line of the arabesque by its own muscular movement   In doing so, it proceeds also step by step, and each step forward that it makes is taken up by it as an indication.

Since, however, the steps that it takes follow a line presented from without, they act as an objective indication, and can unite with those that are optical into one that is objective, without there being anything left over.

The diagram for the steering-mechanism of a receptor action would look like this :— .

First we see the receptor, which is moved by the receiving effector. The receptor transmits its excitation to the mark-organ, while the receiving effector gets its excitations from the action-organ. These excitations are in part turned off from a central receptor, and sent to the mark-organ, where they arrive in company with the waves of excitation proceeding from the receptor.

In the general formula for the action based on experience, the receptor action does not find expression, because this treats all the receptor effects in the same way.

THE IMPULSE IN THE NERVOUS SYSTEM

We have learnt about the invasion of the germ by the impulses, and we know that they affect the genes which lie all together, side by side, in the nucleus of the fertilised egg-cell. But where do the impulses invade the completed animal, when it performs an action ? Even if we restrict the invasion here also to the genes in certain cells, we still have to inquire where these cells are to be looked for. The formulæ for the majority of actions refer us to the two central points—the mark-organ and the action-organ. It is here accordingly that we must look for the cells in question.

To determine on these cells I must first go back to what I said in the section dealing with the theory of indications, concerning the structural principles of the nervous system in animals   Every stimulus that reaches an animal affects it in the same way—a wave of excitation arises in a nerve.   All waves of excitation are qualitatively alike, and do not permit of our distinguishing between stimuli

On the other hand, all the nerve-fibres of the animal are isolated   Each receptor nerve-fibre ends in a receptor centre   The isolated nerve-fibre with its centre may be described as an independent nerve-person.   This arrangement makes it possible to distinguish from one another as many stimuli as there are nerve-persons.   Now every muscle and every gland is connected with a nerve-person   If we consider this arrangement as a whole, we see that, on one hand, the possibility is offered of summing up any chosen combination of stimuli by cutting out certain receptor nerve-persons, and, on the other hand, of making every sort of nervous combination of the muscles and glandular structures, the activity of which then gives a unified response

The binding together of the nerve-persons is effected by net-shaped nervous connecting routes   The nerve-persons themselves are merely representatives, and within the body they transmit, on the one hand, the stimuli to which it is subjected, and, on the other, those which it itself exerts.

In the mark-organ are united the receptor representatives in the combination characteristic for each animal, and in the action-organ are similarly combined the effector representatives.

The combinations of representatives are so arranged, that those of the main receptors are united into special groups, and those of the main effectors into others.   The groups of nerve-persons may again have a representative of their own, which we may call their captain ; and the captains may be united into groups, represented by an adjutant.

If we consider the whole body of representatives (of the

receptor as well as of the effector side) each as a single base
on which the captain or adjutant forms the apex of a
pyramid, we get, as our picture of the whole, a number of
pyramids, arising from a common base, and coming together
by their apices.

If now we connect each receptor captain or adjutant
with a corresponding effector, we get, as the expression of
the steering-mechanism, a bundle of reflex arcs, which, for
the majority of animals, suffices to explain their various
reactions.   The complete structure of representatives as a two-
sided system of pyramids connected together by nervous
routes, will suffice, however, only for reflex actions.   For all
other actions, fresh nervous connections must be made ; and,
to make these, it is necessary that the impulses invade the
protoplasm of the nerve-persons.

The development of new nerve-persons cannot be demonstrated anywhere ; but what unquestionably happens is the
formation of new paths for excitation between those already
present.   So the nerve-persons must have the power to send
out nervous pseudopodia, which serve as permanent or as
temporary bridges for the conduction of the excitation.

This simplifies extraordinarily the problem on which we
are engaged : all we have to do is to imagine the nerve-
persons in question at the moment as little amœbæ, connected together by means of a permanent nerve, whether
receptor or effector, and having the power to send out pseudopodia, which fuse with those of other amœbæ, and with them
form bridges and networks permitting transmission of the
excitation.

The protrusion of a pseudopodium is referable to the
activation of a gene.   The activation of a gene can take
place only through the coming in of an impulse.   But the
possibility of the activation also depends on external circumstances ; for instance, there may be a material chemical

check which hinders the formation of the new framework, and can only be cleared out of the way by the incoming excitation. We may assume that by this means it is possible for free-living amœbæ, whose rhythm in pseudopodium-formation depends on a rhythm of the impulse-action, to concentrate on the stimuli acting from without.

If we wish to form some sort of approximate idea of how a reconstruction of the framework proceeds, let us imagine a series of amœbæ, each with a permanent outgrowth. Each of these projections is connected with a resonator. The resonators respond to the sounds of one octave, and serve as receptors by exciting through their response the nervous outgrowths of the amœbæ in connection with them. Now let us play on some instrument a simple tune, the notes of which lie within one octave. As soon as an air-wave of the corresponding number of vibrations strikes the suitable resonator, an excitation travels to the amœba, which thereupon is freed from the check imposed on it, and becomes accessible to the rhythmically invading impulses that excite the formation of pseudopodia. The pseudopodia of the amœbæ, responding simultaneously, or one after the other, unite to form nervous bridges. In this way, the impulse-rhythm, setting in quite mechanically, can be excited by external interference. If the rhythm of the impulse-melody is determined beforehand, the first onset of the excitation suffices to make the impulses of the amœbæ respond automatically, and, conducted to and fro, further and further, it overcomes the inhibition generally, and permits the impulse-invasion to follow in the given sequence.

If, by the help of the cinematograph, we fix the bridge-formation that arises in this way, we get a picture of a changing tissue, the pattern of which remains the same at every repetition. A skilled musician could then read from the pattern what the melody had been that was played outside.

However the actual process may one day appear to the eye of the observer who succeeds in penetrating the detail of what goes on in the brain, one thing is certain—it will occur in the forms familiar to us, of change of shape and transference of excitation in nervous structures. The arena in which the phenomena we expect to find must take place is already so narrowed down that we need look for no sort of sensational surprises. Everything will appear to proceed quite mechanically ; the super-mechanical invasions will never come to be appreciated by our senses. The only thing that we shall be able to show is the coming in of an automatic rhythm in the bridge-forming—a kind of self-active " Bahnung," if I may use Erner's term.

It must be kept in mind that the impulse-melody is a completely automatic process, which belongs to the subject alone ; and while it can be excited by external circumstances, it can never be formed by these. The capacity of responding, now to one melody, now to another, is limited in the case of each subject. One may play a certain sequence of notes as often as one likes to an unmusical person ; he will not be able to construct a melody therefrom. The same holds good of optical capacity. There are only a few men so artistically gifted that in them other than quite primitive melodies of direction-signs sound forth, just sufficing for recognition of the necessary objects.

From this it follows that the power to form new impulse-sequences through so-called " learning " is restricted. For each creature there is a certain extent of learning power (very different in different individuals) marked out at the beginning. It depends on the individual whether he knows how to exploit this to the full.

THE CONCRETE SCHEMA OF FRAMEWORK-FORMING

So long as we were dealing with framework-forming in
the central nervous system, insufficient knowledge reduced us
to conjecture. Fortunately, however, research in other fields
has advanced so far that it has surprised Nature in the very
act of forming framework.

The body of animals is not merely a machine performing
none but mechanical actions ; it must perform many that
cannot be controlled in mechanical ways. Super-mechanical
actions of this kind are always required when framework
is formed anew ; and the framework already there is quite
incapable of this, in spite of all the physical and chemical
aids that the body has at its disposal.

Growth by cell-division, which in all animals proceeds
in the same way, offers a super-mechanical problem of the
kind. At every cell-division the aim is for the mechanical
apparatus of the cell to divide itself into two parts, which
are equivalent to the first, since they in their turn must
again divide.

The problem of constructing an apparatus capable of
dividing itself into two equivalent apparatuses, is technically
impracticable. No framework can be so built that it can
duplicate itself. By the function of a framework we always
understand its action in an outward direction. A framework
that dissolves or divides itself no longer fulfils a function,
but loses it altogether. But in cell-division a function is
required of the cell-apparatus that shall serve not merely
to divide the cell's own apparatus into two halves, but to
make these halves duplicate.

The dividing cell does actually develop an apparatus of its
own that effects this duplication. This essentially super-
mechanical process has been laid bare down to the finest
detail, and appears to us so logical that scientific men as a

rule do not stop to consider that in it a problem is solved that is mechanically impossible.

I reproduce the diagrammatic pictures that Boveri, in his great work, *Das Problem der Befruchtung*, gives of cell-division, and this will enable every reader to get an idea of this " miraculous " process.

In Fig. 1 we see the resting cell. In its protoplasm is the little centrosome, which is placed above the cell-nucleus. The cell-nucleus is free of protoplasm, and consists of the scaffolding of chromatin, which is spread out like a sponge in the nuclear sap. In Fig. 2 the centrosome has duplicated itself, and at the same time the chromatin is set in motion. In Fig. 3 the centrosomes have separated from one another, while the mesh-work of the surrounding protoplasm arranges itself in rays around them. Within the nucleus the chromatin has clumped together into four strands, the so-called chromosomes. (The number of chromosomes is constant for each species of animal. There may be from four to four hundred.) In Fig. 4 the nuclear membrane has disappeared. The nuclear sap is absorbed by the protoplasm, and the four chromosomes lie free. In Fig. 5 the two centrosomes have separated so far that they stand directly opposite one another. At the same time, the radiation of the protoplasmic network has increased. Four rays have meanwhile isolated themselves completely and on each side they become connected with the chromosomes. In Fig. 6 the chromosomes now split lengthwise in half, and the eight protoplasmic rays each draw a half-chromosome towards the centrosome to which they belong, the centrosome with its rays remaining firmly fixed in the protoplasm (Figs. 7 and 8). In Fig. 9 the degeneration of the division-apparatus begins, the chromosomes are once more surrounded by nuclear sap, and the protoplasm has divided itself into two halves. Fig. 10 shows the two resting nuclei which represent the duplication of Fig. 1.

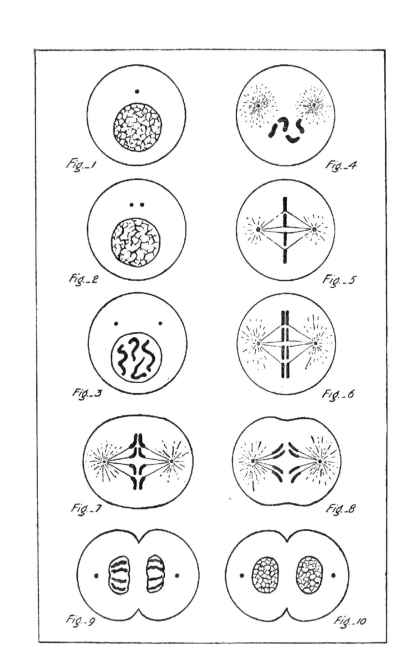

Fig._1

Fig._2

Fig._3

Fig._4

Fig._5

Fig._6

Fig._7

Fig._8

Fig._9

Fig._10

In considering the whole process, we can distinguish two acts—the division and the duplication. The protoplasm of the cell is simply divided into two halves, which form two new spheres. Since the protoplasmic mesh-work everywhere consists of like elements, and the amount of protoplasm plays a secondary part, division suffices here, without an actual duplication coming in. But with the chromatin it is different. The chromatin is the bearer of the genes, and in order to distribute these equally to the two daughter-cells, they must first arrange themselves in rows, and then the opportunity is given for them to become paired by duplication. Then at division there go to each half the same number of all the kinds of genes present in the original cell. At the same time the rearrangement of the chromatin into chromosomes gives a chance in certain cases for the division to result in nuclei with unlike chromatin constitution.

In normal division, however, where the material bearing the heritable properties is equally distributed, there is an actual duplication corresponding to that of the centrosomes. Even in the case of the centrosomes, we cannot speak of a simple division, because each of the two that arise corresponds in every particular to the original one.

The whole process is complicated by the fact that, in addition to the division of the protoplasm and the duplication of the centrosomes and chromosomes, two other processes come in successively, processes involving movement and shaping. The one effects the transformation of the spongy chromatin into four discrete chromosomes ; the other relates to the development of the division-spindle, the protoplasmic threads of which serve to separate the duplicated chromosomes from one another and draw them to their centrosomes. Lastly, the degeneration and the re-forming of the nuclear membrane comes into the process in complete conformity with plan.

These are all independent processes, which are connected

together by a rule. This rule, however, cannot be referred to a hidden framework, because the hypothetical hidden framework must likewise divide and duplicate itself,—a process that is just as insoluble mechanically.

There remains no course open for us but to recognise that here before our eyes a process is going on that is accomplished, not through mechanical compulsion, but through active invasion by a super-mechanical design. Following the line we have pursued up to now, we shall assume the invasion by separate impulses, which are connected together into a system.

The study of cell-division is accordingly of great value to us, since it provides us with a helpful schema for the elucidation of the super-mechanical processes in the central nervous system. There also it is sufficient to assume the appearance of centrosome-like structures with their protoplasmic threads ; and this will give us some concrete idea of how fresh conducting bridges appear between one nerve-person and another. This does not essentially alter our comparison of the nerve-persons to amœbæ, but merely simplifies and deepens it.

The sure and flawless interlocking of the various part-processes in cell-division has misled investigators into regarding it as a purely mechanical process. This is a misconception, for every machine, whether it be one worked by man or a living body-machine, is finally referable to a super-mechanical process,—to that, namely, of framework-forming,—and the mechanical rule of working always presupposes a super-mechanical rule of construction. Moreover, it has been overlooked that every machine in course of time wears out, if there be no direction continually disposing of the damage. So there must always be a super-mechanical rule of direction coming in to keep the mechanical running in working order.

Here we have before us, in concrete form, direct invasion

T

by the control, for cell-division cannot be effected by any mechanical rule of working.

Even where Nature is active in super-mechanical ways, there is no arbitrariness anywhere, but always law. A law, however, which is also design of the most exalted kind, and which casts its spell over the entire process.

DIRECTION

Invasion by the impulses always means a new formation of framework, and consequently is always referable to an influence exerted by the genes on the protoplasm ; the protoplasm, as a result of this influence, either itself begins to move, or else transforms protoplasmic bridges into nervous paths of conduction.

If we look at the entire nervous system of an animal at the beginning of a reflex action, we see everywhere the peripheral routes for excitation and the bridges leading from centre to centre. These structures, however, are invariably accompanied by protoplasm, containing nuclei with genes, ready to repair any damage that may arise by forming new structure.

At the beginning of the non-reflex actions, the intracentral bridges are not quite complete, and accordingly must be re-formed from time to time by the influence of the impulses. It looks like an ingeniously woven net, in which, however, at certain spots, whether in the mark-organ or the action-organ, some meshes are missing that are of decisive importance for the path that the excitation shall follow. These bridges are re-formed each time, and then again broken down. The re-forming of the meshes is not fixed mechanically, and does not follow an automatic rule of working ; it depends on the direction, which is also subject to laws, but of a super-mechanical kind.

Let us imagine that on a ship which is to follow a certain

course, the movements of the helm are mechanically connected with the compass. But in order to meet all the contingencies of the voyage, we place the helmsman between the compass and the rudder ; the helmsman gets his bearings from the compass, though he is not mechanically connected to it, and it is his business to steer the whole ship according to circumstances

In every living organism there is a super-mechanical directing of this kind ; but it is not connected with some person, or director of works, standing outside ; it lies within the works themselves, even if external to the actual frame-work. It cannot invade the works in any way, except by re-construction or by breaking down of the framework Through lack of any analogy, it is very difficult to understand a direction of this kind. Attempts to compare it with a mechanism lead us just as far astray as do those to set it on the level of a personality conscious of an aim.

So far as I can see, the only escape from these difficulties is to imagine some implement, with the framework of which we are very familiar, and endow it with those super-mechanical powers that are the prerogative of the organism.

Let us imagine a two-wheeled iron cart, all the structural parts of which are surrounded, as in a living creature, by a reserve substance, " protoferine," which does not enter into the framework This protoferine has the power, not only to replace a piece of iron if it breaks off, but also to form anew whole structural portions of the framework. Accordingly, it is able, not only to repair substance, but also to restore form. This possibility of restoration of form is the question that interests us here. It is obvious that the form, once destroyed, cannot produce form anew. There must still be present in the residue of protoferine the rule that led to shaping, and this even after part of the framework with its protoferine has been lost. As an auxiliary concept, connecting the rule of shaping with that of substance-forming, I have introduced the impulse. The rule of shaping thereby becomes an impulse-system, extended in space and influencing matter at different places. We must now break up into a number of such systems the protoferine that has not entered into the framework of the cart ; and we shall find that the domain governed by each system corresponds to the spatial extent of the part-functions of the whole vehicle. Two impulse-systems, for instance, would embrace the two wheels. At the common axle, these would pass over into one another. Again, the body of the cart, the seat, the pole, would each correspond to one system.

The several impulse-systems of the cart must in a measure affect one another mutually, for at a number of points the structures they govern fit into one another. At these points the same protoferine will have demands made on it by two impulse-systems.

The impulse-systems have no direct influence on the running of the cart, since they are suited only for the production of framework, and have lost all influence on the framework itself.

Even in those cases where, as in the ship, the compass is not automatically connected with the rudder, but has to be linked up with it anew as occasion requires, the steering does not take place directly through a helmsman, but by development of fresh mechanical connections between the receptor and effector organs. We may imagine that the nerve-meshes at the decisive points in the central nervous system get linked up, now with one impulse-system and now with another ; and this must result in a complete change in the reaction of the whole animal. According to the number of impulse-systems that lie ready to invade the central point, the plasticity of the action will be greater or less.

We can express this, indeed, in the formula for the plastic action. If instead of $\frac{R}{I} - MOI - \frac{AO}{I} - \frac{E}{I}$ we write $\frac{R}{I} - MOI$

$(I_1 \ I_2) - \frac{AO}{I} - \frac{E}{I}$, this means that, in place of the action $\frac{R}{I} - \frac{MOI}{I} - \frac{AO}{I} - \frac{E}{I}$, the action $\frac{R}{I} - \frac{MOI_1}{I} - \frac{AO}{I} - \frac{E}{I}$ can be performed ; and so forth.

In all forms of action is revealed the close connection between the individual organs and their associated impulse-systems But while the connection of the separate parts of the framework within the organ, as well as of the organs among themselves, is obvious to the inquiring eye, this is not the case with the impulse-systems, which can be revealed only by experimental methods.

So long as we content ourselves with including in rules what has been learnt through experiment concerning the inner connections, we require no further auxiliary concept in order to base the connection within a rule.   This is already given by the concept of the regularity of the rule itself   But as soon as we transform the rule into an impulse-system, in the attempt to see how it affects the protoplasm, we have need of some idea which shall help us to visualise the unity within an impulse-system, as well as the unity among the impulse-systems considered collectively. For this purpose, I choose the idea of *internal equilibrium*, which seems to me to express more clearly what one usually understands by correlation.

FUNCTIONAL AND GENETICAL BUILDING-STONES

Before I go on to speak of what has been learnt by experimental research concerning the internal equilibrium of the impulse-systems, I must discuss in more detail an idea that has already been treated of in another connection—the idea of functional building-stones If I write down the simplest action-rule of the reflex $\frac{R}{I} - \frac{MO}{I} - \frac{AO}{I} - \frac{E}{I}$, I have, in so doing, broken up the whole reflex arc into functional building-stones.

$\frac{R}{I}$, for example, means a receptor—an eye, let us say,—together with all its protoplasm and the impulse-system governing that. To the eye also belong the nervous connecting-routes to the mark-organ. But, on the other hand, these belong to the mark-organ itself. Here, therefore, is the debatable ground, which is under the control of two impulse-systems.

$\frac{MO}{I}$ means the mark-organ of the central nervous system, with its protoplasm and the governing impulse-system, etc. But everywhere the connecting-routes from one organ to the next are the integrating portions of each one. The functional building-stones of which the reflex arc is made up, everywhere interlock with one another. In how far the impulse-systems interlock can be decided only by experiment. As concerns the motor nerves going from the action-organ to the muscles, the experiment of severing the nerves has shown that they belong to the impulse-system of the action-organ, for from that organ the nerves grow out again to the muscle after the severance. The impulse-system of the action-organ, and not that of the muscle, is responsible for the repair to the nervous connections.

The uncertainty concerning the delimitation of the functional building-stones one from another exists from the moment beyond which one can speak of functional building-stones at all, i.e. from the critical point onwards.

Up to the critical point there is in the animal body no connecting function, and consequently there are no functional building-stones. Until the critical point is reached, the body is divisible into germinal areas, which I have called genetical building-stones.

In order to make quite clear the rearrangement that takes place at the critical point, let us assume that, in some selected animal, the critical point comes on through the whole body at the same moment   Let us imagine, in an earthworm, for instance, that the development of the germinal areas proceeds so equally that we finally have before us an animal which, in all essentials, already has the form of the completed animal, but consists entirely of protoplasm   A protoplasmic animal of this kind consists entirely of independent genetical building-stones, which, it is true, are spatially contiguous, but do not exercise the slightest influence on one another.   If we remove from one of these a portion of the material, it will restore its own shape from the remains of the protoplasm, without any regard to its neighbours   Indeed, as Harrison showed, one can remove an entire genetical building-stone—for instance, the rudiment for the sciatic nerve—without in any way checking the development of the rest of the limb.

Now the effect of the critical point expresses itself in every cell of each germinal area, in such a way that the gene present in it becomes active and allows its specific framework to crystallise out of the protoplasm.   At one stroke a fully developed earthworm, with all its functions, is got from the protoplasmic worm   And therewith the genetical building-stones have disappeared, which consisted of protoplasm alone : in their place functional building-stones have come in, consisting of framework + protoplasm.

What has now become of the impulse-systems which, in complete independence, each governed a genetical building-stone ?   The boundaries of the completed organs, i e of the functional building-stones, are quite different from those of the germinal areas.   Are the impulse-systems subject to the same rearrangement, or not ?   As we know from Wessely's experiments, at the critical point there occurs a rearrangement of the impulse-systems also   The genetical impulse-systems have vanished ; in their place have come functional impulse-systems, controlling the animal's growth

The earthworm need not fear that when some repair of

a part of its organs is necessary, it will take place without regard to the functional connection with other organs, as happened before the critical point. On the contrary, the requirement is now raised to the normal at each reconstruction of the framework.

During the time that elapses up to the critical point, the direction of construction alone is active With the development of the framework the direction of working comes into its own. It is transferred to impulse-systems separated from one another in space, which influence one another reciprocally.

INTERNAL EQUILIBRIUM

Each impulse-system governing a genetical building-stone constitutes a self-contained unity, which continually strives to repair, after every injury, the protoplasmic structure under its control, independently of the amount of material at its disposal. In the beginning, the genetical building-stones are few in number, and of very simple form. In the course of development, they multiply, and assume more and more complicated forms ; and concurrently there proceeds the distribution of the genes to the cells, which become more and more numerous. As this happens, the impulse-systems belonging to these gradually separate off in a perfectly regular way. But so long as it is active, every impulse-system forms a unity, which is held together by its internal equilibrium. If a germinal area is halved, each half gets half the building-material of protoplasm ; each half remains connected with half the number of impulses, but this in itself forms no unity and possesses no rule, unless the internal equilibrium reconstructs the rule of the whole system. A rule is effective as a whole, or not at all. A rule is independent of the number of times it is used ; accordingly, it may just as well come into effect once or several times in the same germinal area, so long as the material permits

Applied to the auxiliary idea of the impulses, this knowledge must be expressed as follows :—

The number of impulses connected by a rule is unlimited, and so is the number of impulse-systems following a rule. The internal equilibrium alone is effective, which strives to remove the disturbance. This equilibrium, however, is present throughout the entire system, and can make itself felt from every part

Of the experiments that have been made on regeneration (by which is understood the repair of form and content) those performed on the genetical building-stones give us a much less equivocal result than those performed on the functional, because here we are dealing with protoplasm containing the same genes or like mixtures of genes. As long as it is present in the requisite quantity, the material puts no check in the way of repair. Any cell can take up any position within the same germinal area, since its gene-content is the same. With the critical point this ceases. The cells belonging to the same functional building-stone are very different from one another. So we might assume from the outset that repair would either not be possible at all, or only to a limited extent But it has been shown that, especially in the lower animals, the cells, although with regard to their framework they are just as definitely formed as in the higher animals, still bring with them a large reserve of genes, which permits of reconstruction to a very considerable extent

If in a cart consisting of wooden and iron parts, the wooden parts also harbour protoferine and the iron parts a primordium for wood, the quality of the material presents no hindrance to the reconstruction of lost portions

The functional building-stones have this advantage over the genetical, that they are not prevented by the limited quantity of material left over from furnishing parts of the framework in their normal size ; for the circulating stream of fluids enables them to make up the lacking substance.

We have got the fundamental information about regeneration from experiments on earthworms and planarians. Here it appears that each transverse slice cut out of the animal at some selected point is able to remake the whole, right forward to the anterior end and right back to the posterior. In this we perceive clearly the action of an internal equilibrium extending throughout the entire animal.

In these animals the material for the reconstruction of the equilibrium lies everywhere at the disposal of the impulse-systems. An exception is offered only by the head of planarians. If this is cut through transversely, each surface of the wound is capable of regenerating only the anterior half. The consequence is that only the posterior portion of the head regenerates a normal head : the anterior portion duplicates itself, and produces a Janus-head incapable of living.

If we cut a planarian lengthwise, each half regenerates the missing side, and we get two normal planarians. If, beginning at the anterior end, we carry the cut only through the first half of the animal, the edges of the wound gape apart on account of the pull of the lateral muscles, and each half regenerates the missing side. The result is a two-headed planarian.

This experiment (which, after what has been said, holds nothing surprising) has played a fateful part in the history of biology, for from it Vulpian concluded that there could not be any vital force, since vital force would never create monsters. In the state of biological thought at that time, Vulpian could not conceive of a vital force as other than one endowed with reason. From his point of view, there must either be a human-like director in every animal, or else none at all. We have become more cautious, and we speak only

of a direction, the powers of which we endeavour to investigate ; and we find it expressed in the internal equilibrium
which, within the limits set it, effects the reparation. Vulpian's experiment, which was made about the middle of last
century, gave at that time the death-blow to vitalism.
Nowadays we know that it fits in completely with vitalistic
ideas.

Very interesting experiments have been made on the
earthworm   Of these I shall mention one especially, because
it solves the question as to the possibility of competition
between two impulse-systems.   Let us first cut off the head
of an earthworm, and a quarter of the rest of the body   Let
this grow on to the trunk again in the reversed position, so
that now a cut surface is directed forwards that normally
must regenerate the hind end   What is the result ?   The
regenerated part is the missing head.   Here, apparently, the
internal equilibrium controlling the larger portion of the body
has outbalanced the smaller portion, and the cut surface,
which is able to create either the anterior or the posterior end,
is compelled to meet the functional needs of the trunk

To the same category belongs the experiment on a small
crab, which has one small pincer and one large.   If we cut
off its large pincer, the small one grows large, while in place
of the amputated limb a small pincer forms anew.   The result
is a crab with reversed pincers

Of especial interest is the famous experiment of Herbst,
who succeeded in making a crab regenerate an olfactory
antenna in place of a stalked eye.   In the course of this
experiment, it appeared that, when the eye was cut off, it
was always regenerated so long as the optical ganglion was
not removed.   But if the whole functional building-stone
of the stalked eye disappears, that of the olfactory feeler leaps
into the gap and duplicates itself.

All experiments made hitherto agree in this, that we

have to distinguish an internal equilibrium within each
functional building-stone from the internal equilibrium controlling the function as a whole. According to external
conditioning by the injury and the internal conditioning by
the reserve-material present, now the one and now the other
comes into evidence.

EQUILIBRIUM IN TIME

The instances dealt with hitherto all refer to spatial
equilibrium, which expresses itself, now in one functional
building-stone and now in all together. But it cannot be
denied that there are also rules connecting into unities factors
separated from one another in time. The notes of a melody
that we have heard immediately appear to us connected together by a rule. But the melody is not just a rule discovered
afterwards (which would be merely passive) : on the contrary,
it is active in the extreme, as soon as we ourselves sing a
song ; and, in a way unknown to us, it controls the impulses
in the actions of our larynx, which produces the notes. In
this case we are fully justified in assuming an impulse-system
corresponding to the melody, and in seeking for its internal
equilibrium. In the same way, active rules, referable to
impulse-systems, lie behind all those of our actions that are
not reflexes. They must all possess an internal equilibrium.

The way in which we have to picture the invasion of
impulse-systems has already been set forth in detail. According to this conception, there is every time a regeneration of
the central mesh-work. By this means we are enabled to
consider the whole process from outside, without entering on
psychological questions. Before our eyes a natural process
is taking place, which follows an autonomous rule. It owes
its autonomy to an impulse-system, which is held together by
an internal equilibrium.

In order to express in the familiar formulæ also the impulse-systems active in time, we have only to replace the I by a series iii, and to write these one below the other Let the instinct formula serve as an example. It must be written thus :— $\frac{R}{I} - \frac{MO}{I} - \frac{AOi}{i} \overset{i}{-} \frac{E}{I}$. It would be still more expressive, if we introduced the iii as musical notation

A formula of this kind would take account of the fact, that, for instance, the funnel-roller beetle performs its action in melodic sequence, although the birch-leaf on which it does its work does not furnish it with any standard for the action-melody

We shall do justice to the unified action-sequences of instinctive animals, and to the plastic actions of animals that learn by experience, only when we recognise an impulse-melody that determines the action-sequence. The indications of the surrounding-world serve, it is true, to release these, and at times to retard or to quicken their course. But they have no influence whatsoever on the melody of the action. As if on its own hinges, the melody hangs fixed and infallible, within the rhythm determining its internal equilibrium.

RHYTHM

In a melody we distinguish three things—the notes, the sound-sequence, and the beat-sequence. In melody only the last of these is described as rhythm. But it is different as soon as we transfer the word melody into other associations. If we compare some living process with a melody, the beat—the rate at which the process takes place—interests us quite secondarily ; on the other hand, the regular alternation in which the part-processes release one another, comes into prominence, and is then described as rhythm, although it really corresponds to what we describe as sound-sequence in the melody.

Now the sound-sequence in a melody is also the expression of a law, for which we have no exact word. It is true that, in a general way, we speak of the relationship of the sounds ; but for the special law determining the sound-sequence in a certain tune, we have no expression. In this case also we help ourselves out with the word rhythm, although that is intended to describe the special law of beat-sequence.

But it is necessary to distinguish between the two. Accordingly I shall describe the law displayed in the sound-sequence as rhythm, and that displayed in the beat-sequence as " beat-rhythm."

In melody the conditions are extraordinarily clear : the sounds are arranged in a fixed relation, which in all circumstances must be preserved, if no dissonance is to come in. The rhythm of the single sound-sequences, however, cannot be derived from this relation, which has been compared to a seven-sided column, for the law of that relation tells us nothing, for instance, as to whether two related notes are to sound simultaneously or in succession.

The law of relationship deals only with the special nature of the sounds and how they are adapted to one another. The rhythm should reproduce the law according to which the peculiarity is made use of in single instances.

The shape and material properties of the bricks reproduce the peculiar nature of the structural material of a house, and the laws of this must be kept in mind in building. The sequence of construction that causes the house to arise, and with which brick after brick is harmonised in accordance with its special nature—that is the rhythm.

In the development of any structure the same thing can be demonstrated—namely, elementary parts, which are adapted to one another in accordance with their special nature, and a rule, the rhythm, by which the structure arises. The law of peculiarities is called in chemistry the affinity of substances. By affinity was at the same time understood a mutual process of attraction, which was part of the peculiarity. The word affinity was then applied to the relationship of sounds, although these possess no reciprocal power of attraction. Since chemistry has developed more and more into microphysics, concrete, mechanical ideas have begun to break down the concept of affinity. As a matter of fact, nothing nowadays stands in the way of our basing all mixing of substances on a mechanical idea. To understand the fixed arrangement of the atoms in the molecule, we may represent the atom as an already formed spatial magnitude, holding on to its neighbours by means of peg and socket joints.

(An atom of this kind is already a shaped, three-dimensional object, and has lost the original meaning implicit in the word, i.e indivisibility : for only what is without form can be thought of as indivisible. We must so express ourselves that there can be no misunderstanding as to which kind of atom we mean—whether an elementary particle having form in space, and carrying out certain mechanical tasks, or the ultimate sense-quality from which the world of appearance is constructed The latter is always just a local sign associated with a content-sign)

It is possible to refer all chemical processes to the concrete idea of peg and socket joints, if, in addition, we bring in a polar tension drawing the pegs to the sockets and repelling like structures from one another.

For the building up of a living organism from the germ the impulses have at their disposal numerous chemical structures with complicated peg and socket joints, and their polar tensions. What the impulses themselves must bring in is the building-sequence through their rhythm.

The mistake of all anti-vitalistic hypotheses as to the genesis of the organism lies in their regarding the building-sequence as already given in the material. It is just as impossible for a melody to derive its law from the relationship of the notes (even if the related notes should mutually attract one another) as for the building-sequence of an organism to be deduced from the chemical affinity of the germinal elements (i.e. from their peg and socket joints, together with the polar tension).

What seems to us essential—namely, whether or not the rhythm of an action is given all prepared by the framework of the organs—is for Nature of only secondary importance. The process of the building-sequence is not laid down in the germ by a framework of any kind whatsoever ; for the actions of the completed animal the same holds true—the rhythm of the same action that in the one creature is fixed by the framework, in another may dispense with this fixation.

In the majority of animals the process of digestion is conducted along fixed routes by a series of organs, which are joined to one another. Students of the digestive process strive, through exact knowledge of the alimentary canal, to learn how to read off from it, as from a progressive musical notation, the act of digestion, which begins at the mouth and ends at the anus. This is rendered possible, because the food-balls, as they move along, are all the time being conducted past fresh receptors and effectors (glands and muscles). Each section of the gut receives in an altered condition the food-balls pushed forward by effectors of the preceding section, and possesses receptors constructed on a correspondingly different plan, which are able, by means of their effectors, to induce a further change ; and so it goes on. One part links up with the other in unbroken series, and this chain performs a chain of separate actions, which, taken collectively, lead to the disintegration and absorption of the food.

In this process an obvious rhythm is expressed, which it is the task of the physiology of digestion to study in all its details. Nierenstein found exactly the same rhythm in the Infusoria, which have no digestive organs developed. Here, as we have already pointed out, the same food-vacuole goes through all the changes shown by the framework of the alimentary canal of the higher animals. The rhythm of the impulses in the completed organ-chain becomes effective indirectly through a permanent framework, and is directly active only from time to time when that is locally disturbed : in the Infusoria it is expressed directly through a progressive framework-forming

If we look into the matter more closely, we shall understand why the digestive process so easily gets fixed by permanent framework formation, and becomes frozen into a chain of reflexes. Each stretch of the alimentary canal forms, with the food-ball as indicator, a very simple kind of function-circle, which is shut off as a pure reflex arc in the tissues of the animal. The demands made on the steering-mechanism of the nervous system are very slight. The receptors may everywhere lie close to the glands, and convey the excitation to them by simple nerve nets. The secretion from the stimulated glands alters the food-ball in such a way that, when it gets to the next section, it sends forth other stimuli for which there are other receptors.

The onward movement of the food-ball is effected by the movement of the circular muscles, according to the simple law of muscular tension. Round the food-ball they are on the stretch, and so the excitation flows to them, and they push the ball forward

Of course, at each digestive process there occur a number of complications, since the food consists of different substances, which must simultaneously be partially broken down : several function-circles then interlock. But the principle is everywhere the same and everywhere simple.

If we compare the movement-functions of an animal with those of its digestion, we get the reverse picture. Here the

U

animal corresponds to the food-ball, and the alimentary canal to the surrounding-world. This holds good, not only for animals that move along through cavities and passages in the earth, but for all locomotor animals whatsoever. If we follow the track of some selected animal, we can re-create its surrounding-world around that track, by setting up again the indicators with which it came into contact. The surrounding-world of the animal thus becomes a tunnel.

In this indication-tunnel the animal moves forward, in virtue of the antagonistically arranged muscles of its locomotor organs. This is true of progress in the water and in the air, as well as on the dry land. Each forward movement causes an indicator to disappear and a new one to arise. Whereupon a new function-circle begins. The course of the function in each new circle means a new action, and so here also one action connects up with the others into a chain, which winds itself through the whole life.

Now it is true that each member of the chain—i.e. each function-circle—is an independent action on the part of the animal; but the chain itself—i.e. the rhythmic sequence of the function-circles—is a creation of the external world, because the order in which the indicators appear depends on associations that are independent of the animal.

Here for the first time we meet with the idea of an external rhythm which enters into competition with the internal rhythm of the animal.

If the several function-circles are fixed as reflexes, the whole life-course of an animal may give the impression of being a process that unrolls automatically. An indicator, such as the prey, attracts the animal, is devoured, and disappears. The indicator " enemy " appears, and repels the animal, whose flight results in the vanishing of this indicator also. This led Loeb to consider the life of an animal purely from the standpoint of physics, as a chain of tropisms, and to transfer the rhythm of animal life entirely to the exterior

There is an essential misconception here, for the tropisms are not simple physical processes. The appearance of a tropism, which by its nature remains a reflex, necessarily presupposes the presence of an indication. It is true that an indication crops up on the life-path of an animal only when a stimulus affects the receptors. But it depends entirely on the structure of these as to which stimulus is taken up and converted into excitation   There is no physical law, proceeding from which we can say that such and such a physical process must become an indication for the animal, while such and such another one will not.   Much less dare we assume that some particular object must play a part in the life of the animal also. We can only conjecture that it is an indicator . what indications it gives depends solely on the animal.

The life-path of an animal, which we may imagine as a tunnel of indications, holds only such things as exist through their relations to the animal—those and no others. If we wish to enter into the life-path of an earthworm, for instance, we must not forget that it is composed of earthworm things, and of nothing else.

Nevertheless, the inquiry into the presence of an external rhythm and its effect on the animal is justified. The observer can show that the indicators appear on the life-path in a sequence independent of the animal, and he may ask himself the question, " In how far is an inner rhythm of the animal opposed to the external rhythm ? "

It must first be shown that the threshold value of the external stimuli is determined by an inner rhythm based on a periodic change in the steering-gear   Thus, for example, an object will not act as an indication on a satiated animal, though it certainly would on a hungry. In the same way, during the breeding-season there comes in a changing of the steering-gear which is of far-reaching importance for the selection of indications. Animals endowed with plastic power frequently suppress an indication, though it be oft repeated, by raising their threshold-level against it ; and this is especially obvious in the case of actions based on experience.

In many animals an inner rhythm, consisting of waking and sleeping, strives to fall in with the outer rhythm of the life-path that expresses itself in the alternation of day and night. By raising the threshold during sleep, all indications can periodically be suppressed. In the spotted dogfish, which rest all day and seek their prey by night, Beer found a periodic opening and closing of the pupil, which could be demonstrated in animals kept continually in the dark. The rhythm of ebb and flow is responded to in littoral sea-anemones by a periodic change in the reflex activity. In these animals also Bohn was able to demonstrate that there was an inner rhythm, which persisted for days in anemones kept in an aquarium.

The rhythmical change of tone in an apparatus, compelling it to change of work, is an arrangement unknown in machines, and can be achieved only by means of a further mechanical device. The framework of animals, characterised by the presence of a protoplasmic matrix, makes the rhythmic change seem less mysterious. Actually, those who have concerned themselves more closely with the question, see in the protoplasm the cause of this phenomenon.

We might speak of a chemical tide-change in the protoplasm, excited more or less by the external rhythm. These matters still lie so far beyond the possibility of actual investigation that we are reduced to mere conjecture. All that is certain is that there must be a rhythmically active impulse-system at the back of this phenomenon also, furnishing the protoplasm with the power of performing a chemical tide-change.

If we continue to observe the laws that maintain in their mutual dependence the indicators bordering the life-path of an animal, we penetrate deeper into knowledge of the external rhythm that influences the life-course. This law may consist in the spatial connection of the indicators, and yet to the animal this must appear as rhythm, because, as it moves along, it comes in contact with these in time only.

When the funnel-roller beetle cuts its precise mathematical line, the several leaf-veins enter one by one into its surrounding-world. The whole birch-leaf, which to us appears as a definitely outlined object, is broken up for the beetle into a number of indicators, which can be connected together in time only according to a certain rhythm. The inner rhythm must correspond to this external rhythm, if it is to control the fixing of the sequence in which the indicators appear as the leaf is cut through. Here, accordingly, the inner rhythm controls the outer, for the path followed by the animal within a group of indicators fixed in space is not given afresh each time by these as they successively surge up; the reverse is true, for the inner rhythm itself consists entirely of sign-posts, which are obliged to cover themselves with the indicators

The rhythm in which the effectors of the beetle work has not been created from one action to another by the sequence of the indicators; it is formed by the impulse-sequence itself The formula for the instinctive action

expresses this :— $\dfrac{R}{I} - \dfrac{MO}{I} - AO \begin{cases} i\ I \\ 1\ 2 \\ 1\ 3 \end{cases} - \dfrac{E.}{I}$

The presence of a firm external connection, of a spatial or of a temporal kind, between the indicators, forms the preliminary condition for every instinctive action The instinctive action can construct itself only on such a connection. If this is present, then (after the first indication has given the signal for the action to begin) the inner rhythm can set in, to guide the animal confidently through the forest of indicators.

In terms of human thought, the inner rhythm of the animal knows the laws of the outer world, although the animal gets no information thereon through the indications at its disposal It is this knowledge possessed by the inner rhythm that I have called the " wisdom " of organisms. Of course, there is no question here of knowledge or wisdom in the human sense, but of a " congruity " of the internal processes of the animal with the laws of the external world

For the instinctive action in the widest sense (embracing also the tide-change in the protoplasm) it is immaterial whether the law of the external processes consists in a regular alternation of day and night, of the seasons of the year, or of ebb and flow, or whether it is expressed spatially, as in the geographical formation of those portions of the globe used in the migration of birds, or in the organisation of the birch-leaf for the beetle, or in the anatomical disposition of the nervous system of its prey in the case of the ichneumon-fly, or in the chemical reactions of the human tissues in the case of the malaria parasite Everywhere we see an autogenous rhythm at work, which, from the factors held together by the external laws, constructs its own path, a path which is the more securely laid the firmer the external connection of the factors.

Beside these remarkable facts, which I describe as " congruity," the question as to whether the rhythm is given permanently by a corresponding framework, or develops anew as occasion requires, appears quite subordinate. To inquire into the inner rhythm that brings about this harmony involves a far harder problem than the quite secondary consideration as to whether, in a given instance, we have to do with an isolated or with a lasting influence on the framework

In the case of the complicated and prolonged actions

of insects, it is easier to assume that the impulse-systems continually carry on a direct reshaping of the framework. The same holds good with all plastic actions and actions based on experience. With simple actions approximating to reflexes, we may assume the presence of a permanent framework, adjusted once and for all

When we have recognised the inner harmonised rhythm as the determining factor, then it is not difficult to deduce from it the actions that lead to the fabrication of the animal's tools, actions which, almost without exception, belong to the instinctive category.

BEAT-RHYTHM

In comparison with the general rhythm of the impulses which controls the whole life, the beat-rhythm is very insignificant, for it plays an important part only in the higher animals A certain beat, it is true, can be observed in all forward movements by animals, because, in these, antagonistic movements of the limbs release one another in regular alternation. But there is nothing to indicate that the beat according to which these movements are set going, is fixed in the interior. On the contrary, the ease with which the limbs of the animal adapt themselves, in their to and fro movement, to the difficulties presented by the ground, depends on the lack of an internally fixed beat. As a rule, the free extension of the limbs takes place quicker than the pushing back of the ground, by which the body is driven forward.

The rhythm of the gait is, in most cases, so well adapted to the condition of the ground, because the excitation flows to the " antagonist," only when that is actually on the stretch. That happens, however, only when the " agonist " has contracted, and its representatives have been " locked " against excitation, while those of the extended antagonist are " unlocked."

The rate at which the extension and contraction in the muscles of the limbs alternate, depends in considerable degree on the obstacles on the path at the time, obstacles which the muscles must overcome by their contraction. If an internal beat were trying here to regulate the movements, this would only add to the difficulties.

We find an interiorly determined beat only in those effector organs that have always the same obstacle to overcome, such as the hearts of vertebrates, the margin of the umbrella of jelly-fishes and the wings of insects. The hearts of invertebrates move according to the general law of tension; their beat, therefore, is not in constant dependence on the amount of blood they contain. The stroke of the wing in a bird is regulated all the time by the receptors, while in insects it is only the beginning and the end of the rhythmical wing-beat that depend on these; the rhythm itself is quite automatically exerted from the wing-muscle centres.

The effector organs which preserve their own beat-rhythm have for this an arrangement of their own, which is expressed in the so-called "refractory period." The refractory period rhythmically lowers to zero the threshold-value for the regular waves of excitation flowing to the points where the nerves enter the muscles. In what the arrangement consists has not yet been ascertained.

The beat-rhythm in the receptor portions of the steering-mechanism is of quite another kind. It serves to transform the external rhythms in the surrounding-world into an indication, and in this way to fit these into the world-as-sensed. Let us imagine that a chemical tide-change of unequal rate continually controls the mark-organ of an animal; then we should see in this the means by which the animal would be able to refer external rhythms to its own beat, and thereby connect them into an indication.

As we know, the power to form indications is associated

with the possibility of bringing in certain representatives for certain stimuli In a brain that is extended in space, the possibility exists everywhere of using spatially separated centres as representatives for the stimuli coming in from various directions, because the receptors are in a position to pass on the stimuli in the form of excitation to nerves separated in space It is also possible to transform external movements into indications, because these permit the representatives to sound out in a certain sequence, and one captain may stand in place of a certain series of representatives

The arrangement of spatially separated representatives fails, however, as soon as it is a question of more extended sequences of external stimuli Now, as indications, the external rhythms play a very small part in the life of an animal. How few animals there are that can recognise a sound-sequence again ! There are such cases, however, even among the lower animals Unquestionably the beat-rhythm serves as an indication when the female hare warns her young of danger by a rhythmical series of knocking sounds, which she makes with her foot on the ground When the male of the American glow-worm, by a rhythmical " short-long " of its flash, causes the female to react, we see that the power to appreciate beat-rhythms as indications is more widespread than is generally supposed.

For the study of the world-as-sensed, such observations are of great interest, for they give us the opportunity of raising the question, " In what sensed-worlds did ' time ' first appear ? " One thing is certain—that only the presence of a persistent internal beat-rhythm permits the animal to break up time into a series of moments, and thereby make use of it as an indication Animals without a receptor beat-rhythm certainly live in time, like all those we observe (for we see everything in the frame of time) ; they may even perform movements according to a beat : but so long as they have no internal time-standard capable of bringing together in moment-groups events in the outer world, they live without time, without past or future, in a perpetual present.

The attempt has been made to refer the inner beat-rhythm to mechanical arrangements ; but since even these are subject to control of the animal's working, we cannot get on without assuming a beat-forming impulse-system.

CONGRUITY

A carelessly chosen word may cause incalculable harm to science, if it contain an analogy going beyond what is actually known, and so give to research a misdirection. Such a word is " adaptation." Originally by adaptation was meant only the unshakable fact that all animals are suited to their environment.

But the word contains an analogy with human activity, i.e. of the making-themselves-suitable-to-one-another of two objects A and B. So that the word introduced two sorts of principle, which did not arise from observation of Nature. Firstly, it is stated that A and B did not suit one another from the beginning, and secondly, that the business of becoming suited requires a certain time.

By the universal adoption of the word adaptation, men of science were compelled to see in the mutual " harmonising " of organisms and their environment observed in Nature a process which is gradually accomplished. Some relations between organisms and their environment are better adjusted than others.

This assumption, however, was in direct contradiction to the actual facts observed, for which the term " adaptation " had been chosen. But as soon as the word had been assimilated, the contradiction was overlooked, and the factors were sought that were supposed to have brought about a gradual adaptation.

So for decades the word "adaptation" has served as a false sign-post, which has turned research away altogethei from the right path. It is time, therefore, to choose a word that contains no false theories of the kind, but reproduces nothing but the naked truth. "Congruity" seems to me a term of the kind, since it asserts nothing but the undisputed fact that organism and environment suit one another. The question remains open as to whether the congruity was present from the beginning, or whether it was gradually acquired. In the latter case, we should be able to discover relations that are more incongruous than others

As we know, this question has already been decided There is no "more" or "less" as regards congruity. Congruity is always perfect, so far as the means at the disposal of the animal extend. If all organisms are perfectly congruous with their surrounding-world, there is no such thing as gradual attainment of perfection; the perfection of congruity exists everywhere from the very beginning

If this be admitted, the paltry analogy with the human way of doing things collapses into nothing, and we stand face to face with a real law of Nature, as free from exceptions as is the law of gravity.

Every organism, so long as it has all its mechanical and chemical properties, is congruous with its surrounding-world, in perfect conformity with plan. This at once disposes of the doctrine that denies conformity with plan in Nature. At the same time—and this is less obvious—the doctrine of purposefulness in Nature falls to the ground. A purpose, i e. an idea postponed to the future, in no way carries with it guarantee for the complete exploitation of all the available resources; this will always be only more or less completely realised

Karl Ernst von Baer, who in his day investigated this problem very thoroughly, also decided to deny purposefulness in Nature altogether. Instead of " purpose," he declared that " goal " was the decisive thing. We can make Baer's idea clear to ourselves by an example that he selected. When a bullet leaves the barrel of a gun and hits the target, the target is the factor that prescribes the path for the ball. If we imagine the act of shooting to be eliminated, we must ascribe to the ball itself the property of being influenced directly by the target in the direction its movement takes. In such a case the ball possesses what Baer calls " effort towards a goal."

In the same way, Baer declares that the embryo displays effort towards a goal. Considering the time at which he was writing, this presentation of the matter was quite correct. It suffered, however, from the circumstance that the target was placed too near. If what we have in mind is not the full-grown body, but its congruity with the surrounding-world, then the environment becomes the goal into which the body with all its receptors and effectors has to grow. But from the surrounding-world, namely the inorganic medium, no influence can proceed enabling the germ to follow a definite course during its development. A direct reciprocal effect between germ and surrounding-world, such as the doctrine of effort towards a goal presupposes, cannot be assumed. The main difficulty—namely, the congruity of organism and environment—is not solved by effort towards a goal.

If we could ascribe to the environment all properties, and these in their full degree, the solution would be simple. Then every shape assumed by the animal would straightway be in congruity with the outer world. But things are not so. When an animal gets into a strange environment, it is usually unable to make a suitable surrounding-world for itself, and, because it cannot fit in, it perishes. The external world,

it is true, always possesses many more properties than the
animal requires for the construction of its surrounding-world,
but by no means enough to satisfy all animals We have,
accordingly, the remarkable fact that there are actually a
limited number of certain properties present in the external
world, for which the animal, if it is to prosper, must develop
in its bodily structure corresponding counter-properties,
which shall fit in with these like pegs and sockets.

The external world offers to the organism a certain number
of properties separated in space and in time, from which to
select, and therewith the possibility of making a poorer or a
richer surrounding-world But the external world itself takes
no part in the selection, which has to be made by the organism
without external assistance.

We have to come to terms with this fact : on the one
side are the properties of the external world, which exercise
no direction-giving influence ; and on the other is the living
germ, which possesses no organs that could give it knowledge
of these properties. And yet we see how the embryo un-
erringly produces definite counter-properties, which fit into a
definite group of properties in the external world.

Since the discovery of the genes, we know that in the
germinal rudiments all the pegs and sockets of the counter-
properties are present, and these they only have to shape
according to a certain rule, in order for the congruity with
the external world to be complete.

As we know, the rule of shaping is not mechanical, but
is borne by other factors than those with which we are
acquainted through physics and chemistry. I have called
these factors impulses, and have shown that they are enclosed
in an impulse-system, having an internal equilibrium both of
a spatial and of a temporal kind

It only remains to show that the impulse-systems correspond with the groups of properties in the external world, just

as strictly in conformity with plan as they do with the properties of the germ whose shaping they control. Beyond
that, the state of our knowledge at the present day does not
permit us to make any affirmation.

It is only through a diagram that these mysterious relations permit of concrete representation. Let us take as
the starting-point the impulse-system : through the individual
impulses i i i this affects the genes g g g in a super-mechanical
way (as is indicated by the dotted line). In a mechanical
way, which, however, in virtue of the impulse-invasion, is
striving towards a goal, the genes permit the reflex-arc to
arise, which fits into the indicator, on the one side by its receptor, and on the other by its effector. Since the nuclei of
the reserve plasm retain their genes, the influence of the
impulse-system on the body is kept persistent. Now we have

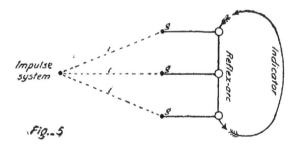

Fig. 5

to assume that, at the critical point, the internal equilibrium
in the impulse-system veers round, for from this stage onwards
the directing of the construction of the developing body
becomes the directing of the working of the finished organism.

Once we have accustomed ourselves to the idea that the
whole direction of the organism, in the species and in the
community as well as in the individual, lies in the hands
of a super-mechanical natural power, which is to be recognised
not only through rules, but itself acts according to rules, all

life on the globe derives a new content, which is accessible to investigation

It is not intended that this shall be the statement of a new dogma , merely that the way shall be cleared for study of the old but ever-new inquiry into the " meaning " of life, a problem worthy the earnest effort of the noblest minds.

Conformity with plan, as the ultimate natural law embracing all living things, is once more laid open for biological investigation Conformity with plan is the guiding law of the impulse-systems, by the aid of which it organises all living matter into subjects, and the coming and going of which it controls, as well as the relations of the subjects to one another and to non-living Nature.

THE THEORIES OF ADAPTATION AND OF CONGRUITY

If we regard the world from the standpoint of the theory of adaptation, then each organism is the product of influences to which it has been exposed for thousands of years Every object, implement and organism in its environment have their share in the transformations that it has undergone. The media, animals and plants set their stamp on it. Its entire organic and inorganic environment, light and rain, warmth and cold, alter and shape the susceptible protoplasm, until at last it assumes the form, colour and consistency that assure it a permanent place in the world.

Through innumerable " errors " the everlasting " trials " of Nature (which permits all the agencies within it to influence each single organism) lead on towards an ultimate product that shall have achieved the suitable form, making it wholly congruous with the other world-factors.

The Darwinian theory offers only an approximate explanation of this dogma. It points out that the production of offspring is so enormous that if each organism should multiply without restriction, it would soon crowd out all the others. That is guarded against by the struggle for existence, in which all animals compete with one another, a struggle that makes for balance in the world, but at the same time permits of a finer and finer selection , for only the " best adapted " organisms are capable of survival.

In order to enter more closely into this idea, let us first of all neglect the super-mechanical properties of animals, and regard them purely as machines, having neither builder nor director : then all the protoplasm in the world appears as a substance undergoing a kind of fermentation, and broken up into a great variety of parts—a substance that, during its changes, is continually being influenced and shaped by physical and chemical agencies, until machines are evolved that are all adapted to one another.

It certainly requires a powerful imagination to assume that any machine capable of functioning could arise in this way. But the Darwinians provide the requisite imagination. Unfortunately, they carefully avoid the more serious consequences of their doctrine.

All the physical and chemical agencies are supposed, by their external influence, to carry out the creation of form on a substratum to which no properties can be ascribed other than great power of reproduction and variability. As soon as we presume any tendency whatsoever in the fermentative process to have a goal or give a direction, we are forsaking the Darwinian basis. In this respect it is essentially different from Lamarckism

The direction followed by the shaping is exclusively dependent on external factors Now animal machines do not consist exclusively of external organs, but also of internal, and these cannot be influenced directly by external agencies. How are we to imagine the genesis of such organs ? Is there a struggle for existence even among the organs ? Roux put this problem very clearly. But he met with nothing but complete silence on the part of the Darwinians.

It is obvious that any machine must fall to pieces if its wheels, instead of cooperating according to the same plan, work against one another, and try to increase at one another's expense. But in no circumstance must there be a plan at work, or the whole doctrine would collapse.

To Nature, however, it is more important that her creations should not fall asunder, than that a theory, however elaborate and ingenious, should come to naught. And so she has constructed all animal machines in full accordance with plan. In all organisms the various organs do not become adjusted to one another by mutual wearing away—a method that no machine could bring off—but, from the very outset, they are quite perfectly " congruous " with one another.

If we proceed from this undeniable fact, and conclude from it that the like congruity also exists between the organism and its surrounding-world, the world takes on a totally different aspect. Each organism is then no longer an impression of the universe, but, like any machine, is inserted in a perfectly definite circle of activity and congruous with the objects, implements and organisms of its surrounding-world. It is not the environing world that has given the shape to the organism by an influence from without ; an inner plan ever causes to arise from out the germ-plasm fresh organisms, which are in harmony with their surrounding-world.

This plan is itself the constructor of the organism, and comes to expression in the protoplasm by the help of the impulses, which it forces to the work of shaping.

There are as many plans as there are organisms The plan of the individual never embraces the whole universe, but just a small, sharply delimited portion thereof. The plan of the individual includes more than the shape of the organism that it creates, but never more than the organism's

X

surrounding-world   It never creates this surrounding-world, but, through selection, binds it, by all its pegs and sockets, into a unified casting-mould, which intimately embraces the organism and its receptor and effector functions.

This mould is the life-tunnel, constructed entirely from indicators arranged in space and time.   Here the existence of the animal is passed, consisting as it does, not merely of struggle, but of all the functions of the life.

It is the task of biology to seek for the plans of the life-tunnels, and to investigate the complicated ways in which they intersect

The plan for each life-tunnel is fixed, and so is the creature within it that takes on shape and power to move.   But the carrying out of the plan depends on external circumstances, which always induce deviations   These deviations bear a delusory resemblance to the variability of organisms, and for the theory they are of secondary importance, although they may come into the life of the individual and determine it.

It was reserved for Darwin to make what is secondary of primary importance, and simply to deny the main feature, namely the definite plan.   By doing this he secured the recognition of physics and chemistry, but he wrecked his own science, biology.

The entire plan of an organism, which surrounds both it and its life-tunnel, is only a part of the plan of the species, which unites related organisms into a whole of a higher order.

The introduction of the plan of the species, which, as the consequence of sex, brings together into one common life the confusing abundance of separate lives, helps us to understand the manifold deviations of the individual plans, which in the species flow together into a whole that expresses plan.   We are then faced with large organisms, stretching through long periods of time and across large spaces, organisms whose parts, the individuals, are fitted into one another.   It is true that we are then still far from the attainment of a real survey of the whole ; but we are on the way to it.

Conformity with plan is never given us directly, but is always yielded up to us. That is to say, it is our task to discover it by studying the associations in the single instance. That alone is *biology*. To deny conformity with plan is certainly convenient, because it relieves us of this heavy task ; but to act in this way is not scientific.

THE PLANS

The peculiarity of every plan that lies at the back of an organism consists firstly in this, that it at one time finds expression in *influencing the shaping of the organism*, and / secondly, that it is manifest in the *selection of the indicators* and their combination into an indication-tunnel.

The first half of the plan forms in the animal's body the pegs and sockets that fit into those of the indicators. The second half itself selects and takes over the pegs and sockets already present in the indicators, and, by fitting them in with the sockets and pegs it has formed in the organism, it connects them all into a unity, the indication-tunnel (or surrounding-world) of the animal.

It often happens that some property of an animal belongs to one plan or to several, according to whether it is merely a member of the organisation of the creature that bears it, or appears as an indication in one or more of the other surrounding-worlds.

Perhaps the presence of the first half of the plan—that which governs the shaping of the animal—will be accepted without contradiction : whereas the second half—which concerns the selecting of the indicators—may excite question.

So long as we are unable to rid ourselves of the idea that the plan is lodged, spatially, in the germ of the organism, we are not likely to credit it at the same time with the power of having such a knowledge of the universe as would enable it to cut out therefrom just the piece that suits it

But we must realise clearly that the very same difficulty exists in the case of the form-giving part of the plan How are the impulses, connected into a system, to acquire knowledge of the substances present in the germ ? And if we are obliged to admit that they do directly control the absolutely fr ign material of the germ, there remains no ground for doubting their indirect control of the indicators through selection, a control which likewise can be demonstrated.

We must try to expand the far too narrow idea of a subjective plan dwelling within all organisms which we involuntarily set in the place of its direct activity We must take a general view of the sphere of that plan's influence as a whole. And then we shall perceive that the plan is able to shape relations in time exactly as it can shape those in space, so that it cannot be transferred to a point, limited in time and space, within the germ. The impulse-systems, which we may call subject-plans, or, briefly, subjects, in their arrangement control the time-relations, not only during the genesis of the organism, but also throughout the rest of its life Youth and old age, sleeping and waking, the period of sexual maturity,—these are just as firmly linked as is the arrangement of the limbs in the body.

In contrast to the doctrine of adaptation, which places time outside the life of the organism, and regards it as the actual former of the species, the theory of congruity regards time as a factor under the control of the organising power.

ORGANIC AND INORGANIC ACTIONS

When we look at a stream hurrying down through the bed which it drags along with it, we know that it is obeying directly the forces of gravity and friction. The resultant of these forces gives us the result directly. We can draw a parallelogram of the forces, and straightway calculate the result therefrom

The same is true of a stream rushing over a mill-wheel that it causes to turn. But in the first case the action of the stream is without plan, while in the second it belongs to a system (to use Driesch's expression), and so expresses plan

The actions of organisms fall into neither of these categories, for in them a new factor, the indication, is interpolated between cause and effect Unlike the stream, many animals run quicker uphill than down ; here the result cannot be calculated from the forces of gravity and friction. Their actions are not determined directly by mechanical forces, but only indirectly by the indication which releases within them their own forces, and gives the direction to their movements

Now let us suppose a self-construction by machines that, in order to execute the action, likewise require a definite stimulus for the releasing of inner forces Machines in which the external stimulus serves for steering can be imagined, it is true, but they have not yet been made.

In a general way, then, we reckon the actions of animals as mechanical, if it can be shown that the forces present in their mechanism are merely released by external stimuli, and then complete the action automatically, as in the reflex. The external stimulus in this case, however, in virtue of special arrangements, serves not merely to release the inner forces for the mechanism, but also to steer the movements, and it is then called an indication

The super-mechanical actions of animals (among which we reckon, along with development and direction, all the plastic actions) are not conditioned indirectly by an indication, for they first create the internal conditions that lead to the selection of the external stimuli. They determine directly what shall serve as stimulus or indication, and what shall not, since they form the internal framework anew, or repair it, or rearrange it.

Seen from this point of view, the difference between machine and organism can be defined quite precisely.

Both machines and organisms show two kinds of actions which are essentially different from one another, (1) the action of genesis, and (2) the action of function. But the action of genesis in the organism (to which regeneration of destroyed tissue is to be reckoned) is direct, whereas that of machines is, without exception and in its very nature, indirect, since it proceeds from the actions of its constructors, which are conditioned by indications. The function-action of the organism is always indirect, because it is built up on indications, whether these be fixed once and for all by the framework that makes the selection, or, as in plastic actions, are conditioned by the newly formed construction of the machinery.

The function-action of the machine is, as a rule, direct, and requires no releasing stimulus, because the whole system is focussed on the effect of one definite external force, whether that be the force of falling water, or whether it be heat, as in the case of steam-engines.

The super-mechanical actions of the organism resemble inorganic actions in proceeding directly. Like the forces of inorganic Nature, they are therefore the outcome of actual natural factors. But they appear to contain a plan, because they create a system, and so, on their side, they must be referred back to a plan system. The Greeks also referred the actions of inorganic Nature to a system, and we cannot maintain that they were wrong in so doing. Even at the present day we involuntarily base the concept of Nature on the idea of a system.

But the system that is expressed in the super-mechanical

actions of the organism we refer to a definite, delimited subject, which, in accordance with its impulses, arranged conformably with plan, is able to create directly definitely organised shapes.

As we saw in the previous section, the difficulty in the way of understanding the actions of the subject lies not so much in their directly producing forms capable of acting indirectly through indications, but in the selection of the indicators that accompanies the shaping, so that ultimately an individual is produced which is perfectly fitted in to an indication-tunnel.

Even we human beings, in constructing our machines, have to consider getting a suitable environment ; for every action, even the simplest, has relation to certain objects, the properties of which must accordingly be taken into account. In doing this, we are guided by our indications, and need only make a selection from these   But subjects stand in a relation to the universe that to us is totally obscure ; they are parts of the universe, like all other natural factors.

We can state confidently only this much,—that there are natural factors acting in accordance with plan, and without these factors organic life would be quite inconceivable.

TRIAL AND ERROR

We have now elaborated our point of view so far that we can easily attain to a critical understanding of the two most important theories of life at the present day, and explain their contradictions

As we know, Jennings built his all-embracing theory of " trial and error " on a single example, which was to be typical of all life's manifestations   A dog, which as a rule could easily jump through a gap in a fence, tried to do so when he was carrying his master's stick held crosswise in his mouth. He failed, because the gap was too narrow.   Then he took hold of the stick at various places, until he managed to jump through with it when he held it by the crook, for now the stick no longer presented an obstacle.

Undoubtedly it is of very great help in biology to seek out typical examples, because only through such can we get visual representation. But we must carefully analyse the typical case down to its ultimate elements, if it is to serve as an explanation of other cases

In Jennings' example, it is obvious that the dog behaves differently from a machine. A driverless motor-car, for instance, would have smashed the stick, or would have come to a standstill in front of the gap in the fence. So in a certain sense we may say that here we have a typical example of a " living " action, as opposed to a mechanical.

We might just as well take the case of a fly, which comes to a window-pane, hits it with its head several times, and then no longer treats it as though it were air, but walks about on it as if on the ground

In both instances, through the coming in of an indication, a rearrangement of the action is undertaken

But Jennings' experiment tells us nothing further. Rightly understood, it suggests that all the function-actions of animals are determined by indications, while those of machines are not. In so far, it is typical. But there is not the slightest ground for trying to make it hold good in the case of developmental actions. And just as little will it serve as evidence of adaptation : for both the old and the new indications were foreseen in the organisation of the dog and of the fly, and the new actions also lay within the normal one conditioned thereby. Moreover, the nervous steering-gear that undertakes the change was already present in both cases.

Meanwhile Jennings himself became convinced that the comparison of the genesis of the organism with the behaviour of the dog is open to objection. For through experiments carried on for a number of years, he had shown that the plan according to which a Paramecium develops remains constant through many thousands of generations, and its place cannot be taken by blind experimenting in Nature.

Although the doctrine of " trial and error " completely missed fire in the case of the genesis of the organism, Jennings and his pupils cannot bring themselves to explain, by recognition of a specific biological factor in Nature, the obvious differences between organic and inorganic actions. On the contrary, they try to get some understanding of the actions of animals on the basis of human psychology Like all psychologists, in so doing they change their standpoint and think themselves into that of the dog carrying the stick. To be consistent, they should also think themselves into the insect as it flies against the window, and put human ideas into it

The outside observer is quite unsatisfied by this. He wants to know an objective reason for the behaviour of the dog and the fly, and he rejects presumptions that he cannot control. Accordingly he seeks for stimuli in the outside world that might serve the dog and the fly as indications. And the knowledge of these solves the problem completely as regards function-actions In so doing, he is conscious that the indications are drawn from his own appearance-world, and he does not seek for the indication-signs that slumber perhaps in the minds of the dog and the fly.

TROPISMS

J Loeb, the founder of the doctrine of tropisms, comes from a far too exact school of physics ever to try to explain the observed life-processes by the aid of psychological hypotheses He never seeks an explanation through the mind of what takes place in space and time in full concreteness.

He is as much averse to explaining the action of an animal through its soul as he would be to inquiring into the soul of a steam-engine.

Nevertheless, he is nearer to biology than are other physicists For him the world does not consist of a haphazard dance of atoms, but is filled with mechanisms and machines, which fit exactly into one another. Loeb is much too much of a professional as regards mechanical problems ever to recognise the doctrine of adaptation. No one could ever persuade him that a motor-car could develop out of a bicycle.

He openly recognises the congruity of organisms one with another and with their medium, without resorting to hypotheses as to uncontrollable series of ancestors, and accordingly he is an outspoken anti-Darwinian and an opposer of Jennings.

The mechanical side of the life-problem has in him its most consistent and logical champion In fighting this cause, he tries to pursue his line of thought to its extreme, and this readily brings him into opposition with well-known biological facts.

As a physicist, Loeb recognised from the outset that, as preliminary to the understanding of the movements of animal-machines, there must be exact knowledge of the steering. Now such of our machines as perform spontaneous movements consist, without exception, of an apparatus that is solely effector, capable of carrying out locomotion in a determined direction only when external forces impart to it the right guidance. Loeb, judging animal-machines from the same point of view, looks for the factor in the external world that shall do this for them. He finds these in the " directed " forces of the external world, and primarily in light and gravity, and accordingly attempts to explain the directed movements of animals by two factors (1) the animal's loco-motor apparatus and (2) the direction-giving agent outside.

In this way he has succeeded in explaining a number of kinds of animal movement as " tropisms " (i.e. a movement directed from without). Heliotropism, phototropism, geotropism, rheotropism, etc., have become useful shibboleths to include a great number of similar movements in very different animal groups.

But Loeb's doctrine has not gained any general recognition, for it leaves out of account essential parts of the animal organisation. A living creature, even if we try to regard it as a mere machine, does not consist merely of an effector portion, as our machines do ; but also of a receptor portion, which first converts all the influences of the external world into an indication which then deals with the steering-gear. And it is not permissible to put on one side this important part of the life organisation, as Loeb has done. Even when externally directed forces are present, these must transform themselves within the animal into an indication, which then, in accordance with these external stimuli, prescribes the animal's own direction.

If we wish to compare machines with animals, we must first, then, construct them to correspond with the animal body. It is not enough to assign to them elastic forces of their own, which can be released by selected external forces and so perform actions This is found also in the effector portion of the animal organism. The part that makes the selection must be fitted up before the steering-apparatus, if the external stimulus is to act as the direction-giving indication. Even in this case, the resemblance would continue to be purely external, because every organism consists of cells, which are all of them active, both as receptors and as effectors

And in addition to all this, the super-mechanical capacities of the organism are not taken into account

Apart from these shortcomings, Loeb's doctrine remains

a serious attempt to manage without any amateurish acces-
sories It has a firm mechanico-physical basis, which it
has expanded in a remarkable way, and it scorns to borrow
insecure support from psychology and the doctrine of
adaptation.

Unfortunately Loeb gives his case away, as soon as he
comes to speak of the human soul, the activity of which
he undertakes to explain through the chemical processes of
the brain. If he repels the encroachments of the psychologists in explaining the mechanics of the body, the
psychologists have equal right to set aside as amateurish his
mechanical explanation of the life of the mind. Even if we
recognise law and order in the life of the mind, and so speak
of an organisation of the soul, there are no mechanics of the
soul or the mind. Loeb's attempt to ascribe to an acidifying
in the brain the appearance of an idea in the human spirit
is positively grotesque, although it is not actually less in accord
with the facts than is the statement that the writhing of an
earthworm trodden under foot is caused by its pain.

THE SENSED-WORLDS OF HUMAN BEINGS

If we wish to apply to human beings what we have learnt
from biological consideration of animals, it is of the first
importance to choose the right standpoint, permitting us to
view not merely human beings themselves, but also their
surrounding-worlds.

If we mount up in a captive balloon, human beings at
first recede from us, and then, at a certain point, this changes
into their reduction in size. They seem nearer to us again,
but very much smaller Let us choose the moment when
they have assumed the size of a large insect, such as a dragon-
fly or a grasshopper Now at our leisure let us consider these
little creatures which occupy but a tiny action-circle in the

vast horizon.   We see the rivers, as on a map, branching away
like blue ribbons , the mountains have become mere mounds,
and the cities playthings.   Within these the homunculi
move to and fro.

Unlike what happens in the majority of animals, the
sensed-world of the human being also embraces his effector-
organs and their activity.   So it is possible to form real
implements based on a human action-rule, around which
certain properties arrange themselves under compulsion by
the schema

In early childhood the implements are still few in number.
As the man grows, they become more numerous, and soon
in his world-as-sensed we can distinguish from one another
implements, objects and organisms.   As observers, it is true,
we have always to form the implements of the people observed
on the lines of our own diagrams and action-rules   But in
spite of the monotony of the material, it is quite possible for
us to detect great differences in the sensed-worlds we study.

If we begin with the external envelope of the space of
the senses that surrounds each human being—the extended,
which encloses every world-as-sensed—we find, up to the
Middle Ages, a definite wall, an actual firmament, which shut
off the men of those days from the universe   Behind this
a deity was enthroned, dwelling in the incomprehensible.
Everything beneath the heavens obeyed his laws, which at
that time were horribly arbitrary, and kept men in a constant
state of fear and dread

Then (as Troels-Lund convincingly explains) came the
period of astrology   The sky, with the fixed stars, became a
vast clock-face, in front of which the planets circled like the
hands, and to him who knew how to read gave information of
his fate.   The worlds-as-sensed acquired rigid laws ; everything within them moved in time to the everlasting clock.

Then Giordano Bruno rent open the roof of the heavens,

and in its place put space, infinite and meaningless. In this boundless space, existing only in thought, the small earthly dimensions could find no explanation. Their place was taken by light years, and light centuries. And everlasting space engulfed these too.

The deity enthroned above the sky disappeared ; there was no place for him in the infinite expanse of space. But with him disappeared the idea of the universe. For now the world-as-sensed really embraced everything that was there, and did not, as formerly, seem to stop at the limits of what could be apprehended by the senses.

The newly discovered telescopes seemed to be trying to master the infinity of space, and yet they only pushed back the visible a little further, without ever being able to burst the bonds of the extended. In the same way, microscopes seemed to open up the world of the infinitely small, but they also were able to expand the limits of the visible only a small way. Even between the smallest points the extended always reappeared, enveloping them like a firm wall. Even here the limited perceptive faculties had always to be corrected by the aid of a " thought " space in which the whirl of atoms could spin.

The infinite space of thought, combined with the infinite time of thought, prevented men from recognising a universe lying beyond the possibility of their own perception. Everything, positively everything, ought to be and must be carried out in the world-as-sensed of each individual human being.

Since that time a kind of megalomania has seized men, and they will no longer recognise limits to the possibility of knowledge. To the observer in the balloon this megalomania has something comical in it ; human beings seem to him like flies gone so mad that they believe they can command a view of the entire universe and master it.

With the shape of the world that they marked off from

the universe, its planned construction and the control of its working disappeared, and now everything was handed over to physical necessity. The first thing that resulted was the complete withdrawal of interest from the starry heavens. The sky, which once was able to embody the idea of a providence enthroned above it, became a wearisome mathematical problem. In most human sensed-worlds to-day there is no distinction between fixed stars and planets : in their place have come irregularly arranged bright points, which are somehow connected together physically.

Beginning with the heavens, the physical process of decomposition has gradually invaded the whole of the world-as-sensed. If we assume from the beginning that there is no conformity with plan hidden behind natural phenomena, but always just the same mathematical calculation, complicated, it is true, but utterly stupid, then all interest in these things must die out

A sort of rot has set in in the sensed-worlds, and everything within them has been handed over to disintegration. Since Darwin's day, we see not only the inorganic objects, but also the living things in the sensed-worlds of our fellow-men, fall to pieces. In the majority of sensed-worlds, animals and plants have become nothing but assemblages of atoms without plan. The same process has also seized on the human being in the sensed-worlds ; even the subject's own body is just an assemblage of matter, and all its manifestations have become reduced to physical atomic processes.

If we look down attentively from our balloon on this ever-spreading epidemic in the worlds-as-sensed, we get the impression of a dangerous infectious disease. The joy in the search for new indications has quite slacked off What is the use of searching, if we know beforehand that the whole thing is just a dance of atoms ?

On the other hand, we perceive an alarming reduction in

indications. The world of most people whose calling does not oblige them to pay regard to Nature, is hopelessly impoverished. Instead of the thousand different plants and animals, we see a deadly, monotonous repetition of the same tree with the same indications of " green " and " high," and among animals even the dog and the horse are scarcely distinguishable as regards their indications. Almost everything else is simply and monotonously " animal." It is not surprising that landscapes differ from one another merely quantitatively. The most famous view-points are always those from which one can see " as much as possible." We are able to see " many " mountains or " many " rivers, it is true ; but fundamentally they all look alike.

If we look into the worlds-as-sensed of the pygmies that tear through the world in motor-cars, we find, with the exception of indications for the hotels, scarcely any by the aid of which we could distinguish between towns or between landscapes.

Such people, dwelling in the most dreadful wilderness, where only a few of the commonest objects repeat themselves again and again ad nauseam, are called " rich," as though in mockery ; although in comparison with any peasant or shepherd, they are as poor as beggars.

This regrettable laying-waste of the worlds-as-sensed has really arisen from the superstition started by the physicists, which would induce each person to consider as the universe his own small and often inferior sensed-world, a universe composed of nothing but points revolving round one another without plan.

The physicists have a good reason for spreading this belief. What would become of their indestructible continuity of the world as a whole, if once it were understood that the millions of worlds-as-sensed are completely independent, each with its heaven, its stars and its sun ? These innumerable firmaments have no physical influence on one another. The law that forms and binds them is not physical, but biological, constructed on the activity of impulse-systems arranged in accordance with plan.

We must clearly realise that, when we leave the balloon that gave us a general view over the sensed-worlds of other human beings, and yield our place to another observer, our whole world with its heaven and stars shrinks together into that little opaque saucer which, looking down from above, we discovered in the case of all our fellow-men.

But if we have once enjoyed the wide and universal view, we shall carry away with us the conviction that all the many millions of animal and human worlds are in the control of a great universal law, which governs in full conformity with plan. It is true that we are able to recognise this law only by the aid of the means at our disposal, in the shape of our order- and content-qualities and the laws pertaining to these (such as the law of regular increase), but, in employing this means, we shall be obliged to recognise in Nature the pervading conformity with plan.

All worlds-as-sensed are composed solely of the relation to their indicators that are attached by the subjects themselves. The nature and the number of these relations is decisive for estimation of the individual worlds-as-sensed. To illustrate the relations radiating on every side from the subject, we may choose the image of a tree with branches ramifying far and wide The healthy tree will always be sending out fresh twigs, while the sick tree loses one twig after the other.

It will then appear as the task of each man's life to develop his tree into full foliage and blossom. And it will also be realised that even the tallest tree does not grow up to the sky, and that there is an absolute limit to the world-as-sensed, behind which the universe begins Even the subject of a man's neighbour lies on the far side of the boundary

Y

THE COMMUNITY AS AN ORGANISM

If we mount up still higher in the balloon, there become defined below us the boundaries of a small community-being, which we are able to survey in its entire expanse. We now employ the method of geographers, who are able to construct an entire portion of the world on their mapping-table—the method of macroscopy, which, unlike microscopy, makes the details subordinate to the framework of the whole—and we try to detach carefully from the substratum everything that belongs to the human community-being, so that we may spread it out on a small scale on our work-table. We get then a delicate tissue, filled with life. The railways intersect the tissue as firm, straight threads, with which the network of streets and roads connects. Towns, villages and country-houses, interspersed in the network, are filled with little human creatures, which we have carefully detached from the earth, along with all their tools and machines, so that we can study the whole of human production as one complete framework.

The underside of the tissue is the most interesting, which shows us all the apparatus that, like a system of roots, penetrates the ground for the exploitation of its treasures. Everywhere we see ploughs and harrows at work, scratching up the ground. Deeper than these penetrate the shafts that bring up to the surface metals and coal. These directly rob the earth of its treasures, while the ploughs and harrows continually enable it to bear fresh fruits, which are then harvested. All products of the soil move into the interior of the tissue, which they renovate and develop. As well as food and clothing, they provide men with dwellings, and with means for communication and for work.

All this is effected through the ceaseless labour of a thousand tools and machines, which are worked by human beings.

At the first glance, the men seem part and parcel of their apparatus, so closely do their actions correspond with the movement of the machines. If that were really so, then the resemblance to an animal-community would be complete, and we should only have to look around for those inhabitants who, like the queens of ants and bees, see to the business of reproduction, which is necessary to ensure the perpetuation of the community.

Here we see the fundamental difference between the animal-community and the human. The human community has no sexless individuals, dedicated exclusively to the affairs of the community, and therefore grown to their tools like the workers and soldiers of the ants. All human beings can free themselves from their apparatus, their clothes and their dwellings, and still remain capable of exercising the functions of the individual life and of reproduction. It is only among human beings that we can separate the community and the people.

The community shows human beings as associates in work ; the people shows them as founders of families, devoting themselves to reproduction and the rearing of children. Each human being has a twofold task assigned him, as member of the people, and as worker for the community. The community requires that the people shall provide it with suitable workers ; the people demands of the community that it shall create for it suitable conditions of life. And thus both complete themselves, though they are essentially different from one another.

Let us consider first of all those organs of the community, the task of which is to bring to the individual beings the fruits of the earth in a suitable condition.

If it is to be fully exploited, the spatial extension of the earth requires a spatial distribution of the individuals that everywhere attack it. But the workers distributed in space have needs greater than the products of their own work can satisfy, and so they are referred to those of other workers, likewise distributed in space   Accordingly there must be an exchange of products or goods   For this exchange roads and railways serve, which, on the one hand, accumulate the goods and, on the other, distribute them again. A centralisation of the products becomes necessary, as soon as separation in space makes direct exchange impossible. We see how, in this way, the goods come into the hands of the few, although they are made by the many and used by the many.

Moreover, very few products are capable of being used in the form in which they leave the hands of the workers on the soil. (Corn, for instance, must first be ground and then baked, before it can be used as food) The consequence of this is that there is a further assembling of goods in the hands of the few who are interposed between the many workers and the many consumers.

To demonstrate these relations, let us make a simple diagram (Fig. 6) ; then we see how the goods first flow from the producers P' to the centre C', before they reach the con-sumers P"   But these, in their turn, are producers of other goods, which must be conveyed to C" before they reach the producers P'. We get from this the impression of a circulating stream, which rhythmically broadens out and then narrows again. But we must not forget that each stream of products dries up as soon as it gets to the consumer ; and so the stream can circulate only if the consumer is also a producer.

Now there is one product that cannot be consumed, but is in continual circulation, because it serves as the means of exchange—gold. Gold circulates in the opposite direction to the stream of products, but follows that faithfully in all its ramifications, flowing, like it, in great abundance towards the centre, and so passing from the hands of the many into those of the few   The centralising of gold, however, goes further than that of goods, because it can circulate independently. Thus special gold-centres develop, which are able to control the exchange of goods over a wide area

The amassing of the gold-stream in the hands of a few

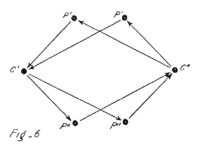

Fig - 6

individuals gives these a great advantage over their fellows in the community, and may result in injury to the community as a whole.

The community, however, has organs of its own which determine its peculiar framework, and they are called on to safeguard the normal course of the functions against the encroachments of individuals Such are the organs of the administration of justice and of government, and to these is allotted, as executive organ, the police.

While we may compare the stream of goods and the stream of gold with the streams of blood and fluids in the body, the organs of the administration of justice and of government form the bones of the community, which, by their stability, serve as support for the ever-changing streams of goods and gold.

If fixed rules for government and the administration of justice had developed in a community, and the individual beings forming these organs automatically accommodated themselves to these rules, it is possible that the community might get on without further centralisation, provided that the earth on which it had grown furnished it with all the necessary products. Since, however, every state is surrounded by neighbours, and is perpetually at the mercy of their encroachments, it always sees itself faced with new contingencies, towards which it must take up a position as a whole.

Accordingly, like every organism, it requires sense-organs and a steering-apparatus and special action-organs, in order to ward off hostile attacks, if need should arise. All these organs must be formed out of individuals

Only such individuals are suited for sense-organs as are specially developed as observers ; otherwise they would only involve injury.

At the present day we need not waste words on the necessity of having an army as action-organ, all ready to strike.

Very various views are held as to the best kind of construction of the steering-apparatus   There has been miserable failure from all attempts to set in the critical place a large number of individuals who decide by a majority.   Individuals are like qualities, the values of which we can weigh one against the other : if we treat them as quantities, the result is always meaningless   So we shall probably continue to place at the head of the community a single being who, freed from youth upwards of all special vocational interests, and concentrating on the interest of the whole, is able to weigh against one another impartially the individuals whom he entrusts with the directing of the community.

Yet none of these considerations go to the heart of the question—how it is possible to compare a community, consisting entirely of separate individuals, with an organism, which, like the body of a living creature, is solely composed of intergrown cells ?   On the one hand, we have an anatomical framework, closely knit by means of pegs and sockets ; on the other, a free company of individuals, which, at the sexual mixing of their properties, effect interchange according to the rule of probability and without regard to the functions of the whole.

Nevertheless we see that this free company does not form merely a people-unity, but also a function-unity, which is able to carry on like clockwork   So, even if invisible, there must be pegs and sockets there, for only a framework will ensure the trustworthy cooperation of the separate parts.

Let us make use of a very simple illustration   Two blacksmiths are working at the same rate with their hammers on a piece of iron   We can show that the sound of the first man's hammer, as it hits the iron, releases the action of striking by the second. If we realise that each of the men is surrounded by a world-as-sensed and a world of action, then it is obvious that the rhythmic cooperation of the two comes from the deed in the world of action of the first appearing as an indication in the world-as-sensed of the second, and, by stimulation of the steering-apparatus focussed on this activity, producing the same action of striking in his world of action also.   This again serves as indication in the world-as-sensed of the first blacksmith ; and so it goes on   One effect of the action of the first blacksmith, namely, the sound, fits like a peg exactly into the socket of the world-as-sensed of the other, which is concentrated on the reception of this sound   If the sound-reception by the second man is diverted by any circumstance, external or internal, then the rhythmical stroke of the hammer ceases.

This example explains to us very completely how the framework is constituted in all human beings who are collaborating. Performance in the world of action of the one worker always serves as peg for the socket in the world-as-sensed of the next. In this way we are enabled to consider the machine of the community as though it were a wheel-work, in which a peg on one cog-wheel fits into a socket in the next, so that the whole mechanism gets going

This simple idea, however, can be taken as a substitute for the whole process, only if we bear in mind that here we have to do, not with a mechanical but with a biological framework. In every case, from the action of the one collaborator a stimulus must proceed, which is converted by the other into excitation, and this then leads to release of the corresponding action.

Accordingly the whole process must be described as a transference of excitation from organism to organism, which proceeds along fixed paths, because in each organism the steering-apparatus is focussed on a certain excitation-indication, and after that appears, hands on the excitation to certain effectors.

The means whereby the excitation is transferred from one human being to another in speech and writing become so complicated, that we usually forget their significance as effector pegs which fit into receptor sockets.

The power to concentrate the steering-apparatus in the individual man both on the receptor and on the effector side with the degree of delicacy and accuracy required for most sorts of work, is not present from the beginning, but must be acquired through executing certain movements, and through working out certain indications, which often appear above the threshold only after others have been suppressed.

And so it happens that the worker must be specially trained for each vocation, before he can serve as a cog-wheel in the community-machine.

When we have succeeded in forming a picture of the community-machine, we shall be able to show that here, as in every other machinery that has to run smoothly, the same basic principles are in control ; namely, compulsion, variety and subordination.

We shall also learn to estimate the variety of form of the worlds-as-sensed, which have to change with the vocation, and which give to each human being a different stamp according to the place he assumes in the community. Thus the community itself sees to an ever-increasing progressive differentiation of human beings

The danger that ultimately the members of callings far removed from one another will not be mutually intelligible, is obviated by the fact that each individual belongs to a family as well as to a profession Since the needs of all families are in the main alike, these provide that a similar human foundation is retained, from which renewed understanding can always proceed ; for in all questions affecting family life and the life of the people, the sensed-worlds must exhibit like indications.

The fact, so characteristic of human beings, that they belong both to community and to people, has led to manifold ✓ misunderstandings. Men have tried to raise to the position of the ideal of the community the ideal of the people, which may be formulated as *liberty, equality and fraternity ;* whereas the community ideal cannot read other than *compulsion, inequality and subordination.* The reconciliation of these two antitheses is the chief task of humanity

THE ORGANISM AS A COMMUNITY

In comparing organisms with machines, I have pointed out that, in contrast to the majority of tools and machines made by man, they consist of very small units, the boundaries of which by no means always coincide with the mechanically conditioned boundaries of the organs. I have referred this state of things to the organism's mode of genesis, and shown that there are " signs of genesis " in the cell-boundaries

Apart from bones, hairs and similar cell-products, which show no cellular structure, the whole body is composed of cells which persist throughout the entire life. They all show the familiar twofold structure,—a mechanical portion, which shares in the performance of work by the organs, and a protoplasmic portion, which carries out the repairs. This residuum of protoplasm is the means employed by the control to make injured organs once more capable of functioning.

From this it appeared that the cellular structure of the organs and tissues was sufficiently established, and the fact that remote portions of the body, such as the lens of the eye, while consisting of cells, yet behaves like a polished, homogeneous lens of glass, seemed to raise no further problems. The skin, consisting of thousands of cells, and with it the connective tissue, divided up according to the mechanical requirements of the body-machine into strands or flat surfaces, works like a lens, quite irrespective of the number of cells that go to form the parts.

But in other respects the cellular structure of the tissues is exploited to its utmost by the body-machine. The single muscle-fibres are connected by single nerve-fibres to their representatives, which are able to stimulate the muscle-fibres one at a time ; just as the keys of a piano cause the strings to sound singly. And each single muscle-fibre can influence its representative, which, as each fresh excitation comes in, can lock or unlock, according to the state of tension of the muscle-fibre. Even in this case we might continue to regard muscle-cell, nerve-fibre and the motor-centre serving as representative as an isolated part of a machine. Indeed, the comparison has even been pushed so far that the whole reflex-arc, from the receptive sense-cell to the effector muscle-cell or gland-cell, has been described as a self-contained electrical apparatus.

But in this respect the comparison of the community-being with an organism requires caution. As we see, the transference of excitation from one individual to another often takes place quite automatically, as in a machine, without the individual losing its independence in so doing, an independence expressed by the fact that an indication referring to the individual must always appear in its sensed-world before it can perform the action.

If we imagine the world-as-sensed to be so restricted that it contains only one indication, then the activity of the individuals will assume an increasingly mechanical character. According to the structure of the individual, this may be of a very special kind, if only one external stimulus serves as indication ; or of a general kind, if many different stimuli act as the same indication.

Regarding the reflex arc from this point of view, then the sensory cell that responds to a single stimulus represents a specialised individual, e g the auditory cell responding to a certain atmospheric vibration, the optic cell to a certain etheric vibration

The nerve-cell follows the sensory cell. It also is an individual which can conduct excitation only when it has received from the sensory cell a stimulus, which becomes an indication as soon as it releases a nervous excitation at the peripheral end of the nerve-cell   But the nerve-cell is able to convert into excitation other stimuli, such as mechanical and electrical shocks, and it can do this at any point on its elongated body.   A nervous excitation, however, must always be aroused before it can be conducted further.   The simple steering of the nerve-cell consists in conduction. It must hand on by stimulation to the central cells an excitation transmitted to it by the sensory cell.

In this way the transference of excitation proceeds in the reflex arc, whether we have to do with nerves, centres, glands or muscles. In each case a very restricted sensed-world forms the socket into which fits the action from the similarly restricted world of action of its neighbour.

The community-mechanism, based on the transference of

excitation by individuals, appears with especial clearness in the white blood-corpuscles, which move about freely through the tissues of the body, collecting together at the stimulated parts, in order to efface there the injuries that produced the stimulus.

Recently it has been shown that a whole network of excitation-transference by individuals runs through the body, and plays a very important part there, especially in the digestive processes. " Hormone " is the name given to these substances, which are cast into the blood-stream by certain cells of the alimentary canal ; they form a special stimulus for certain other digestive glands, which thereupon pour out their secretion into the gut. For the most part, this chemical transference of excitation accompanies the nervous one, but it remains quite independent thereof.

Further, it has been shown that there are a whole number of internal glands, the secretion of which, cast into the blood-stream, affects other cells as a stimulus, and activates them.

Finally, the whole taking up of food by the cells from the blood-stream and the body-fluids must be referred to stimulation of individuals and the action that ensues.

To the same class of facts belongs the power the tissues have of reacting to poisons by throwing anti-bodies into the blood-stream. But in this the protoplasm seems to play a part, and the direction itself seems to come in.

The action of vitamins on the tissues also points to an " individual " reaction, the omission of which has harmful consequences.

Although this field of investigation is still very obscure, and we are dependent on vague conjecture, especially as to the stimuli that accelerate or restrict cell-multiplication, we shall not go far wrong if, instead of trying to solve these newly-discovered relations by referring them to simple mechanical or chemical processes, we rely on the transference of excitation by individuals that is furnished us by the analogy of the community. Part of these processes takes place in the differentiated, mechanical portion of the cell; but another part initiates an invasion of the protoplasm by impulses. From our study of the life of the community, both are familiar to us, for there also the co-operation of the individuals depends partly on simple reflexes, and partly on plastic actions.

There still remains much to be done before we can succeed in revealing the higher mechanics of the relations of the individual somatic cells to one another. But only when this is brought to light, shall we be able to say that we have a real insight into the functions of the body.

The time is past when we could compare living organisms with machines; it may be that we shall succeed in constructing machines that, in addition to the familiar mechanism, possess a special excitation-mechanism for the interchange of differentiated substances. But even so, if the analogy with living organisms is to be complete, it would be necessary for the machines to be built up of individualised parts of the framework, converting only certain stimuli into indications, and then performing certain actions. But even all this would not suffice, for we should not be able to endow our machines with the internal constructor and director. These remain the lasting prerogative of the living organism.

On the other hand, a more profound knowledge of the life of the community will beneficially affect our understanding of organisms The community is itself a living being, possessing an internal constructor and director. All its organs are composed of individuals. Its functions take place in the realm of higher mechanics, by means of the transference of excitation Its success depends on the faultless focussing of the sensed-worlds of individual beings on the indications that accord with their special vocations, and on the flawless execution of the actions pertaining to these. For both these tasks *discipline* is above all necessary. For the rest, the super-mechanical principle of the community is expressed in those plastic actions of its members endowed with protoplasm, which form the community and maintain it.

THE LIFE-ENERGY

The comparison of the organisation of the community with that of the body of the living creature has revealed a pervading property which is determinative for all living organisms—the presence of functioning individualities or " indivisible units ", having their own irritability, their own conduction of excitation (or steering), and producing their independent effect.

Each individual well deserves this name, for only so long as it contains the undivided, tripartite chain, can it fill its place as living member of an organism

An individual may consist of one cell, or of an association of cells. In the latter case, the single cells have so far fitted themselves into a whole of a higher order that they have specially developed a portion of their function-chain in the interests of the whole, without, however, surrendering the other portions The sensory cells have had to develop especially their receptor part, the nerve-cells their conducting or steering part, and the muscle-cells and gland-cells their effector part, in order that, for instance, a reflex-arc may be formed. The nerve-fibres, which conduct the excitation further *in one direction*, have the simplest kind of steering, which permits the excitation to proceed always along the same routes ; while the nerve-cells of the centre are able to conduct it now into this outgrowth and now into that It is immaterial whether we speak of steering as a complicated conduction, or of conduction as a simplified steering. Both expressions describe what is done by the connecting portion between reception and effect, an action which is sometimes more simple and sometimes more complex.

The three links in the function-chain of the individual may be described as " reception—conduction of excitation—effect," or as " observe—steer—act "

Each individual must form an indivisible whole, because, on the one side, it serves as the peg part of the machine, and, on the other, as the socket, while at the same time it makes the connection between the two. Any cell will serve as an example of an elementary building-stone of the kind. The simplest piece of framework we can think of consists of a peg and a socket, with a single connecting-route between them. The simple reflex-arcs, in spite of being built up of several cells, nevertheless form simple pieces of framework, when, by means of one single path through the centre, they effect the connection between a nerve-cell and a muscle- or gland-cell.

As soon as several receiving cells are connected through a centre with several effector cells, the steering in the centre comes into its own, and guides the excitation, now into one route, and now into another. The steering, on its side, is influenced by the " tone " of the whole, which may change periodically. This decides the appearance of thresholds, which divert the excitation, and so invade the steering. In the same way, the threshold in the centre can be influenced by the effector-organ We know of muscles that are rhythmically " locked," and then " unlocked " (towards excitation). In this case we speak of a " refractory period."

The impulses, as we have seen, also influence the centre and, within modest limits, enable the body to perform new actions, which we call " plastic " The plastic actions also are restricted within a predetermined frame, and never go outside the limits set for the individual.

This limitation, again, results from the congruity which

binds the organism to a definite life-tunnel, with which it is dovetailed, on the one hand by its receptive organs (as sockets), and on the other by its effector organs (as pegs).

In this way there develops, everywhere that life extends, a closely coherent framework, built in full conformity with plan.

If we consider the framework of life as a whole, we come everywhere on individuals, which constitute its organs, and serve the life-functions so long as they form a whole Accordingly they are to be regarded as the elements of the living. Since undoubtedly they must always be renewing themselves, we must conclude that there is a *life-energy*, which perpetually produces them This life-energy is subjective, in the sense that it puts autonomous subjects into the world. We may therefore infer that the several impulses are already united into subject-systems when they begin their activity.

As soon as living organisms are made, their organisation enables them to lay hold of the world and systematise it. The genesis of their own organisation, however, lies outside their scope, and requires special natural forces, to which, in the last resort, even the machines and tools of man are referable, since these owe their existence to organised beings.

And so it is a mistake to conclude that organisms should be treated as mechanisms Fundamentally, the genesis of a machine is harder to understand than that of a human being. The genesis of the latter involves the former, since the machine is a secondary product of a being that has arisen through primary forces of Nature

Superficially considered, the constructing of a machine seems easier to grasp, because, as personal observation tells us, it arises from unorganised forces of Nature and unorganised substances, on which organisation is imposed by the organism Man The conclusion that has been drawn from this is that in Nature there are only unorganised substances and forces.

Men have tried, in the face of all known analogies, to refer to unorganised forces and substances the organisation of organisms themselves.

Quite consciously they have turned away from recognition of natural forces imposing order, and in this way they have attempted to dispose of the problem of life.

We know now that this is not possible, but that behind every living creature lie elements that are not disorderly but arranged, consisting of pegs and sockets that fit into one another.

The organising forces of Nature are, in their essence, specifically constituted otherwise than are the unorganised forces of physics   Accordingly we are quite justified in speaking of " *specific energies,*" or life-energies.   Their specific nature consists in their existing only in an organised condition.   Their specific singularity, organisation, does not come under the law of the conservation of energy, which has only to do with quantities, and not with arrangements   In contrast to this, organisation in the world of the living, which expresses itself in increased complexity, is a process of perpetual shaping.

It is true that the simplest organisms are just as congruous as are the highest.   But the congruity of the highest is very much more many-sided.

The manner in which the specific energies are associated dispenses with mechanical compulsion, but is, in its nature, an imperative.   All living beings develop, not in accordance with a causal " thou must," as is characteristic of the unorganised forces, but according to a biological " thou shalt."

As we know, since Kant's day the ethical command " thou shalt " is referred to a transcendental influence on the empirical character of the human being, and the empirical character, with a " thou must," forces the decision

On this analogy, we may describe all actions of the body

z

as " thou must," so long as they are based on the compulsion
of the developed biological organisation, and all super-
mechanical invasions as a " thou shalt," proceeding from an
impulse-system.

This way of considering things permits us to say of the
impulse-systems that they are " imperative " in respect of
form, which they always relate to the development or main-
tenance of the individual.   This individual is always a subject,
because it always forms a new world-centre.   Everything
that happens, happens for the individual only in so far as
the phenomenon becomes a new indication within it.   The
indications are, so to speak, the lighthouses of the individual,
from which it gets glimpses of the world.   Each individual
has only so much world as is subjectively accessible to it.

Objectively considered, each individual, whether large
or small, is an element in the framework of the whole, into
which it fits by pegs and sockets.

Accordingly the impulse-system, to the imperative of
which the individual owes its development, must, from one
aspect, be described as a subject, because it creates a world-
centre.   But from the other aspect, it is arranged as an
objective factor in the plan of the world as a whole, in order
that the new world-centre may become part of the framework
of the whole.

We get a survey of these difficult and complicated relations most easily, if we proceed from a universal conformity
with plan, in which the subjective impulse-systems are woven
in as objective factors along with the other objective factors
of Nature.   For the conformity with plan of life embraces
both inorganic and organic forces, even if it directly influences
only the organic shaping.

The impulse-systems continually form in the individuals
fresh world-centres, large and small ; the worlds belonging
to these centres mutually embrace and cut across one

another, but at the same time unite into one splendid
framework.

The direct influence of the impulses on the protoplasm
is specifically different from the reciprocal influence that
other natural forces exert on one another ; for the impulses,
which do nothing but organise, act on physical and chemical
factors already present in the protoplasm.

Protoplasm is almost unlimited in its formative possibilities, and so is almost ideal as a plastic medium.

But at the present day we do not know why the impulses
affect the protoplasm only, nor how they do it.   They connect
themselves with substances that release processes, and they
activate these substances.   That is all we can say about it.

And so the impulses differ from other natural factors
in two respects—by the way in which they affect the protoplasm, and by their association into systems.

The great question of the future will be whether it is
possible to isolate the impulses, and force them to influence
substances other than protoplasm.   Already there are indications that an isolation of the impulses may be effected.   Many
instances of gall-formation point this way, seeming to suggest
the transference of a form-giving impulse from the insect to
the plant.   The discovery made in Spemann's laboratory by
Wachs when working on Amphibia has a like significance :
he found that the cells of the upper iris, which do not
themselves possess the power to make lens fibres, can be
endowed with that power by a secretion coming from the
retina.

I am convinced that cases of this kind, accessible to
analysis, will become more numerous as soon as attention
is more generally directed to them.

It is impossible to say whether we shall attain to the ideal
I have before me, of inducing form-making to take place
within a test-tube   But at any rate we can get much closer

to the problem, as soon as we have found the right way of putting the question.

It is not a question of making something living out of dead matter. That is doomed to failure. It is a question of breaking up the protoplasm activated by the impulses into separate genes, and then investigating their effect, singly and together, on a second substance that is not necessarily protoplasm itself.

Since there can be no doubt that we have to do with real natural factors, it must be possible to get on the track of their mode of operation and their interlinkings. In so doing, the more we employ the methods elaborated by physicists and chemists, the sooner will biology win the recognition of these two sciences, which hitherto have been her implacable enemies.

If my statements as to the life-energy be compared with those of Reinke, it will be seen that they agree almost completely with his theory of dominants. Only that I emphasise more strongly than he that, when I refer to genes and impulses, I am talking of actual natural factors. And I refuse to obliterate the boundaries on the psychical side, since I reckon the impulse-systems to an objective conformity with plan, instead of to a universal world-intelligence. The world-intelligence always remains a psychical factor, and no one would dream of trying to inject single intelligences into matter, however plastic.

SELF-OBSERVATION

For a biologist, observation of his own body does not differ fundamentally from observation of other living organisms. He shows that there is a surrounding-world in the case of his own body also, divisible into world-as-sensed and world of action, and set over against an inner world within the body itself And his functions, too, are made up of numerous function-circles, with reference to the medium, enemies, food, family life, the business of the community, etc.

The world-as-sensed, discovered through observation of the body, contains a greater number of indications than the world of the senses can afford us directly. The stimulus producing the reflex closing of the eyelid is often so trivial and so fleeting that we are not conscious of it at all, and yet we shall admit that even this releases an indication, though, for our consciousness, it may remain below the threshold. The nature of this indication belonging to the reflex-arc is as much out of the reach of our knowledge as though we were dealing with that of some animal; and yet it belongs to the sensed-world of our body. The same is true of all the indications that appear in the countless reflex actions of our organs, especially the organs of digestion, respiration and circulation. We know absolutely nothing about the indications of our innumerable body-cells. What we are conscious of are only those that appear in the mark-organ of our brain, when we perform plastic actions. This is the whole material that serves for the construction of our conscious sensed-world.

The proof of this lies in the fact that only those nerve-fibres that run from the organs of reception to the cerebral hemispheres cause sensations to arise in us when they are directly stimulated : when any of the other nerves are so stimulated, we have no sensations. Accordingly it is only on stimulation of the mark-organ that sensations arise in us, and not on stimulation of the action-organ of the central nervous system Moreover, if the process runs on reflex or instinctive lines, no sensations are experienced. From which we may conclude that sensations are connected with the onset of super-mechanical processes in the mark-organ.

Only when this has been recognised, can we attain to a right understanding of the fundamental doctrine of Johannes Muller, who described as " specific sensory energy " the appearance of certain qualities in our mind after stimulation of certain sensory nerves.

His theory goes beyond the mere physiological demonstration that the same steering in the centre is connected with the excitation of the same centripetal fibres. It speaks of a " specific," non-mechanical energy, which is active when the qualities appear in the mind; and only in the second place does it point out that the nature of the quality that appears is connected with the person of the nerves in which this " super-mechanical " energy becomes effective.

Now, as I have stated, in super-mechanical processes, impulses always come in determinatively; they are specific life-energies. If we wish to follow Johannes Müller, we must assume that the impulses which invade our mark-organ determinatively and create new forms, are in essence qualities.

For the representational idea that we made of these processes, this assumption is unimportant. It is of no interest to the outside observer whether the amœba-like centres in stretching forth their pseudopodia to make new bridges for excitation, receive the order to build the bridge in the form of " a way for blue " or " a way for red." The content of the subjective mark-sign in the active brain during the building of new bridges is a matter of indifference to the observer. He need only pay regard to the nature of the external stimulus to which the bridge-building gives the opportunity of entering determinatively into the steering of the action. From these objective indications he will construct the sensed-world of animals, i.e. he will always employ his own qualities, from which he constructs the world, to describe the sensed-world of animals. In so doing, he will make no distinction as to whether the indications released by the stimuli determined the actions in a reflex or in a plastic manner. All indications are equally necessary for the construction of the world-as-sensed.

These indications, taken collectively, are subjective mark-signs of the observer. That being so, when they play the part of objective indications or external properties in the sensed-world of the animal observed, the observer will be obliged, as we have already said, to confer on them the laws governing his own subjective indications or qualities. So he will always surround the living organism with space and time, since these constitute the formal laws of his order-qualities. In the same way he will always endow them with the laws of relationship and of the regular increase in colour, sound, etc., since these are the formal laws of his content-qualities.

But the conclusions to be drawn from Muller's theory are of great interest, if, as observers, we follow what goes on in our own central nervous system. Excitation is transferred in the familiar way, and arrives in the mark-organ of our cerebrum. Now the impulses become active, the bridges are built on which the excitation will be conducted on to the action-organ. But in this case we know the impulses ; they say, for instance, " a way for blue." At the same moment, the indication " blue " appears in our world-as-sensed The *subjective* mark-sign " blue " forces a place for itself as *objective* indication in our appearance-world It acts as an imperative on the properties of the external world, which it transforms and enriches.

The command given by the super-mechanical impulse acts on the world like an enchanter's wand. By a stroke of magic, the sum of the impulses that appear creates around us the whole vast world of colour and sound.

From the standpoint of the outside observer, the task of the impulses is to steer to the action-organ the excitation produced by the external stimulus, and so to convert it into an indication. We must therefore try to discover whether the psychical mark-signs also show a steering. If we consider the three great works of Kant from this point of view, those

incomparable guides to the associations in our subjective
life, we may say that the *Critique of Pure Reason* deals with
the forming of indications, while the *Critique of Practical
Reason* and the *Critique of Judgment* deal with the steering
by means of judgments, which are exercised both by the
ethical and by the æsthetic impulses.

To go further into this matter would take us beyond
the scope of biology, and into the realms of psychology and
the critique of knowledge.

There is just one more point to which I wish to direct
attention. Why did Kant write no *Critique of Will-
Power*? Because we know nothing about will-power.
When the excitation leaves the mark-organ and enters the
action-organ of the brain, we see the impulses likewise making
their active invasion. But this releases no mark-signs in
our mind. We have only the vague sensation that impulses
of the will are in play, but we do not know them.

That is why the organisation of the subject remains so
incomplete. It shows us qualities which are arranged by
schemata and group themselves round actions (i.e. round the
typical movements of the body transmitted to the mark-
organ by inner sense-organs) in order to make objects. Concerning the impulses of our will, which alone make the formation of actions even possible, we learn nothing.

This hiatus is very regrettable ; it appears in the case of
all actions. Suppose I ask myself the question, " What
really called forth my action ? " It was not the indication,
neither was it the judgment ; it was a something which I
call " will," but which I do not know. The gap becomes
most unfortunate when we inquire into our memory. For
instance, I can repeat a poem without omitting any part
of it ; before I repeat it, I know nothing of it, and yet, as I
speak, a whole chain of will-impulses reels off without inter-
ruption. The chain must have been there already, if it

could be run off like that. But it is quite unknown to me.

If we could observe our action-organ during the repetition, we should see no more in it than when we looked at the mark-organ. A number of impulses become active in accordance with law, and they make bridges ; but they give us no mark-sign. The command that dwells within them evades our consciousness.

Small wonder if the impulses that build up our bodies elude our knowledge.

And so it is self-evident that the whole impulse-system, which is at once the architect and the director of our body, is forever hidden from our view. As Kant would say, we have to do with a transcendental subject (i.e. a subject lying beyond what we can experience) far wider in its embrace than the spirit, which embraces only the life of our ego.

And so it is quite hopeless to try to explain through our psychical experiences the life of other living organisms. We do not even know the quality of the command given by the impulses active in the mark-organ of another, which nevertheless do permit of a certain analogy with the impulses of our own mark-organ. And for all the other impulses we cannot rely even on this very insecure analogy.

There certainly are realities which remain inaccessible to investigation, and of which we are able to form only a very dubious image, deduced from their activities. But fundamentally biology, in so far as it is obliged to deal with the organising factors of Nature, is in exactly the same case as physics, which is able to judge of the unorganised forces of Nature that form its province, only from their activities.

But biology has a far more secure foundation than physics and chemistry, proceeding as it does from the only stable basis, the sense-qualities ; from these the surrounding-worlds, with all their substances and forces, things, objects, implements and living organisms, are wholly and solely built up, and in accordance with enduring laws.

And so the theory of biology must always proceed from these elements of intuition, if it would seek to bring the phenomena of life into a comprehensive association.

The present book contains the first attempt of the kind. How far it has been successful, my readers can decide for themselves.

PRINTED IN GREAT BRITAIN BY
THE EDINBURGH PRESS, 9 AND 11 YOUNG STREET, EDINBURGH

Lightning Source UK Ltd.
Milton Keynes UK
UKHW022019091221
395394UK00006B/1573